NIEUWPOORT
SECTOR 1917
THE BATTLE OF THE DUNES

Kristof Jacobs

UNIFORM

First published by Uitgeverij De Krijger
This edition first published by Uniform in 2018
an imprint of Unicorn Publishing Group

Unicorn Publishing Group
101 Wardour Street
London W1F 0UG

www.unicornpublishing.org

A catalogue record for this book is available from the British Library

ISBN 978-1-910500-88-0

Printed and bound in Great Britain

Cover design by Unicorn
Typeset by Vivian@Bookscribe

CONTENTS

FRENCH AND FLEMISH NAMES

In this book the author refers to the current Flemish spelling of place names in his narrative but, where contemporary sources are used these may also be found in French, as whilst Flanders was bilingual, French was the administrative language at the time in Belgium.

The following should aid the reader in confirming locations mentioned.

Flemish	*English*
Hoek	corner
Bos	wood, forest
Molen	mill, windmill
Berg	hill

Flemish	*French*
Brugge	Bruges
Diksmuide	Dixmude
Koksijde	Coxyde
Lombardsijde	Lombardsijde
Middelkerke	Middlekerke
Nieuwpoort	Nieuport
Oudenburg	Oudenburg
Oostduinkerke	Oostdunkerke
Oostende	Ostende
Passchendaele	Passendale
Pijpegale	Pypegaele
Poperinghe	Poperinge
Raversijde	Raversyde
Staden	Stade
Veurne	Furnes
Ieper	Ypres
Zuydschoote	Zuidschote

FOREWORD

It is curious how a few casual words can create a trail of fascinating research and unexpected events. This book is the culmination of just such a situation.

It was more than two decades ago in Liverpool that the then 98-year-old Lancashire Fusilier veteran Bert Fearns explained to my surprise that the most terrifying period of his Great War career was not at Passchendaele (*Passendale*) or even the Somme in spring 1918 (where he was wounded and taken prisoner) but at Nieuwpoort in the summer of 1917.

To reach the front lines, he said, he and his comrades had to pass through a town targeted by German artillery. The streets were often infernos of singing splinters of red-hot razor-sharp steel, flying fragments of brick and timber, tumbling masonry, and clouds of pungent smoke and dust. The troops of every unit dreaded the ordeal, and suffered many casualties.

On approaching the town one day, to their delight and relief Bert and his pals were led into a tunnel which carried them secretly and securely beneath the streets to emerge near the river. Their torment was over – solved by the skills of the Royal Engineer Tunnelling Companies.

Research revealed not just one or two tunnels, but a vast network of workings both in and around Nieuwpoort, throughout the dune area along the coast and at neighbouring Nieuwpoort Bains. The scheme included subterranean accommodation for several thousand men and even underground hospitals.

It was about this time that news appeared of structural complications in numerous buildings in Nieuwpoort town. At one address the problem was so serious the house had to be demolished.

The cause was subsidence, but the source was unknown. Was there, I wondered, a correlation with the wartime activities of the engineers – I had encountered numerous similar situations elsewhere on the old battlefields?

Overlaying the original Nieuwpoort tunnel plans upon modern maps revealed clear associations, to the point where evidence of structural problems (in the form of cracks in walls) could be predicted simply by following the routes through the town.

My colleague Kristof Jacobs took up the research, adding his own professional architectural expertise and spent years digging ever deeper into town records, military archives and local memories. He expanded the scope of investigation to produce this excellent and valuable volume on an overlooked but dynamic, always animated and strategically crucial sector: the northern extremity of the Western Front.

This splendid book, full of surprises and revelations, is a significant addition to the canon of World War One research, reminding us especially of the unexpected and often hidden consequences of conflict with which the peoples of France and Flanders must forever live.

PETER BARTON

PREFACE

'Nieuwpoort' (*Nieuport*) – many of us associate this name with beach holidays, conviviality, sun, sea and sand. For some it has been their home for generations, or the home port of their boat or ship.

For others Nieuwpoort equates to abomination, misery, fear, death … war. Unfortunately the last living witnesses of these wretched times have sadly passed away and we must start to use writings and documents as our sole source of information.

One of these last witnesses was Bert Fearns (1898–1997) and his tale is one of our main guides throughout this publication. Both current events and historical facts corroborate the story of this man, who, at only eighteen years old, was thrown into the violence of war.

In 1999, Nieuwpoort again made the headlines in the national and international press with reports about the subsidence of homes. British academics referred to the history of under-

ground war within the town. Local politicians and a professor at the Royal Military School completely dismissed this.

With this book I wish to give you some insights into the situation at Nieuwpoort in 1917, by using historical documents, regimental reports and witness statements. This will make the relation between the current issues in and around the town and the historical facts indisputable.

This book is therefore dedicated to the memory of Bert and all the other boys who fought, both above and below ground, at Nieuwpoort. May their presence, their work and their struggle continue to be commemorated.

'…We will remember them.'

CHAPTER ONE
THE HISTORY OF NIEUWPOORT

The oldest document concerning the town of Nieuwpoort dates from 1112. It concerns a grant by Robrecht de Fries, Count of Flanders, of the recently heightened dune-lands to the Abbey of Bourbourg. In a charter dating from 1150, a commercial settlement is described, situated at the end of the 'Zandhoofd' on the left bank of the mouth of the river Yser. The deepening and banking of the shipping canal in 1160 made the harbour more accessible. The surrounding salt marshes were slowly protected against flooding by the monks of the abbeys of Oudenburg and Koksijde (*Coxyde*).

In 1163, Philip of Alsace founded a new town at the mouth of the Yser bay. The town was named 'Novum Oppidum', meaning New Town. Moorings were constructed and the town was surrounded by water and earthen fortifications. Nieuwpoort developed into a reasonably important commercial port which even then had a Saint-John's hospital for pilgrims and travellers.

During 1165, the Church of Our Lady was consecrated by Nilo, Bishop of the Morins at Teruanne. During this time fishing in and around Nieuwpoort was the most important commercial enterprise in the County of Flanders. To help stimulate this industry, Count Philip of Alsace granted the burghers of the town a dispensation of market and passage taxes for all of Flanders. This privilege was challenged many times, yet Nieuwpoort always retained this right through the Courts of Appeal, even centuries later.

The town underwent its first siege in 1213, after a conflict between Philip II Augustus, King of France, and Emperor Otto IV, ally of the Count of Flanders.

In 1240 the borders of Nieuwpoort and Oostduinkerke (*Oostdunkerke*) were determined by Pieter, Bishop of the Morins.

During 1284, large building projects were carried out in Nieuwpoort to expand the town. A second parish church, Saint Laurentius, was built, as well as a stone 'Vierboete' (lighthouse) on the coastline. A second lighthouse was later built slightly further along by the western port access.

In 1299 a second siege and subsequent occupation by the French, during the reign of King Philip IV the Fair, took place. Under the feudal system, the French King was the liege lord of the Count of Flanders.

After 1302 a perilous period started for the whole area, as there was an anarchic period from 1323 with collective revolt against the heavy taxation imposed by the French King.

For the first time Nieuwpoort offered active resistance against a legitimate ruler, and during the Battle at Kassel on 23 August 1328, 174 inhabitants of Nieuwpoort perished.

Shortly afterwards Nieuwpoort was captured by the French for the third time.

An English expedition in 1383 attempted to conquer Ypres (*Ieper*), but were forced to retreat and arrived to capture Nieuwpoort. The town was partially destroyed, apart from the Draper's Hall and part of the Saint Laurentius Church.

For the first time Nieuwpoort acquired full fortifications with earthen embankments, fortified walls, corner turrets, gates, draw-bridges and star-shaped waterworks. The new Count, Philip of Valois (Philip the Bold), wanted to protect his border on the coast by his own means by using aggression against the English. The Hundred-Year War between France and England had started.

In 1489, Nieuwpoort successfully endured its first real siege. Nieuwpoort fiercely resisted, but in the enemy camp disarray had broken out between militias from France and Ghent. Up to a point Nieuwpoort had become a competitor to the Shippers Guild of Ghent for the transportations between France and Brugge (*Bruges*), and they rebelled against their legitimate ruler.

The new governor, Maximilian, granted Nieuwpoort many privileges as a reward for its loyalty. The town had a hey-day. The ruins of the Saint Laurentius Church were refurbished and transformed into a castle, a fourth nave was built in the Church of Our Lady; in short Nieuwpoort became a flourishing garrison town with a military governor.

Because the town held a key position, especially during the period of conflicts known as the Religious Wars, in 1576 it was for a while given in pledge to Prince William of Orange-Nassau, in order to secure a truce with the Spanish rulers.

The conflict between the Spanish rulers and the Northern Provinces mainly took place on Flemish territory. In June 1600, a Dutch expeditionary army led by Prince Maurice of Nassau was sent to take control of the coastal port town of Dunkerque. It marched past Brugge and Oostende and besieged Nieuwpoort. He was pursued by another force, hastily assembled under the command of Archduke Albrecht.

On 2 June they arrived in battle array at the dunes, just a short distance from Nieuwpoort.

After the battle, the Spanish troops had to fall back after many troops succumbed on both sides.

In 1606 calm returned thanks to the twelve-year truce which was signed between Holland and Archduke Albrecht.

From 1646, a long period of conflict between Spain and Louis XIV began; many of the confrontations taking place in the Low Countries.

Before the end of the 17th century the French Army besieged Nieuwpoort at least ten times.

The garrison, made up of mercenaries and Spaniards, always managed to keep the besiegers at bay by using inundations. Only on the western side of the town supplementary fortifications with artillery had to be used.

Now Nieuwpoort found itself on an international border. The river Yser was considered to be the northern border of France, but Nieuwpoort remained Spanish. King Philip IV rewarded the burghers of Nieuwpoort for their loyalty by exempting them of all military billeting for fifty years. But even *that* the sovereign could not guarantee!

At the start of the 18th century the Flemish territory was under the control of an allied coalition against the French. Finally Nieuwpoort was transferred to the Austrian Habsburg authorities from 1715.

But in 1745 the French entered Nieuwpoort following a short period of resistance. On 22

May 1745, the French conquered Tournai and all of Flanders fell into their hands. The attack on Nieuwpoort by Löwendal on 31 August ended on 5 September. Notwithstanding the floods which surrounded the town, it had to capitulate.

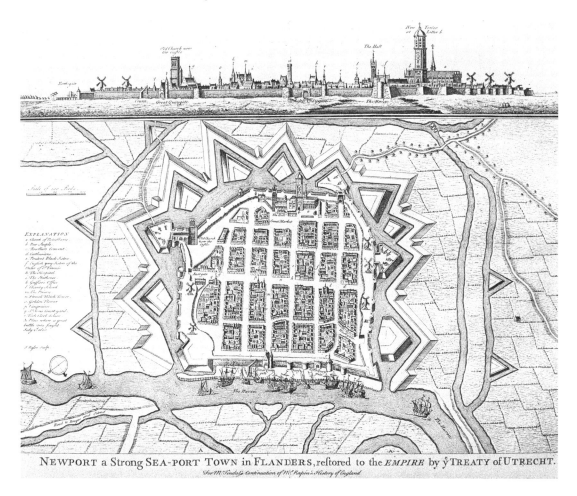

NEWPORT a Strong SEA-PORT TOWN in FLANDERS, reſtored to the *EMPIRE* by y͜e TREATY of UTRECHT.
For Mr. Tindal's Continuation of Mr. Rapin's History of England

In 1748 the Treaty of Aix-la-Chapelle resolved the situation. Nieuwpoort is Austrian once again.

The destruction of all fortifications was ordered in 1782 by Joseph II; Nieuwpoort could only keep its embankments. During the French attacks the fortifications of Nieuwpoort were partially rebuilt and with the help of the flooding of the surrounding area, the town managed to resist the attack by the French General Vandamme, who had to retire from the field on 26 October.

The year after the defence failed one last time and France colonised the Nieuwpoort area.

In 1815, Nieuwpoort became an undefended port within the Kingdom of The Netherlands. At the urging of the Duke of Wellington – on behalf of the allied coalition against France – the Dutch authorities turned the town into a garrison town once more. From 1820 it housed caserns [a small, temporary building for housing a garrison of troops], fortification walls, embankments, arsenals, a military bakery, abattoir and artillery on the walls. After Belgian independence, Nieuwpoort remained a military town. However, in 1857 the demolition of the fortifications was started.

When, in 1914, it became clear that the Belgian Army was exhausted, very diminished and therefore could no longer resist the German armed forces, it was decided to flood the front facing the enemy but in a controlled way. A demarcated area to Dixmude (*Diksmuide*), and even further, was flooded…

The strategic location of the town would also play an important role later in the war. A less well known, but nevertheless very important part of history, the British-Australian defence of Nieuwpoort during 1917, is the subject of this book.

NIEUWPOORT-BAD

On 21 July 1864, the town of Nieuwpoort fêted the official opening of its design seaside resort. A Royal Decree of 26 August 1864 gave the town permission to install a service for sea bathing over a length of 500 metres of the beach west of the harbour channel. One year later the first stone of Nieuwpoort-Bad was laid. The Crombez family played an important role in the growth and development of the resort.

NIEUPORT-BAINS. — *Villa Crombez.*

The building of the villa Crombez, and the residence of the family during the summer months, started further development of the resort. The saleable land with building permission was divided into parcels. In the dunes, the Place Henriette (Hendrikaplein) and some parallel roads were put in place. Commercial and drinking establishments were at first rejected. Only large hotels and selected private houses could be built. During World War One Nieuwpoort-Bad would play a strategic role as the endpoint of the Western Front.

CHAPTER TWO
SECTOR NIEUWPOORT

Before June 1917, Nieuwpoort was defended by units of different nationalities. One of the most remarkable actions during 1914 was carried out by the French 7e Tirailleurs de Marche and the 1e Regiment de Marche of the Zouaves.

7e RMT 1914 – ATTACK OF 'LA GRANDE DUNE' AT LOMBARDSIJDE

On 20 December 1914, at 15.00 hours, the Jacquot and Sacquet battalions leave Steenvoorde by car. They arrive at Oostduinkerke where they join the Mensier battalion.

The French naval fusiliers arrive by train

The regiment receives information confirming that the 7e Tirailleurs de Marche have officially been allocated to them. The 7e de Marche, which inherited the well known 1e Marche and 2e Mixte, will soon make its name in military history. After a number of battles, the enemy has been forced back on the right hand bank of the Yser. Two battalions of the regiment are tasked to continue this progress. On the left near the sea, the trenches they use run at the foot of the 'Grande Dune' and then continue through the Polder towards Lombardsijde.

'La Grande Dune' before the war

'La Grande Dune' seen from the French side

'La Grande Dune' before the war

'La Grande Dune' in 1915, seen from the French side

The German side of the Apenberg

The rambling trenches (notice the struts and sandbags holding back the sand)

The trenches, dug in dune sand, are practically usable, but tend to collapse at the slightest tremor; in the Polder the water stands on the surface and work is carried out with rickety struts and sandbags.

The regiment concentrates all its efforts on taking 'La Grande Dune'. A first attack starts on the 22nd but is halted by a phenomenal fire fight which caused a strong reaction by the enemy. The German artillery rains destruction on the trenches which collapse and bury the men in them.

A German artillery projectile in the French position

It is in this way that on the evening of the 24th Captain Frossard is killed by a bullet through the heart while crossing through the sector occupied by his company.

An operation during the night of the 24th is partially successful. The allied first line is pushed back and some units take the 'Grande Dune' but cannot hold it. In the meantime most of the south-westerly occupied point is part of the trench 'Le cratère', which remains in allied hands. The enemy, who is only some thirty metres away, completely dominates this area. It continuously rains grenades and bombs throughout the day. The allied troops, armed with defensive artillery, are not able to shelter in the moving terrain and suffer great losses. In a single morning, Lieutenant Francescetti's section loses twenty-two men because of the incessant artillery barrage. In the meantime there was no weakening of the units which had each been tasked with holding out under this fiery barrage. The situation does not change during the first two weeks of January. The troops try to keep morale high, but the cold and snow add to their woes. Also, there are more postponements and the battalions which relieve each other only spend two days in the first line. The units cross the Yser by the 'Général Joffre' bridge which has been installed by the Engineers. The enemy artillery grimly fights on and finally destroys the bridge.

German artillery in the dunes of Lombardsijde

German artillery at Westende-Bad

The river must now be crossed in flat barges to avoid a large detour, alternatively ramshackle footbridges without handrails would have to be navigated. When they arrive at their quarters in Nieuwpoort-Bad and Oostduinkerke-Bad the troops find neither comfort nor security.

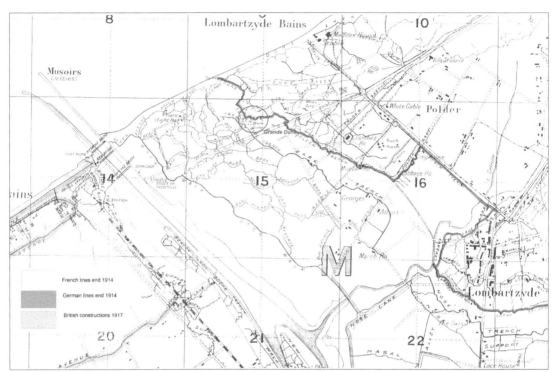

The market in Nieuwpoort

The German artillery bombs Nieuwpoort every day and causes major losses in the resting battalions On 3 December the machine gunners of the 3rd Battalion are nearly all killed by a shell.

1915

On 1 January, while the non-commissioned officers of the 9th Company are celebrating the New Year in their kitchen, a shell explodes in the middle of the room which results in three casualties. A new attack is being prepared.

The preparatory works are being encouraged and the fully reinforced allied artillery takes the advance on the batteries of the enemy. On 24 January the Marine Fusiliers Regiment takes a brief rest before the attack. On 26 January the unit commanders make a last reconnaissance. At the moment the officers of the 3rd Battalion cross the bridge across the Yser, a grenade explodes in the middle of the group, gravely wounding commander Mensier and Captains Camus and Simon. On the same day Lieutenant-Colonel Demetz replaces Lieutenant-Colonel Levêque at the head of the group, as Levêque was wounded some days before. Commander Jacquot, who had assumed his replacement and had given orders to start the attack next morning, continues to lead the operation.

On the morning of 27 January the regrouping has finished. Three companies of the Toulet Battalion[1], aided by three companies of the Jacquot Battalion, have to attack the trenches of the Polder while a company of the Sacquet Battalion has the 'Grande Dune' as its target. During the night the sappers have prepared attacks on the network of the enemy. The explosions take place at first dawn and make four wide breaches in their defence works. The allied artillery arrives and at 8 o'clock a heavy bombardment starts. The elements of the first line are grouped behind a bank only a hundred metres from the enemy trenches. The 75mm cannons are very accurate. The shells clip the edges of the trenches and the arc backs fall in the allied positions.

At 9.10 a lull in the firing identifies the threatening presence of a trench full of intact machine guns. A revolving cannon is placed in the battery. The chief of the squadron of Luget, the cavaliers who have to hold the lines on foot during the operation, points out the emplacement himself. At 9.20 the artillery recommences with increasing violence, and the enemy positions disappear in a cloud of sand.

At 9.30 the attacking companies, divided into two groups, jump off the parapet.

They quickly land in the first enemy trench taking everyone by surprise. Not a single person alive emerges from the heap of warped plates, broken shields and ripped sandbags. The first line has been removed without any fighting. But nearby, undamaged shelters hide the German garrison which, surprised by the speed of the attack, has no time to resist and flees in disarray through the trench leading to the 2nd line, which has held and which has not suffered under the well prepared allied artillery.

---

[1]Commander Toulet had replaced Commander Mensier at the head of the 3rd Battalion.

German shooting range at Lombardsijde

These tough fights inspire the company to do more. They hold on to a parapet which they install under a hail of bullets. The enemy plans a counterattack, after having hidden in a small wood. This counterattack is rebuffed by the allied artillery. Sergeant-Major Dellupo leads the artillery of his section, standing on the parapet, until a bullet kills him. But his bravery transcends courage. It is impossible to advance, but the positions are held.

German sailors near their shelters in the dunes

The enemy artillery swiftly intervenes. The batteries of Lombardsijde fight for the captured terrain by shooting obliquely. In a terrain totally sodden by water it is impossible to dig five foxholes. The sections along the parapet do not weaken, but not without losses. They undergo this terrible barrage of shells.

While all this takes place in the Polder, the 'Grande Dune' is also the scene of hard fighting. At 9.30 the three attacking sections of the Fricolet Company had only one goal: clear the 'Grande Dune'. Breaking through the artillery placed by the enemy, Sergeant Bruneau had avoided a catastrophe.

An unexploded German 380mm shell

The Germans, momentarily overwhelmed, increase their efforts to retake 'La Dune'. After many counterattacks they manage to close in on the flanks, and take the allied line under crossfire. From that point they open a serious fire fight. In a short time the three heads of the section are killed and almost all commissioned officers out of action. Nevertheless, the troops hang on but at the cost of many casualties, so the retreat is sounded at 11.30. Sergeant Bruneau's group is not subject to this order and holds on in a trench until 18.00.

The situation of the units in the Polder is endangered by the loss of the 'Grande Dune'. From their dominating position the Germans fire at them from behind.

The German machine gun shelter in 'La grande Dune'

Lieutenant Weisbecker's section of gunners is massacred by the bullets. His chief and all aids, except two, are killed.

The Delorme Company receives the order to retake the 'Grande Dune' at 13.30. A second attempt does not have any success. Despite everything, the remainder of the Company starts to undermine the enemy positions. The artillery showers a rain of shells but these cannot stem the allied progress. However, soon the enemy aims a revolving cannon at the miners. This relentless attack tears the sandbags and horribly mutilates the workers. Every time a group is destroyed it is replaced, all looking death in the face without protest. But this bloody slaughter must urgently be stopped. The situation continues all day. The enemy artillery doubles its efforts. Complete unprotected sections are killed by the shells.

The weapons, impaired by sand and mud, are nearly all out of commission. Only a miracle will allow the men to hold on. At last, as night falls, Command orders the retreat. This is carried out in regular order. The wounded, the equipment, even the bodies, are brought back to the allied lines.

The victims of the violent artillery bombardments

This looks like an escape from the enemy. The cavalry on foot, who carried the wounded all day and brought supplies, help the evacuation.

The regiment is replaced by marine fusiliers and will regroup at Nieuwpoort. The companies have suffered great losses.

The balance of the operation: 121 dead, 206 wounded, 46 missing.

This effort must be the last for the regiment in Belgium. After a short rest in the section, in the Sacquet and Jacquot, the 7e Tirailleurs de Marche is founded on 1 February.

After a troop review at Uxem by the Generals, the brigade embarks for a new sector.

(From the *Historique du Régiment*, Librairie Militaire CHAPELOT)

HISTORY OF THE FIRST 'REGIMENT DE MARCHE' OF THE ZOUAVES AT NIEUWPOORT.

During the first days of February 1916, the altered 38th Division Infantry (the marine fusiliers replaced by the Algerian gunners) takes the sector Nieuwpoort. The 1st Zouaves, shielded on the left by the sea, uses the sector in front of Nieuwpoort-Bad, across from the 'Grande Dune'.

They carry out a continuous fight for five and a half months, placed in the most disadvantageous positions with no trenches, no shelters worth being called a shelter, and with communication arrears due to links which can only be used at night, marked by two glorious incidents for the regiment.

The Zouave regiment

First there is the German attack on 9 May during which the first line keeps its positions, completely overwrought by ten hours of bombardment, and kills the enemy as soon as they appear over the parapet.

Then, on 11 June, aided by a group of the regiment and a division of the Engineers (19/2 Company), an attack on and short capture of the 'Grande Dune', a strongpoint for the Germans, and a nightmare for all those who knew this sector. From this dominating point, progressing into the allied lines, the enemy can spot the smallest movement and makes the allies pay heavily for the smallest carelessness.

Unfortunately many fell in the 'Dune'. It is in this sector, supposedly the quietest one, that the regiment has the most losses.

THE FOURTH ZOUAVES AND THEIR STAY IN BELGIUM
Nieuwpoort-town – Lombardsijde

The regiment leaves the area of Bergues-Quaedypre on 31 January 1915 in two stages, via Hondschoote and Veurne (*Furnes*) they approach the area of the 'dunes'. Fortunately for the officers and troops they find the first sand hillocks, and after their experiences in Pijpegale (*Pypegaele*) and Ypres, clean trenches free of mud and water in which they can sleep.

Their luck was short lived. The 'Dunes' sector was assigned to the 1st regiment of the Zouaves.

A short break after their arrival in the 'Dunes' sector

Up until the 4th, on the right, the Polder area between the 'Dunes' and the road to Lombardsijde–Nieuwpoort town was assigned.

The famous Brigade de Marins (Brigade of Seamen) of Admiral Ronarch follow the line to Saint Joris and Ramscapelle.

Admiral Ronarch in his command post (in the 'Admiral House') along the road to Nieuwpoort–Oostduinkerke

After having crossed through the ruins of Nieuwpoort, two battalions of the regiment, the 11th and the 3rd, take their positions in their new domain during the night of the 4–5 February.

A monotonous square lays under a dark sky, with here and there some rare houses of market gardeners, trees, but nothing that obstructs the view between 'Les Dunes' and the inundation caused by the Belgians during their retreat.

German marines at the ruins of a 'gardener's post' in the Polders of Lombardsijde

The soil is like a sodden sponge and cannot be dug. There is not a single trench.

The defences are behind a parapet of sandbags, almost too narrow to stop the bullets, behind which one can walk doubled over.

No shelters, the sector is new and still has to be organised, there is work here for many months. The resting places of Koksijde-Bad and Camp de Mitry near Oostduinkerke are better, especially Koksijde with its town, shops, sympathetic population and its lovely beach, where the spectacle of the English Fleet which stands guard in front of the Belgian coast can be enjoyed. It becomes the preferred resting place for the Zouaves, a kind of small paradise where they come for a while, always cheerful, to walk on the beach or in La Panne to play a game of football.

Spahi's on the steps of De Panne

It is during the same night, while they are taking their positions in Lombardsijde, that the Zouaves get to know the German mines. Their results were serious, extraordinary; whole parts of the parapet were gone, wiped out, taken away by the blast of the projectiles. The troops who were hit were torn apart. During the night the dead had to be were buried, feverishly quickly, under a hail of bullets. Fill sandbags, close breaches and in the morning help to demolish the painful work of the past night.

In this fight between the destructive Germans and the organising Zouaves, the latter slowly manage to gain the advantage, much to the vexation of the enemy.

The width of the parapet grows, with a double load. A second parallel line was almost finished when the work was suddenly halted.

SECOND BATTLE OF YPRES

On 23 April 1915, at 5.00 o'clock, the Pruneaux and Bonnery battalions, resting at Koksijde, are called up.

They walk to Veurne, take a train to the stop at the Lion Belge near Woesten and are deployed in full scale fighting at 15.00 hours.

In the morning the Germans use a new attack process for the first time. It will become well known to the allies: gas is thrown and they manage to penetrate the allied front north of Ypres. Time is of the essence, the breach widens, the allies must prevent a German success at all cost. The two battalions of the area north of Zuydschoote (*Zuidschote*) arrive just in time to reduce the gap between the Belgian Army and the remains of the division. At 17.00 they form a line in front of

Lizerne and Steenstraete. They search for connections, the machine guns are placed, the Germans will not be allowed to make progress.

French soldiers, at rest near the farm 'Ten Bogaerde' in Koksijde, are getting ready for their departure

On 24 April at 4 o'clock, under the light from the burning Belgian farms, the Bonnery Battalion attack towards Lizerne. They advance 300 metres but, heavily harassed by machine guns, cannot advance any further. The Sub-lieutenant Trinquart, sixty years old, and a veteran of seventy, Lieutenant Pietel, are amongst the dead.

During the 24th, 25th and the morning of the 26 April the battalions get installed, dig in and organise the terrain notwithstanding a heavy bombardment. The 9th line has many dead. Lieutenants Soulié and Rey are killed by the same shell. These losses annoy the Zouaves and urge them on in their fervour. Patrols are launched and the murderous reconnaissance takes prisoners. They ensure that the village of Lizerne is preserved and on the 26th at 15.30, after a short artillery barrage, the 3rd Battalion finally receives the order to attack. In the crackle of the fire fight the men of Chéchia kaki suddenly appear with a tearing enthusiasm. The moment the enemy can get payback has finally arrived. The gas kills, but so do the bayonets. The first German trench is reached, those in it are soon corpses, nothwithstanding their pleas. The Zouaves tot up their account.

French troops leave Koksijde, in the direction of Veurne

Lieutenant Pellegrin, who urges the men on, is killed by a pistol shot straight in the face; the Aspirant Dénivaux falls in the same way. They are avenged!

The battalion regroups on the other side of the trench and, reinforced by 11th Company, it leaves to attack the village. The first houses are hit and the firing is extreme, in the trenches, in the *boyaux* and other *pare-éclat*. For ten minutes a great battle ensues. Sergeant Houet, Leutenant R. d'Hulières, corporals Riffet, Balussou and soldier Valéro fall, but the Zouaves have sworn to take the village and they keep their word. At 16.30 they take the last houses. The war booty comprises two machine guns and 130 prisoners, soldiers of the infantry and the Württemberg Hunters.

This splendid triumph, after the hard and depressing days at Nieuwpoort, considerably contributes to the soldiers regaining their composure after a long stay in the trenches.

From 26 April to 4 May the two battalions are occupied in the

The Zouaves with a machine gun

village, which the Germans, furious about their defeat, are bombarding incessantly. The losses are considerable and only a handful of men are found by the 418th RI on the evening of the 4 May. The remainder of the battalions arrive back at Koksijde on the 6 May. The population, having heard about their glorious success and the ramifications thereof, gives them an enthusiastic welcome.

THE GERMAN ATTACK OF 9 MAY

The second battle of Ypres is felt all the way to Nieuwpoort. From the 25 April 1915 the Germans have kept the 4th Zouaves in front of Lizerne. They believe the moment has come to attack the line Nieuwpoort-Lombardsijde, knowing the objective of the holding regiment had been shifted to Northern Ypres. The 9 May, from 4.00 o'clock, the 2nd Division of the German Navy starts heavy shelling from 'La Grande Dune' at Lombardsijde, using artillery and trench mortars.

Heavy impact in de Polders

Badly protected by their narrow parapet, the Zouaves and the Territorials suffer great losses. The gunners are at their embrasures, the machine gunners at their positions, fearfully waiting until the flat caps appear. At noon the attack commences, the Feldgrauen break through the parapet, towards the French lines, which they believed destroyed. Suddenly a heavy battery lets fly, frightening the attackers and stopping them in their tracks. They regroup and set out again, encouraged by their first officers, but to no avail. On 50 metres of the allied line, which they thought would be easily taken, they are stopped. The German battalions separate and collapse. The most courageous Germans come to die at the foot of the parapet. The others run hither and thither, and the allied machine guns fire into this mulling mass of men. They kill as many as they can and cut the Feldgrauen down completely.

In this way the Germans are driven back on the largest part of their line of attack. To the right of the allies they manage to infiltrate all the way to the first allied trench, notwithstanding heavy losses. They capture 300 metres between Mamelon-Vert and the road to Nieuwpoort.

At 18.00 two companies of the 5th Battalion and two companies of the French Navy Gunners carry out a counterattack, and manage to recapture the terrain and take prisoners. By 19.00 the allied line is completely regained. The German attack has failed.

The grey bodies are lying everywhere, in the grass or on the barbed wire. They will remain there for many months as an ominous testimony to the value of the Zouaves, a spectre for the allies. They remind what it is to insult the French in these places where the machine guns are working very well.

Victims of the attack by the Zouaves

Nothing can trouble them now, and the Zouaves use this interlude to finish the organisational works.

The trenches allow safe movements from Nieuwpoort to the Polder and to Mamelon-Vert. The rickety parapet used at the start is no longer used as lookout point. The main parallel trenches

The consequences of the retaliation by the Zouaves

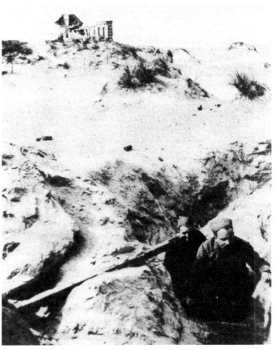

One of the bunkers built by Zouaves in the dunes

Zouaves on the road between Mamelon-Vert and the Polder in Lombardsijde

are finished during June, the maintenance trenches by the end of July. The Redan in Nieuwpoort is used to stock weapons for the 1st battalion. The Zouaves are still as active as ever at the rear. Helped by the division's Engineers they restore Camp Mitryn, making it inhabitable, build Camp Rinck, build horses tables, install washbasins and a platform between two dunes. Everywhere, from Oostduinkerke to Koksijde, that part of the Belgian coast shows evidence of their activities.

Spahis on horseback in the vicinity of Oostduinkerke

Commander Richaud of the 1st Zouaves is promoted to Lieutenant-Colonel in July and replaces Lieutenant-Colonel Eyché of the Ministry of Defence as head of the regiment.

At the start of August the 8th Gunners come to replace the 1st Zouaves, who are leaving the area around Nieuwpoort. The Gunners have been merged with the troops of the 4th Zouaves, forming mixed sections. At the start of September the Algerians regain their autonomy. They are very well informed about the system of trenches. The 8th Gunners hold the Polder and Mamelon-Vert, the 4th Zouaves take the 'Dunes' and Nieuwpoort-Bad, left of the sea.

Once they have taken their positions they can see that further works have advanced well. The men especially appreciate the shelters which have been built in the flanks of the sand hills. These are formidable and indestructible compared to the barracks and sandbags at Lombardsijde. 'Let the shells come,' they laugh, and they are unsparing in their praises of their predecessors, the 1st, who have worked unceasingly to maintain the position of their regiment.

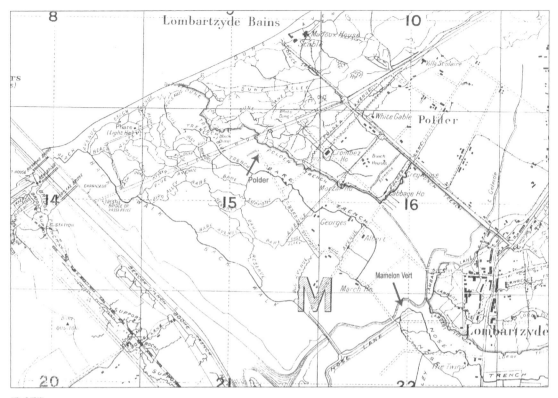

View from Mamelon-Vert towards Polders

Site manned by Zouaves on the beach of Lombardsijde

Pierre Valet, 4th Zouaves, died at Nieuwpoort on 15 July 1916

ORGANISATION OF NIEUWPOORT-BAD

During this period a lot of work takes place in Nieuwpoort-Bad. Everyone works hard to be able to resist the worst bombardments. Nieuwpoort-Bad is transformed into a military support station.

The buildings Marin and Neacon are fortified towards the enemy.

Two covered trenches are built in the main street, and fitted with electricity. These, and some shrubbery, allow access from the road Groenen Dijk to the Yser. The trench can also be used by gunners.

All the basements of the villas are connected with a central trench, which in its turn is connected with various shelters and command posts.

It takes four months to complete these works. All battalions and pioneers help, and are led by Commander Lagarde and his adjunct, Captain Reynes. The former concentrates on the first lines and the defence of the Yser, the latter on the works in the centre of Nieuwpoort town. A lot of courage was required for these works during the worst bombardments by the Germans. The sector was equipped to answer these bombardments: 58mm, 150mm and 240mm cannon are

Above and right: Panoramic view of Maison du Marin, Nieuwpoort-Bad

The end of the west front with a concealed wooden passage on the right

brought in and installed on the dunes. They are partly manned by the Zouaves and partly by the Artillery, with rivalry between the two about who destroyed the most enemy trenches. Quiet days passed, but suddenly heavy calibre guns were fired by the Germans. The allies answer and a terrible, indescribable bombardment lasts for an hour. Shells and splinter bombs fly through the air everywhere. Just as suddenly calm returns. Everyone regains his collapsed hoarding, repairs his shelter, picks up new ammunition. After a few days a fresh bombardment takes place, first for the allies, then for the Germans. The Zouaves call these days the days of *bamboula*. The great days of *bamboula* are the 7 and the 15 October, the 10 November, the 27 December 1915 and the 1 and the 21 January 1916.

GERMAN ATTACK OF 2 JANUARY 1916

The bombardment of 21 January was carried out by the regiment. Right from the start the Germans replied with such violence that it was almost impossible for the allied bombardiers to fire all their projectiles.

It was calm during the night of 22 January. The Germans started to fire at the trenches and connection points. On the 23rd the German artillery is more active. It was normal that they adjusted their guns and nobody was surprised when the *Trommerfeuer* started on the 24th at 10.40. Everyone had been prepared for two days.

Nobody had ever experienced the duration and the intensity of the bombardment, nor the size of the projectiles fired at the French trenches. It was even worse than the bombardment and devious tactics the Germans were later to use at Verdun.

Sudden, at 13.30, there is silence. Nobody wanted to get trapped and apart from some guards everybody stayed in the shelters.

At 13.40 the German artillery resumes, this time accompanied by charges which nobody had ever seen. Shells are everywhere, and the smoke is so thick that the men think they have gotten lost, separated from everyone in the hell in which they have to stay. The beach is hit worst, then 'La Grande Dune' and next the Polder. It is in the Polder that the Germans attack around 16.30. A small attack, as apart from about ten men who leave the 'Grande Dune' and some forty who arrive at the Polder, nobody moves in the German trenches. The allied artillery kept everyone rooted. In the Polder the attack is easily rebutted after a short counter-attack by the 15th Company. The attack of 24 January, as well as the one of 9 May 1915, fails. The terrain under the Zouaves remained intact. Although the losses in the Regiment were heavy, the German losses were much worse. As the Allies later learned, more than 900 men were put out of action.

The allied trenches were severely disturbed; the trenches were almost non-existent and had to be rebuilt. The parapets and defences had to be rebuilt too. The Germans, who were nurturing larger wounds than the allies, did not interfere.

On 25 January, Commander Vernois, adjunct to Colonel Richaud, becomes Lieutenant-Colonel. He leaves the regiment in order to take command of the 4th Mixed of Zouaves and Gunners, who have just arrived at Nieuwpoort.

— FÊTE DES ZOUAVES. — Théâtre en plein air.

Theatre performance by Zouaves in Stavele

A new camp is built near Koksijde, named Camp Bador in honour of one of the fallen Zouaves of the 11th Battalion, at the end of February. The new camp is built with every necessary comfort. The barracks has a reading room and a sergeant's mess and in the middle is a theatre with 800 seats. The regimental theatrical troupe gives many performances here and are known throughout the whole garrison of Koksijde.

The musicians and singers give a concert every day in the officers' mess. They play a revue under general acclaim, both tragic and comedy, which help to pass the long winter months without the men getting too depressed.

On 15 March, the calm was disturbed by the allies. Forty grenadiers, led by the sub-lieutenants Beaudoin and De Ghest, manage to penetrate into the German's third trench, which they found had been evacuated. In April a second raid is carried out by the 1st under Lieutenant Papillon but with the same result. These subsequent actions and the incessant bombardments slowly have their effect on the regiment. The men have self-doubts. As a tool being forged they are getting used to the red glow of the shells, the noise of the trench mortars, the rattling of the bayonets and the whistling of the bullets. But in order to have a suitable instrument for war, hard but flexible, it is necessary for this tool to undergo the ultimate test on a great battlefield, in order to know the value of its character. This justifies the 1st being an elite regiment.

The regiment leaves Belgium, the 'Dunes' and Nieuwpoort-Bad on the 20 April, parading amongst the population of Koksijde. They take their leave and are loaded into trucks to be driven to Dunkirk and the area around it. They have fought for fourteen months in the most appalling circumstances, at first without even any hand grenades to throw at the Germans who were firing at them with heavy artillery. They fought without shelter, without trenches, in the water and mud. The Zouaves had held on to that little bit of Belgium; they had bravely defended a country that was not theirs even though the Germans twice tried to take it.

All of this was happening with a lot of sorrow and grief. They left the area with regret, because many comrades they had known, loved and appreciated slept their last night under the many small wooden crosses which had been placed in the Belgian rose gardens.

From 20 April to 10 May the regiment took part in the offensive in the 'Dunes' of Dunkirk. Training units are formed, manned by company commanders, section chiefs, grenadiers and gunners, and the lessons are attended, with great results, by the officers, non-commissioned officers and Zouaves.

On 10 May the regiment leaves Dunkirk by rail. The 11th lands in Breteuil in the Oise near the training camp Crèvecoeur le Grand. The training of the troops and officers is resumed.

The 4th Zouaves takes part in the manoeuvres of the Brigade and the Division.

Notwithstanding the Battle of Verdun, which costs the allies a part of their forces, the French General Staff prepares an offensive in the north. The 38th Division must take part. In the meantime the Germans redouble the ferocity of their attacks, not on the banks of the Somme, but towards the river Meuse, which will be held by the regiment until the final victorious offensive.

The Zouaves move towards the front

THE FOURTH MIXED REGIMENT OF THE ZOUAVES AND GUNNERS.

(From *L'Armée Tunisienne*, by Commandant R.DREVET, 1922, Weber Editions)

In Belgium

The regiment is embarked by car, they are given a few days respite and are then sent towards Belgium; on the 28 December 1915 the battalion of the Zouaves enters the sector in front of Nieuwpoort, three and a half months, alternating with the Colonial Regiment of Laroc.

The regiment remains in the vicinity of Nieuwpoort. Its sector near this small town is the one of Lombaertsyde and Passchendaele (canal Nieuwpoort – Oudenburg).

Again it is a marshy area, a small inhospitable piece of Flanders. To clear everything is impossible but the works have been intensified. The depth of the trenches and the boyaux is increased, and they are supplied with a parapet of sandbags but many are only rickety fences. The enemy activity is almost incessant. Without there being large attacks, the regiment loses 160 men, of which thirty-one dead amongst whom three officers and three officers wounded, notwithstanding its energy and courage.

On 28 January 1916, Commander Vernois of the 4th Zouaves, appointed Lieutenant-Colonel, takes over command of the 4th Mixed Regiment. Lieutenant-Colonel Levêque is appointed head of the 142nd Regiment Infantry.

Brilliant in attack, clinging to the ground in order to persevere, ready for the ultimate sacrifice, always with the word 'valour' on their lips, the 4th Mixed Regiment of Zouaves and Gunners was worthy of the greatest ordeal.

CHAPTER THREE

THE STORY OF THE TUNNELLING COMPANIES, ROYAL ENGINEERS, DURING WORLD WAR ONE, ON THE BELGIAN COAST

NIEUWPOORT 1917

The failure of general Nivelle's (Commander-in-Chief of the French Army) plans, and the regular mutinies in the French Army, resulted in the majority of any offensive actions against the Germans resting on the shoulders of the British. This problem will be further elucidated in this chapter.

Sir Douglas Haig planned a series of ambitious operations in order to chase the enemy from the Belgian Coast.

Though this would never have had much influence on the U-boot campaign (although it would have deprived the German destroyers in the Channel of a very convenient base of operations), it would certainly have been a great success, probably the greatest of the whole war. The value of an operation, however, cannot be measured purely by its definite success.

Sir Douglas Haig

The raid on Zeebrugge on St George's Day, 1918, had a relatively small impact on the activities of the German U-boats, but was amply justified by its heartening effect on the very low moral of the Allies. The map of Flanders showed for the first time, and importantly, the 'the Messines Ridge', the hill range near Messines, which controlled the southern flank of the Ypres Salient. Once this was acquired a large attack had to be carried out just before Ypres. After breaking through the defences of the Germans, the Fourth Army would push through to the coastal area, whilst a division would disembark near Oostende. It was assumed that once the enemy forces were withdrawing, they would find it difficult to stop and take up new positions. During the preparations of this offensive (in June 1917) the British took over the coastal sector from the French. It was, without doubt, a tranquil area. The front was narrow and scant. On the one side was the sea and on the other a manmade ocean, the flooded area which had inundated part of the German advance during the first days of the war.

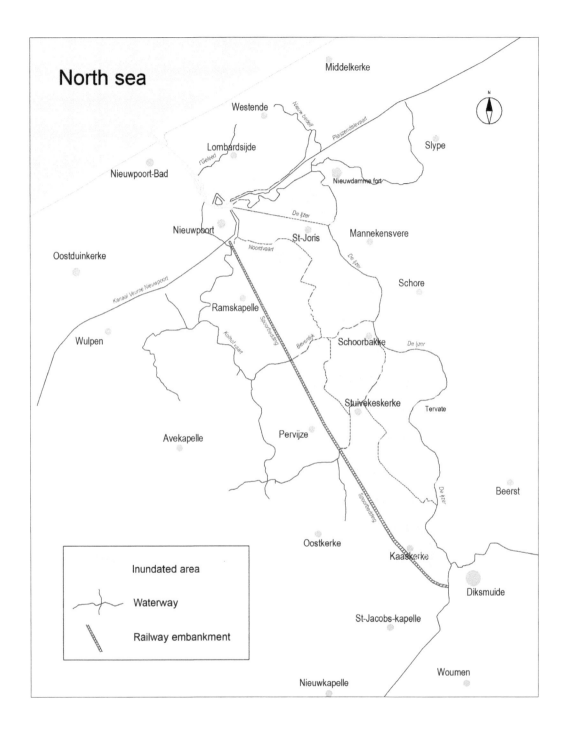

The supply line was immediately east of the Yser, across which all materials and supplies were delivered by using three wooden emergency bridges. These were also used as entrance and exit to the front lines by the troops.

An aerial photograph of the area under water

In July 1917 three Tunnelling Companies were sent to this sector: the 2nd Australian, 256th and 257th. Later the 184th Tunnelling Company followed them. The Australians immediately began offensive earthworks near 'the Grand Dune', and started to construct tunnels to and from the front in order to support the lines, as well as the mining of dug-outs for Battalion Headquarters.

The 257th Company was tasked with the construction of tunnels with the building of tunnels near Nieuwpoort town, and the 256th Company with the construction of shelters in the dunes and the sinking of wells. All this was to happen in sand, and the circumstances were totally different from those they were used to near Ypres on the other side of the front.

Everything went smoothly (apart from the fact that the British were not keen on sharing their plans with the other allied armies).

On 10 July 1917 the Germans started an extremely heavy bombardment of the sector, using 42cm calibre cannon, and paying special attention to the bridges and the system of locks and sluices.

View of the channel port

A projectile hitting the area near the destroyed lock complex

By the middle of the day these had all been destroyed, and the few surviving troops east of the Yser were isolated. The bombardment continued. By evening, after a full day of bombardment, the Germans attacked. A section of the tunnelling troops and some infantry sought shelter in a tunnel; their fate was of no importance to the Germans, who started dropping shells in the ventilation shafts and directed a flame thrower at the entrance.

D.C.M. (DISTINGUISHED CONDUCT MEDAL)

Sapper James O'Connell, an Australian, was one of the unfortunates who was severely wounded by the shells as well as by the flame throwers, but he still managed to disarm a few bombs when he managed to make his way out of the tunnel to the Yser, keeping the Germans on the bank by using some grenades. He was shot in the head and fell in the water. Nevertheless, he managed to

Demolition at the locks

get himself out of the water and to find shelter in a dugout, where his wounds were treated by Second-Lieutenant E. P. Hargraves.

The situation was now critical. Staying would mean being captured, but an attempt to escape would almost certainly mean death. Nevertheless, O'Connell decided to take a chance. In his severely wounded state he walked down to the destroyed pier of a bridge, dove into the water and swam to the other side. Just as he clambered from the water, a cry of help arose from the water. Confused by the precarious situation, he went back into the water and managed, with great difficulty, to bring the drowning person to shore, where he collapsed with exhaustion. He was then taken to a dressing station. He was awarded a D.C.M. (Distinguished Conduct Medal), which he certainly earned, for his bravery.

```
No. 2425 Spr. James O'CONNELL,
  2nd Tunnelling Coy., Aust. Engrs.

   During the attack on the 10th July 1917, East of the YSER
RIVER, he was very badly burned on the face with Flammenwerfer
was also wounded in the head, and his hands were badly torn
by shrapnel; he was lying in a dug out on the river bank
and was apparently in a very critical condition.  Late in
the evening it was apparent that the Germans had command of
the situation right down to the river bank, and it was a
question of either being taken prisoner or swimming to the
other side of the river.
   He in spite of his condition entered the water and made his
way across, and when on the far side went back into the
river to the assistance of another sapper, who was exhausted
and sinking and succeeded in bringing him to shore.
   His conduct is worthy of reward, and his example of steadine
ss and self sacrifice under extremely trying and unnerving
conditions, magnificent.
```

An important area was still being held east of the Yser. Communication was maintained by means of floating bridges made of linked cork plates. It needed acrobatic skills to cross these.

So even if the British attack on the 'Passchendaele Ridge' had been a success, it would have been extremely difficult to launch a counter-offensive on the coastal sector. Compared to others, the actions there were insignificant, but the importance of the sector was such that it could be vital. One thing was certain, a British intervention in the sector did not improve the cooperation between the Allies, and the British troops were treated with suspicion by the French and Belgian troops present. They had defended the bridgehead of Nieuwpoort for nearly three years, and the British lost it in three weeks.

In the struggle for power many forgot the underlying military efforts. The British on the one hand had meant to carry out a forward-looking offensive. The German on their side grabbed the inestimable advantage of surprise. It was also generally known that an army with a strong offensive bent tends to neglect its defence. The French had learned this lesson, as they had already experienced it to their cost. The British had been on the offensive for nearly two years and had forgotten this important fact. The German, who gave this lesson, forgot it themselves on 8 August 1918, 'the black day for the German Army'.

As a result of the abrupt stopping of the British offensive, work was now being concentrated on installing shelters and the construction of underground corridors in Nieuwpoort and Nieuwpoort-Bad. The whole area was the target of very heavy bombardments, during which much use was made of gas grenades. The British losses were considerable. One Tunnelling Company had more than a hundred casualties in one week. As the tunnels were finished and movement on the surface diminished, the German artillery lessened. 256th Company managed to sink 'elephant shelters' in the dunes. These offered bombproof accommodation to a large number of soldiers by means of a fast and cheap method, compared to the usual cut and cover trench.

The subterranean work offered colossal problems, though. The fine dry sand ran out through the smallest opening between two planks. Due to a bombardment near the place where the tunnelling was taking place, work had to cease and the end of the tunnel nailed shut in order to avoid its collapse it being filled with sand because of the shockwaves of the exploding grenades. Once a man was rendered unconscious and half covered by the sudden ingress of fine sand and it took one and a half hours to rescue him.

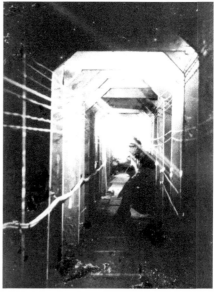

Top right: Members of the 2nd Australian Tunnelling Company carry out repairs to an obscured France 'cut and cover' covered trench in Nieuwpoort-Bad on 12 August 1917
Right: The inside of a covered trench

184th Company provided the coastal sector with dug-outs, from Nieuwpoort to La Panne. The Australians undertook a number of test drillings on both sides of the Yser and determined the suitability of the subsoil for possible tunnels under the river. The suitable *bleu* clay was found at a depth of 24 metres, but the tunnel was never started.

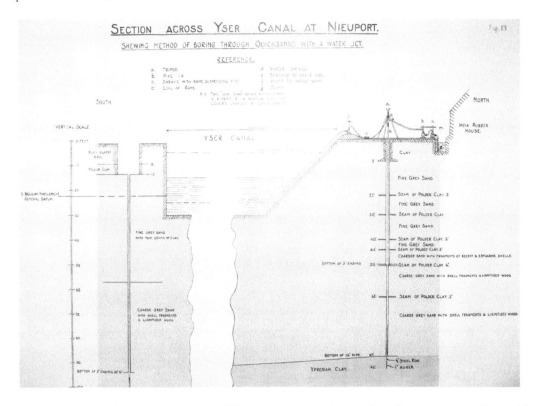

Working in the dunes was very troublesome, because the sand really crept everywhere. The food was sandy, and more or less everyone had sand colic. The horses died because of the sand, and during the vivisection of one horse, 25 kg sand was found in its stomach.

When command of the coastal sector was transferred to the French in November 1917, these were surprised to see how much work the British had carried out. The artillery units especially were delighted to have bomb free shelters at their disposal. A large part of the work done by the British in Nieuwpoort was laid waste during the coastal offensive, or not maintained any further. In the mean time the British had left the sector. They were redeployed in the marshlands near Passchendaele.

The British constructions were scarcely or badly maintained, and after the war the troops left Nieuwpoort. Together with the memories of the horror and deprivations of the past years, the French also took with them the knowledge of the existence of the numerous underground constructions.

Nobody could suspect that the presence of these constructions would still cause commotions nearly eighty-five year later.

CHAPTER FOUR
THE HISTORY OF THE EAST LANCASHIRE ROYAL ENGINEERS

42ND DIVISION ROYAL ENGINEERS

After their training, the Division was deployed for three weeks in the lines near Ypres. There they were involved in the somewhat unsuccessful attack on a modest part of the front in the Salient on 6 September 1917. The 427th and 428th Field Companies also took part in this attack. Their wiring platoons were tasked to equip the new front with barbed wire fences as soon as the capture was confirmed. Unfortunately, the front did not reach the planned site and the sections of the Royal Engineers responsible for the fences were not deployed.

A heavy gas bombardment of Ypres took place during the night of 5 September 1917. Most of the grenades landed on and around the fortifications near the Menin Gate. As the 427th and 428th Field Companies had their joint quarters in dug-outs in the fortifications very near to this point, they found themselves in the centre of the attack.

Dug-outs of the 427th and 428th Field Companies in the fortresses near the Menin Gate in Ypres

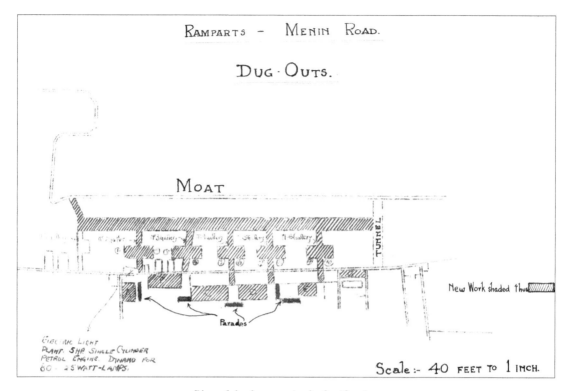

Plan of the dug-outs in the fortifications

It was their first experience of mustard gas. It was noted that the effects of the gas only became fully clear on the day after the attack, when it did not blow away but the clouds lingered for a considerable time. The dug-outs were equipped with gas resistant curtains and no signs of illness caused by the gas were noted in the troops who had been inside the dug-outs during the attack. The troops who were outside during the attack, or who had emerged shortly afterwards, did not suffer any effects from the gas as they were all wearing gas masks. The men who were on duty near the dug-outs next day did not used respiratory protection and subsequently suffered from the effects of the remaining mustard gas.

One had the impression that the 42nd Division had been sent to Ypres in order to take part in a tremendous attack, and for a while this was indeed the plan. Whether the losses of the 125th Brigade on 6 September changed the plans is not known, but the 42nd Division was never a part of an attack in this sector. On 18 September, they were relieved by the 9th Division and retreated behind Poperinghe (*Poperinge*), from where they took over the coastal sector from the 66th Division and the East Lancashire 2nd Line Division. On 5 and 6 October 1917, the units of the Royal Engineers were moved to the Nieuwpoort Sector where the lines were taken over from the 32nd Division. Nieuwpoort was generally known to the men as 'a sticky place' where one could be fired at around every corner.

British soldiers on their way to Nieuwpoort on the Veurne-Dunkirk canal

In view of the large number of bridges which had to be repaired on an ongoing basis, the work of the Royal Engineers at Nieuwpoort was heavy and exhausting.

Condition of the locks at the end of the war

In the summer, during quiet moments when one could afford silliness and amusement at the cost of those who landed in the water from the bridge, the work was pleasant.

Moment of relaxation during the summer. Engineers take a dive in the fresh water at Nieuwpoort

A water polo match in the Veurne-Dunkirk canal

In October and November it was a lot less pleasant to fall in the water, and the work had to continue during all types of weather and under enemy artillery attacks. The 428th and 429th Field Companies each had the supervision of more than thirty bridges of varying sizes.

The reason for this enormous number of bridges is easy to understand when one looks at the map of Nieuwpoort and the surrounding area.

Nieuwpoort is nearly totally surrounded by canals, and to the north east of the town is the Ganzenpoot, where six streams flow into the harbour channel. In 1917, the current 'Long Bridge' had not yet been built, and the road from Oostende to Nieuwpoort crossed the six streams of the Ganzenpoot. Notwithstanding the fact that there were six bridges, the British knew the area as 'Five Bridges'. No one ever found out what the cause or reason for this name was. To the south and west of the town lay the Koolhof-canal, which was used to drain the lower laying farms and fields, and which flowed into the harbour channel at low tide through sluices and locks northwest of the town.

In order to reach Nieuwpoort from the land side, the Koolhof canal had to be crossed, and in order to reach the forward lines from the town, the harbour channel had to be crossed, or the detour via the Ganzenpoot, 'Five Bridges', had to be made.

A floating bridge had been installed across the harbour channel, connecting the front lines with the north of the town. This was used as the main route for the transport of troops. The bridges

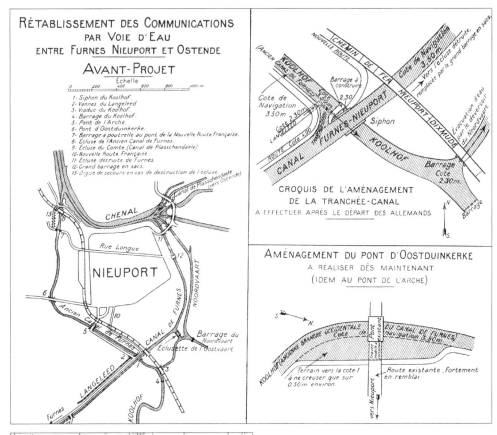

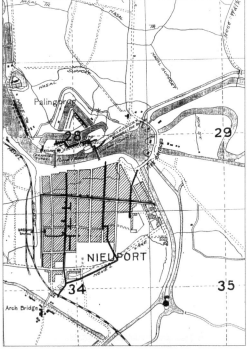

at the Ganzenpoot were only occasionally used. The Brigade which occupied the lines to the north east of the town had a wider choice of lines of supply.

The work done by the Royal Engineers in this sector was usually carried out under the most difficult circumstances, causing various victims to fall during the works. The 429th Field Company did have the situation in hand at first, but when they were all later charged with the repair of the three pontoon bridges across the harbour channel, and also given other tasks for which they seemed most suitable, some jobs had to be given to the 427th Field Company.

Map of the Ganzenpoot ('five bridges')

The Koolhof canal

North bridge over the Koolhof canal

A soldier of the 429 Field Company Royal Engineers surveys the destruction at the lock complex,
'de Ganzenpoot', 1917

Each of the three Field Companies present in the area took on a part of the works in concrete, and needed large supplies of building materials for the building and repairing of the bridges. As a consequence the number of supply vehicles sent to Nieuwpoort each night was enormous.

Apart from supplies and materials for the Royal Engineers, these vehicles also contained the rations for all units near the front. The road from Koksijde to Nieuwpoort was solid with transports from dusk till midnight, when all the vehicles, now empty, returned. This road had to take a large number of artillery barrages during the day as well as during the night, but the transport columns were never substantially damaged. Those trying to cycle down this road in the dark while it was full of transport vehicles, soon discovered that this was one of the nightmares of the war.
Most of the main streets of the town of Nieuwpoort had covered trenches, installed by the French, which ran almost the full length of the street.

Trucks bringing material for the construction and repair of pontoon bridges

German shelling of the coastal road from Nieuwpoort - Oostduinkerke, just past Groenendijk

A view of the covered trenches in the Sint-Jacobsstraat in Nieuwpoort. The photo was taken in the direction of the city with its back to Yser (inset: the place where the previous photo was taken, today)

The same covered trenches with the entrance at the intersection of the Langestraat and the Sint-Jacobsstraat in Nieuwpoort. The photo was taken in the direction of the Yser (inset: the place where the previous photo was taken, today)

These were put in place so people did not have to use the streets, which were often perilous. Some streets did not have trenches, such as the Valkenstraat (Falcon Street) which led to Crowder Bridge (a temporary pontoon bridge which had been installed across the harbour channel in order to connect the town with the Redan). Walking down this street one got the most unpleasant feeling of being spied upon, as the street ran towards the enemy lines.

Fortunately many of the houses in Nieuwpoort were very sturdily built, and living in their cellars and basements was relatively safe. The warehouse which the 427th Field Company took over was an old gunpowder store, with enormously thick walls and roof, meaning the whole building was impervious to bombing and that they could live in it without having to worry about finding suitable basements.

Above: German prisoners of war near a shelter to the left of the old gunpowder magazine Bombproof
Below: The Sints-Laureinstoren, 'Devil's Tower', with the old gunpowder magazine to the left, before the war

Bombproof in 1918

Middle left: The actual Bombproof

Middle right: Inside view of the ground floor

Left: Interior view of the floor

A similar building was known as the 'India Rubber House' (the population of Nieuwpoort knew it as the 'Caoutchou') which was the remains of the old fortifications around the town. It was situated on the other side of the harbour channel (the current location of ''t Zand') and its name was due to the fact that the shells seemed to bounce off the building. It was in use as the headquarters of one of the frontline battalions of the Brigade on the left.

The 'Caoutchou' during the war

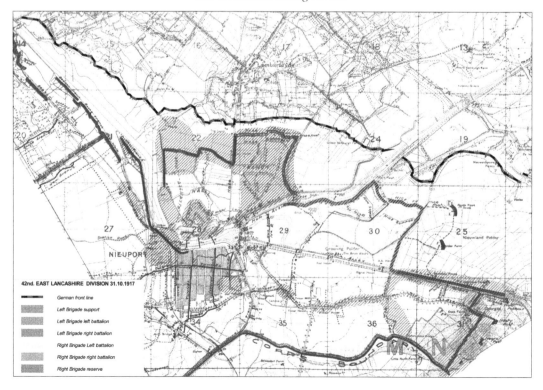

The 42nd Division was relieved on 18 November 1917 by a French Division, and the three Field Companies were relieved by the 42nd Régiment du Génie (French Engineers). A long march followed, ending at the 'La Bassée' Sector, where the 42nd Division relieved the 25th Division. Being stationed in this sector varied from two and a half months, as for the 429th Field Company, to three and a half months for the 428th Field Company. In this sector they undertook the most practical work ever undertaken on the French border. The work at Nieuwpoort mainly consisted of maintenance, which was interesting for a while, but soon started to get boring even under the most positive circumstances. The artillery barrages in the 'La Bassée' sector were less heavy than in Nieuwpoort and a lot of new work had to be done. Even before the arrival of the 42nd Division in the area at the end of November 1917, it was suspected a large enemy attack would take place during the coming months. As this area had little or no bombproof shelters, the immediate large-scale building project of such shelters was started.

427TH FIELD COMPANY ROYAL ENGINEERS

The Divisional Royal Engineers were relieved by the 9th Division Royal Engineers (Scots) on 17 September 1917. The Company came to the Nieuwpoort sector by train and on foot, and were quartered near Brandhoek, Sint Jan-ter-Biezen, Couthouf Farm and Ghyvelde, after which they arrived in Oostduinkerke-Bad on 25 September 1917.

The quarters reminded one of the Middle East, as they were situated in the middle of the dunes. They were wooden huts which had originally been built by the French troops.

The original camp 'Jean Bart' constructed by the French

ᴹ ᴹ   LA PANNE-COXYDE   La Garde du camp " Jean Bart "
ᴮʳ.

Above: The extended camp 'Jean Bart' in Koksijde, in use by the Belgian Army
Below: The camp 'Jean Bart' in Koksijde during the British occupation in 1917. The camp was located along the
R. Vandammestraat where the quarters of the air base are now situated

Above: Panorama of the quarters in the dunes in Koksijde

There were few artillery attacks because of the location, but the site was the target of various air attacks. The instructions were to build an Advanced Division HQ in the sand dunes, with cut-and-cover offices (a system of digging, shuttering and covering) which were connected to a deep dug-out, dug by a tunnelling company, shelters for the horses of a single artillery brigade, and the maintenance of the camp.

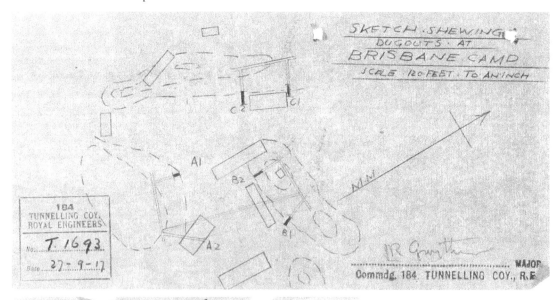

Above: Sketch of the underground quarters of 'Brisbane Camp' with a capacity of about 300 people, under the 'Witte Burg' in Oostduinkerke

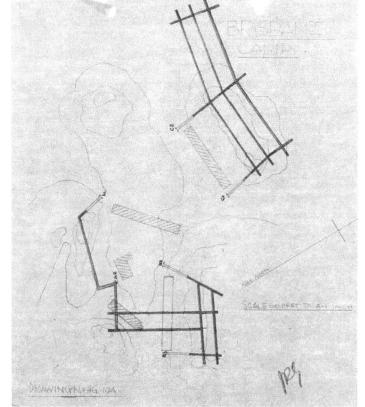

Left: Sketch of the advanced underground quarters of 'Brisbane Camp' under the 'Witte Burg' in Oostduinkerke

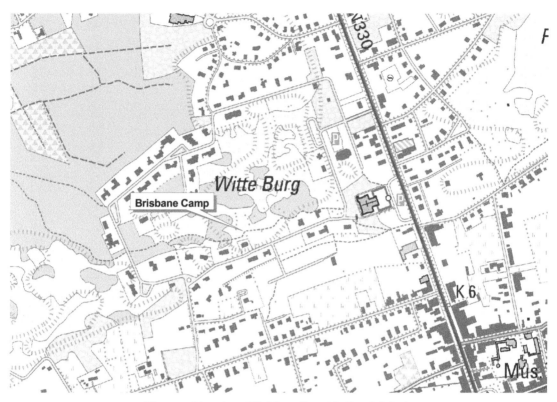

The actual location of 'Brisbane Camp' in Oostduinkerke

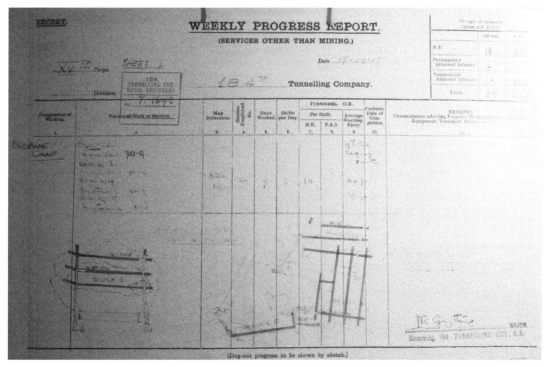

A page from the 'Weekly Progress Report' from 'Brisbane Camp' in Oostduinkerke

The Company left, without transport, for Nieuwpoort on 5 October 1917, in order to relieve the 206th Field Company of the 32nd Division. The Company was stationed in the town, all together in one building which turned out to be an old gunpowder warehouse (we are talking here about the building which is known as 'the bombproof', which was in the past a store for gunpowder), some walls of which were two metres thick and which could resist shells of any calibre. Although they worked mainly at night, the shifts were short and all troops had sufficient sleep. The men were generally healthy and the damp and cold did not cause any problems, apart from a few cases of rheumatism and trench fever. The added infantry, consisting of three officers and seventy troops, had separate quarters mainly in basements in the town. Baths and an airing room were installed after a short delay.

The horse lines were situated some 10 kilometres from the quarters, in the dunes between Koksijde and La Panne.

Major Bridge of the Royal Engineers on horseback between Oostduinkerke and Wulpen in 1917

Special measures were taken to prevent sand colic in the horses. The company were mainly required to do the maintenance and improvement of land drainage, and the strengthening of the dykes of the Yser, in order to maintain the inundation at the north east of the town, and to keep control of the tides. The area occupied by the British troops north of the Yser was cut in two parts by the road from Lombaertzyde to Nieuwpoort.

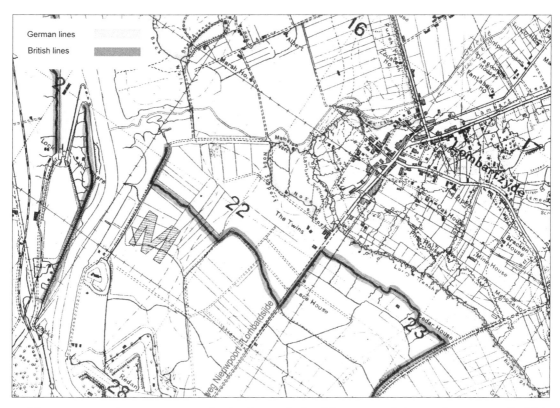

The most easterly part, rectangular in shape, drained into a canal the southern part of which was called 'Evacuation Canal of Vladslo' (known as Het Nieuw Bedelf). The front line was the northern and eastern sides of the rectangle, giving a good view of the lower fields, which could be, if necessary, flooded. The water was controlled by a lock called Bath Dam, formerly known as Bridge number 66 (lock of Het Nieuw Bedelf).

Soldiers of the 427th Field Company Royal Engineers carrying out repair works on Dam 66

The condition of the lock that was called 'Bath Dam' and previously known as Bridge No. 66 (lock of The New Bedelf) on 11 July 1917

And the condition mid-August 1917

The condition of Nieuw Bedelf in mid-August 1917

The western part of the area was drained through the former embankment moat of the Redan. The water was further drained, through a couple of smaller sluices, to the Yser. The mouth of the river Het Geleed (*Geleïde*), which lay in the middle of the British front, was heavily bombed by the German artillery which tried to divert the water in order to cause an inundation in the middle of the British lines.

Reinforced lock at the mouth of the river Het Geleed

The mouth of the river Het Geleed

To cause a serious flooding it was necessary to destroy the other sluices and locks. These constructions were therefore heavily bombed at the time of the spring tide, which occurred at the start and the middle of each month, and each time German observation balloons had noticed repairs. Hidden escape routes were designed, one from the Redan and one from the Oyster pit (Huiteries basin).

Visibility screens placed at the entrances and exits of the tunnels to deceive the enemy lookouts

Tunnels had to be dug to the sluices, in order to stay out of view of the enemy. The entrances and exits were camouflaged and all dug out earth was thrown into the water. This type of work was carried out by a Tunnelling Company of the Royal Engineers. The Hull Dam was damaged twice by enemy artillery during October, each time blocking the mouth of the sluice. This was of course repaired and the sluice was completely reconstructed using sandbags. The York Dam had just been finished by the 206th Field Company and was also completely built out of sandbags. The opening of the sluice mouth was 65 x 65 centimetres. The western side of the sluice wall was connected to a dyke by a wall of sandbags. It was pierced only once by shelling, but soon repaired so that only a small amount of the water of the Yser could penetrate into the Redan.

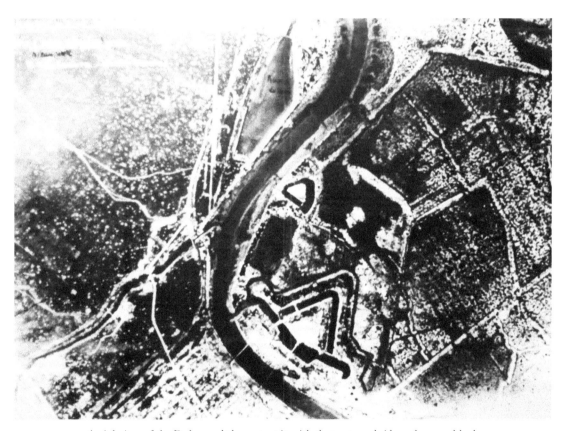

Aerial view of the Redan and the oyster pit with the pontoon bridges, dams and locks

On 17 October 1917, while the construction of the enclosure in reinforced concrete was going on, the Bath Dam (No. 66) was taken over by the 429th Field Company. The sluice was shelled with 20 centimetre-calibre grenades on 31 October. These made a breach of 5 metres across and 2 metres deep, causing the fields to flood all the way to the trenches of the third line. The breach was quickly closed with sandbags, forming a dam of 3.5 metres width at the bottom and 1.8 metres at the top.

The result of the heavy German shelling

During the repair of this breach, the C.R.E., Lieutenant Colonel D. S. MacInnes, insisted on taking command of one of the relief groups, and it was mainly through his fine example of cold-bloodedness and courage that the breach was closed before the rapidly rising tide had a chance to do even more damage. Lieutenant Mellor was awarded the Military Cross for his outstanding organisation of the repairs whilst under continual fire. Corporal F. E. Taylor and Lance-Corporal J. Mullany were also awarded military honours.

It was decided to start building the Mellor Dam on the tidal side of the Bath Dam. Due to its positioning this could not be seen by the Germans and could only be observed from the air. The design was a dam built from sandbags resting on a raster of steel girders. The top layer of girders was put in parallel with the direction of the stream, so the water could flow in between them. The spaces between the lower girders were filled with rubble.

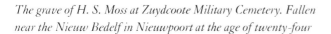

The grave of H. S. Moss at Zuydcoote Military Cemetery. Fallen near the Nieuw Bedelf in Nieuwpoort at the age of twenty-four

In total about 22,000 sandbags were used for the construction of this dam, which was mainly built during the night by 15 Royal Engineers and 150 infantry troops. Various victims fell during the works, amongst whom Sergeant Moss, an invaluable commanding officer. He died on 5 November 1917 at the age of twenty-four. He is buried at the Zuydcoote Military Cemetery in Northern France.

Zuydcoote Military Cemetery in Northern France

15 November 1917 was a clear day, giving the Germans the chance to carry out aerial observations. As a result both the Bath Dam and Mellor Dam were blown up by heavy and concentrated shellings. During the same night, an attempt was made to repair the damage to the dams, but the work was seriously hindered by the high tide. This meant the dams had to be handed over with severe damages to the French troops who had arrived to relieve the British.

On 3 November 1917, the York Dam came under fire and was heavily damaged, but Lieutenant Eastwood, together with a large group of men and 2,000 sandbags, managed to close the breach that same night, and to get the sluice back in working order. Nevertheless, the York Dam and the Hull Dam came under heavy fire on 13 November and were put out of commission, but the ruined chunks of masonry formed a new dam, although less effective than a sluice. The drainage of the Redan was now completely dependent on the tunnelled sluice.

In the course of this month Second Lieutenant Arkieson joined the Company. The repairs and clearing of the drainage channels up to the front lines were undertaken, which greatly improved the general living conditions in the trenches.

Lord Athlone, Brigade Major, and Lt-Colonel A.C. Macdonald (Royal Engineers) on inspection near the Koolhofvaart in Nieuwpoort in 1917

Water level indicators were placed, which were checked at regular intervals. They were of great help to the maintenance teams to assess the level of damage done by enemy artillery.

On 18 November 1917, all the works were handed over to the French Engineers and the British troops were lodged in the camp where the horses they used for pulling the Decauville rail carts were kept, near the windmill between Koksijde and La Panne.

Shortly thereafter, the Company, together with the 125th Brigade, left on foot for the area around Béthune and arrived at Le Préol on 29 November. There they took over from the 106th Field Company Royal Engineers of the 25th Division.

429TH FIELD COMPANY ROYAL ENGINEERS

The experiences of the 429th Field Company Royal Engineers in Ypres was limited to three weeks, but that was sufficient for them to realise what a desperate place it was. There were no events of any importance during their stay in Ypres. The use of the motorbike, which was usual for Field Companies in that area, formed a continuous source of relaxation for Colonel Lawford. He could usually be found with a valve in one hand and a socket wrench in the other. Conversations with him usually concerned carburettors more than camouflage, and oil pumps more than military maps.

Most of the work consisted of clearing old German dug-outs, which was a terrible job as they were in a dreadful state.

After Ypres, the next place they were sent to was the coastal sector. The Company HQ was set up in Nieuwpoort-Bad. where they took over the duties of the 66th Division. The quarters were in relatively good condition and were located in cellars and basements of hotels and such, which were all connected to each other by means of tunnels. These were accessible from a covered trench about two kilometres long, which ended at a depot of the Royal Engineers. There was talk about an advance in the near future with a view to taking part in the crossing of the Yser. A group led by Lieutenant Hughes went to Veurne to practise placing pontoons in the canal there, and the use of gas masks. After a while there was no more possibility of an advance and in early October 1917 the 429th Field Company Royal Engineers left for Nieuwpoort town, relieving the 32nd Division, while the 41st Division took over the coastal sector.

They stayed in the Nieuwpoort sector for six weeks. The company was quartered in barracks along the railway line which had been built by the French.

Railway track incorporating living quarters

Actual photo of the former railway bridge

Places that were built by the Belgian Army along the railway between Nieuwpoort and Diksmuide

*The railway strip today with the remains
of the barracks*

The remains of a shelter

Fortunately these shelters were robustly built and had thick, strong roofs, as they were often the subject of long and heavy artillery barrages. The arrival of rations during the evening was often the favourite moment for the Germans to show their hatred, and it was a very difficult time for the drivers of the supply vehicles. The whole length of the road from Koksijde (where their was once donkey tracks) to Nieuwpoort was the target of enemy fire, but no serious incidents ever took place. The 429th Field Company Royal Engineers were lucky. It was sometimes by the smallest of margins, as during the night the supply vehicles arrived and were heavily shelled during the unloading near the company HQ. Lance-Corporal J. Robinson, who supervised the unloading, was later awarded the Belgian Croix de Guerre for his actions during this time.

When Corporal Hamilton arrived with his load of rations, he was unfortunate in having chosen a bad night. A splinter from a grenade sheared across the side of this face while he was waiting at the Company HQ. Colonel Lawford and the Company Sergeant Major were nearby, and while he ran over to them he shouted, in a panic: 'What should I do? What should I do?' 'What you should do,' said the CSM while laughing 'is to wash it off'. 'It is all very well for you to stand there laughing,' said Corporal Hamilton, 'but I have been hit in the face.'

Two British soldiers carry a wounded person near the lock complex in Nieuwpoort; on the right Capt. Robert Thys, Belgian Engineers Company

Corporal Stafford Charles Mort, 429 Field Company,
Royal Engineers, aged 37

Lance-Corporal David Wright, 429 Field Company,
Royal Engineers, aged 17

The 429th Field Company Royal Engineers had only been in Nieuwpoort for one day when they lost Corporal Stafford Charles Mort and Lance-Corporal David Wright, a loss they could not really afford. Corporal Mort was an extremely good NCO and had shortly before been transferred from Section No. 4 to No. 1 to serve as acting Section Sergeant. Apart from the fact that Wright had not long been a Lance-Corporal, he was one of the most promising junior NCOs. Together with Lieutenant Hughes they were visiting a patrol which was tasked with observing the bridges which were the target of enemy attacks, reporting any damage, carrying out of small repairs, etc.

While walking through a trench the whole group was nearly blown out of it by an exploding shell just behind them. Lieutenant Hughes survived with minor cuts and was only shortly out of action, but the other two were killed on the spot.

They were buried at Koksijde the next day.

Today Corporal Stafford Charles Mort and Lance-Corporal David Wright are still buried at the Koksijde Military Cemetery, along the Robert Vandammestraat at Koksijde. Both died on Saturday, 6 October 1917 at Nieuwpoort.

The accompanying infantry at Nieuwpoort was not quartered with the Company, but were stationed in the town, in a building with sturdy basements. Fortunately there was no shortage of such buildings but it was still an unpleasant town to live in.

In general, the works at Nieuwpoort were probably the most tiring the Company ever carried out. Its task was to do the upkeep of a number of bridges, of which the most offensive were three horrible little floating pontoons made from cork floats and duckboards.

Because these bridges were vital for maintaining the front line they regularly underwent heavy firing by enemy artillery, and as they were about a hundred metres long they were easily damaged. Almost not a single day went by without a bridge here or there being damaged, and even if they were not there was enough maintenance work to do to keep them usable. Night time bombardments often caused heavy damages to bridges and dams, requiring the men to get up in the middle of the night in order to carry out repairs. When going to bed they were never assured of a god night's sleep.

The three bridges across the harbour channel at Nieuwpoort, known as Putney, Crowder and Vauxhall bridges, as well as a whole series of other bridges had to be kept open at all cost.

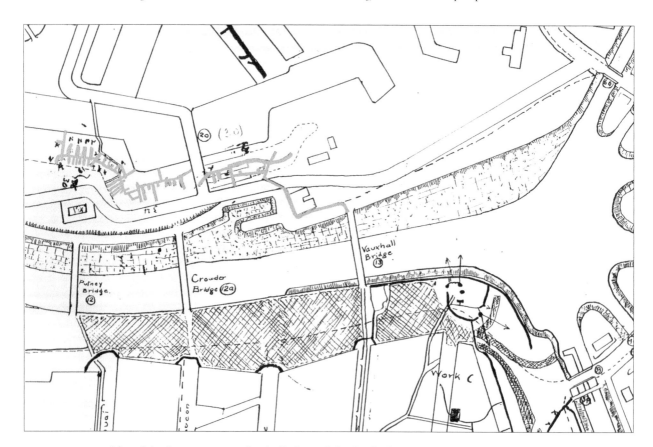

Map of the dugout system under the Redan and floating bridges Putney, Crowder and Vauxhall

Aerial view of Nieuwpoort in early 1917 with already two of the three floating bridges over the Yser

The other bridges were not the subject to such heavy firing as the three across the harbour channel.

Lieutenant Nicolson was awarded the Military Cross, and Corporal Brightmore, Sappers Rylance and Bennet were awarded the Military Medal for repairs under heavy enemy fire on a day all three bridges were damaged. On Friday, 9 November 1917, Sapper Galpine was lost, killed during the repairs to one of the bridges. He is buried at the Koksijde Military Cemetery.

One day Vauxhall Bridge was out of use and it was necessary to stretch a cable from one bank of the Yser to the other in order to carry out repairs. Such a bridge was made from four gables that were stretched over the water to which the pontoons were fastened.

Sapper Harold Galpine, 429 Field Company,
Royal Engineers, 42 years

Crowder bridge over the Yser. Note the construction consisting of four cables stretched over the water that hold the pontoons in place

All cables of Vauxhall Bridge were broken. Sapper T. Wright volunteered to swim across with a rope. It was certainly not a pleasant task, in view of the temperature of the water, but he managed to reach the other side and the works could be started. These could now be finished much earlier than planned.

A diary was kept of all damages to the bridges and of all repairs carried out, recording all artillery attacks, damage sustained and repairs, on a day to day basis.

Another task which was just as unpleasant was the maintaining of Dam 66 (Het Nieuw Bedelf) which they soon had to hand over and which was taken over by the 427th Field Company, which lost several men there.

Apart from the activities mentioned above, the 429th Field Company R.E. had built a sort of rope walk across the Yser. One day in October, Lance Corporal Edsforth noted, to his surprise, that halfway across the rope walk the water reached his knees. The reason for this was the men who were tasked to pull up the ropes. Because of the heavy shelling they thought it too dangerous to continue working and left the Lance Corporal in the middle of the river.

The Company sustained a number of wounded at Nieuwpoort, but these were usually lightly wounded.

Colonel Lawford and Sapper Spaven were awarded the Belgian 'Croix de Guerre' for their work during their stay at Nieuwpoort.

The 429th Field Company Royal Engineers left Nieuwpoort on 19 November 1917 and handed the sector to the French.

Great Boogaerde Farm, Koksijde

Barracks near Ten Bogaerde Farm, Koksijde

CHAPTER FIVE
THE 135TH SIEGE BATTERY

In July 1917, the Fourth Army moved to the Belgian coast to take over the front line between Diksmuide and the North Sea, which was held by the French and Belgian armies. The front line ran north of Diksmuide along the Yser to St-Joris, and from there east of Nieuwpoort to the sea. The reason for this change was because the British, together with the British Navy, were planning an attack from here to connect with the planned offensive from Ypres (Passchendaele) and force a breakthrough towards the North Sea (Operation Hush). If successful, it might justify the hard fighting and probable heavy casualties.

The XV Corps were holding the front line and their Heavy Artillery ('HA') headquarters was located in Oostduinkerke, about twenty kilometres north-east of Dunkirk.

The 135th Siege Battery ('the Battery') left Arras on 7 July 1917 and arrived the following afternoon in Dunkirk, where they rejoined their Commanding

Major-General Sir Gerard Moore Heath

Panoramic view of the dunes between Koksijde and Nieuwpoort

Ten Bogaerde Farm, Koksijde

Officer, Major C. P. Heath who had travelled by car. The guns and their caterpillars were unloaded on site, and moved to De Panne before nightfall. Later that evening the men were transported in lorries to the HA tented, rest camp located in the grounds of 'Groot Boogaerde Farm' (now Ten Bogaerde Cultural Centre) about 2.5 kilometres south-west of Koksijde.

The coastal strip between Koksijde and Nieuwpoort is comprised mainly of dunes sand. The dunes strip is about 1.5 kilometres wide of very uneven terrain with high dunes and deep hollows.

Upon joining the XV Corps, the Battery was posted to the 34th Heavy Artillery Brigade. A battery position had already been selected by the Brigade, located behind a row of dunes known as the 'Blekker'. These dunes ranged in height from twenty to thirty metres. Another battery had started to construct two new gunpits, under cover of yellow sheeting to camouflage the work from hostile aerial observation. Today, this location can be found in the 'Ter Yde Reserve' adjacent to Cottagelaan, Koksijde.

Pulling the heavy guns over the long sand strip promised to be a difficult task. There were two possible routes. Taking the coastal road towards the Blekker involved negotiating a relatively short strip of sand, but it also meant that everything had to be pulled over the dunes. This was rejected in favor of the alternative, namely, pulling the guns along the Oostduinkerke – Nieuwpoort road, a distance of about one and a half kilometres, over sand, but which was largely flat and held firm in places by strips of grass.

To reduce the weight of the guns and minimise the risk of accidents, it was decided to dismantle each gun-barrel and carry them separately on a 9.2 gun-wagon. The dismantling of the guns was

Three British officers observe the Nieuwpoort-Oostduinkerke coastal road during German shelling

carried out in De Panne by a party of soldiers under the command of Lieutenant Wood. However, there was a nasty accident, which resulted in the loss of a very dedicated and resourceful Sergeant-Major, Battery Sergeant-Major Falconbridge. The rope of the hoist snapped whilst one of the gun-barrels, weighing a few tons, was being lifted and it fell on the Battery Sergeant-Major's foot. He suffered serious fractures and had to be evacuated to base camp and from there to England.

On 9 July, the men who were not deployed in De Panne were sent to the Blekker to take over construction of the two gun-pits and lay the platforms. Others unloaded lorries at the site where stores were transferred on to a Decauville railtrack and transported to within 180 metres of the gun-pits. All of this work had to continue despite the area around Koksijde and Oostduinkerke being subject to constant shell fire. As if this shell fire was not dangerous enough, 500 crates of ammunition arrived for unloading, but still the men had to continue working throughout the night, pushing and pulling carts to and from the battery position. Enemy shell fire increased as the night progressed and a large number of gas shells were fired into the dunes. The gas worried the men and and work had to be stopped for a time and gas-helmets worn. When the enemy became so active during the night it usually preceded an attack.

The following morning the Germans attacked the British lines between Nieuwpoort and the

A heavy gun is pulled to the front by a caterpillar in Trones Wood near Longeval, France. A similar gun and tractor were used at Koksijde

COXYDE-BAINS -   CAMP FOCH ,, CORPS DE GARDE ET BATTERIES

Rest Camp in Koksijde

COXYDE-BAINS - " CAMP FOCH ,, - BARAQUEMENTS

Rest Camp in Koksijde

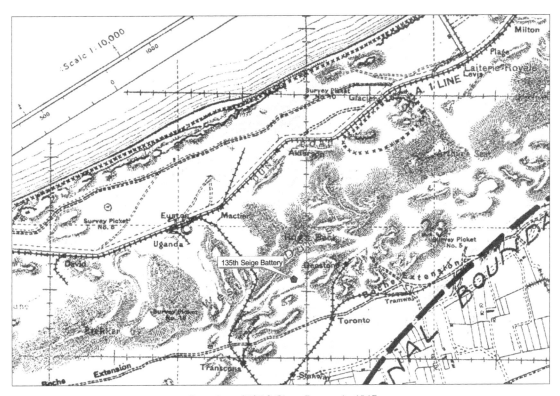

Location of 135th Siege Battery in 1917

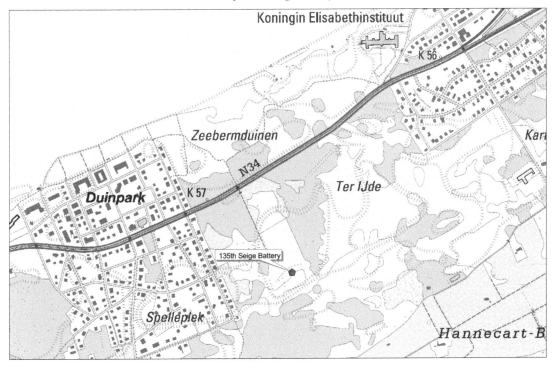

Present day location of 135th Siege Battery

In the dune-cover of the 'Ter Yde' Reserve are the remains of dug-outs of the 135th Siege Battery

View from Nieuwpoort towards the former position of the 135th Siege Battery

sea. Except for the Divisional Artillery, the British had few guns in position, made worse since the French artillery had withdrawn a week earlier. The enemy attack was overwhelming, and there was little support available for the British infantry. At Nieuwpoort-Bad, north of Lombardsijde, the enemy attack almost wiped out the British forces and succeeded in pushing the line back across to the other side of the Yser. Further inland to the south of Lombardsijde the enemy attack was repulsed. The British maintained their original lines as well as holding the town of Nieuwpoort (Operation Strandfest).

The following night, the Battery's guns came up into position. They were each pulled by two caterpillars from the road to the gun-pits in the dunes.

Using two caterpillars in this way, the four guns were brought to within a few metres of their platforms. The caterpillars could do no more because of the final steep slope at the edge of the gun-pit. The guns were now camouflaged and the caterpillars sent back to De Panne, while the working party used the remaining time to cover the caterpillar tracks in the sand. It was far too risky to do any work on the guns and gun-pits during daylight, so after a few hours of rest, the men had to undertake 'shell duty'. Some of the men were loading and unloading ammunition onto trucks and pulling them along the Decauville track; other men were employed in the very heavy work of carrying, or in some cases with shells of larger calibre rolling the ammunition all the way from the narrow-gauge to the gun-pits, a distance of approximately 350 metres.

There was only one hoist and so it took two nights to mount the guns and fix them onto their platforms. On the second night, the caterpillars came up to remove the 9.2 gun-carriages. This involved some delay and the task was only just completed a short time before daybreak. Whilst hurrying to camouflage the gun-pits and obliterate the caterpillar tracks in the sand, a low flying German bomber, returning from a raid, noticed the British, and dropped a number of bombs as he flew over. During this bombardment, three men were injured, Gunners Crewe, Hughes and Mitcheson.

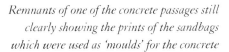

Remnants of one of the concrete passages still clearly showing the prints of the sandbags which were used as 'moulds' for the concrete

The Battery environment still shows the traces of heavy damage. The place is covered with shell fragments of all calibres as can be seen below

That night, 'the Right Section', under the command of Captain Phillips, arrived at the rest camp.

The following day, the Right Section went to the Blekker to prepare two gun-pits for their guns. These were to be located about 500 metres further to the rear of the 'Left Section'. The track from Oostduinkerke-Bad to the gun-pits was fairly safe and so it was decided not to dismantle these guns for transport, but to bring them to their positions in their entirety.

On the night of 14/15 July 1917, the guns were moved to their positions, once again using two caterpillars to pull each gun across the sand to its platform. Both guns were safely in position before dawn.

Very few dug-outs existed in this area. There were two narrow concrete passages close to the guns, which served as temporary shelters for the gun detachments.

The only other dug-out, constructed of wood and protected with tree trunks

Wireless communication aerials in the dunes near Koksijde

The location of the barracks relative to the Battery

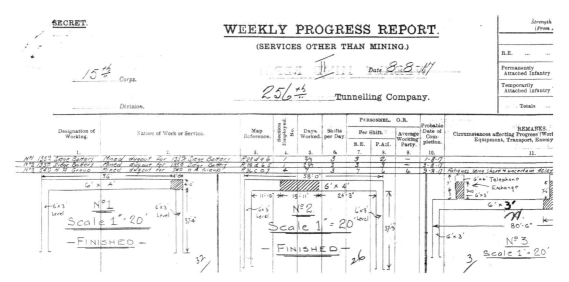

Extract from the Weekly Progress Report dated 8 August 1917 of the 256th Tunnelling Company, Royal Engineers with plans of the two finished dug-outs for the 135th Siege Battery

and sand, was used as a Brigade Command Post, with the telephone exchange and wireless station in wooden huts and the antennae all located nearby.

The remainder of the Battery was housed temporarily in a number of wooden huts about 850 metres south of the guns. These billets were regularly the target of enemy artillery and therefore were very unpleasant quarters. Safe shelters for the men were built as soon as the necessary materials became available.

In a matter of weeks, the billets were moved to 'elephant shelters' constructed in the sand about 650 metres behind the rear guns. One shelter was assigned to each detachment and one to the Signallers. The men were now relatively comfortable, but an infantry track in the vicinity often attracted enemy harassing shell fire at night. One of these shells hit a shelter when it was fully occupied with men sleeping. The entrance door was blown away and the room was completely filled with dust and smoke. When the smoke had cleared a candle was lit and it was discovered that Gunner Davis had been killed and three others wounded.

Panorama taken from the observation post 'Beer Emma' near the Nieuwendamme Creek

Ruines de Nieuport   1914-18   Tour d'observation et l'Yser vers Dixmude.
The ruins at Nieuport   Observation tower and the Yser towards Dixmude.

A similar observation post alongside the Yser

Sappers from the 256th Tunnelling Company, Royal Engineers assisted in the construction of the dug-outs located near to the guns. Galleries with two entrances were constructed under the sand dunes. These were the only really safe dug-outs, given that without skilled workers it was impossible to build anything safer than bullet or splinter-proof shelters.

The gun-pits were also in need of constant attention. Blowing sand would fill the pits and hamper access to the guns.

To prevent this happening, wooden revetments were constructed around each gun-pit, but without much success as the pressure of the sand was too great. The revetment structure that achieved most success was constructed from barrels filled with sand and strengthened with wooden beams. However, barrels were scarce and difficult to obtain so 'scrounging' was the main source.

The Observation Posts ('OP') in this sector were close to the front line, making them very interesting and frequently used. The most popular was the very high 'Beer Emma', a strong

Café de L'Yser. A concrete-reinforced observation station was built inside the ruin of this building

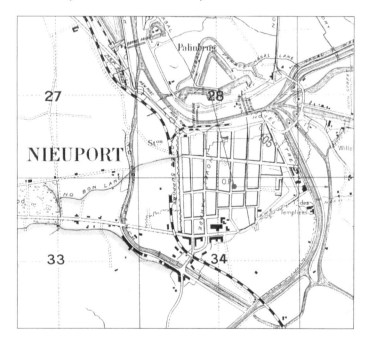

Location and field of view of one of the most important observation stations in the Marktstraat in Nieuwpoort

Panorama from the observation post in the Marktstraat

Ruines de Nieuport
The ruins at Nieuport   1914-18   Poste d'observation.
Observation post.

The notorious observation tower in the Recolettenstraat which survived the war

*Location and field of view of observation
post PP in Nieuwpoort-Bad*

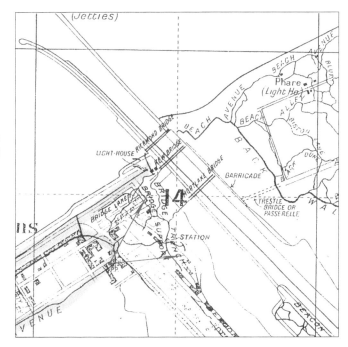

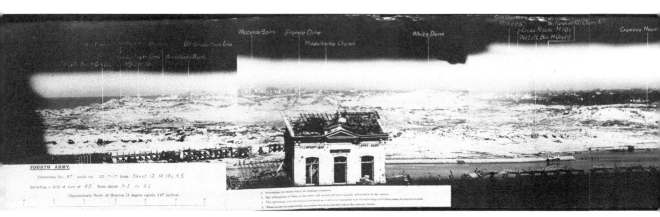

Panorama of Lombardsijde from the observation post PP

concrete tower built inside a house in Nieuwpoort and standing high above the surrounding countryside. Beer Emma provided an exceptional view of trenches and fortified houses in and around Lombardsijde and also a wide panorama of the enemy's territory.

On a clear day, it was possible to see beyond the enemy's front as far as Oostende (*Ostende*). Flashes of hostile guns could be seen quite easily and occasionally it was also possible to observe troop movements on the roads in the back areas.

Observation post PP in Nieuwpoort-Bad with dune OV behind

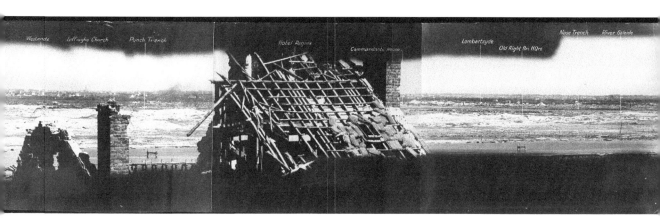

The Beer Emma observation post was almost continuously manned. It is probable that Lieutenants Allen and Wood, who were doing most of the forward observations, knew the countryside by heart!

There was an OP in Nieuwpoort with a good view of the bridges, which connected the town to the front lines (the pontoon bridges from the Quay to the Redan) and this was sometimes manned. The pontoon bridges were a favourite target for the German artillery and attracted a great deal of shell fire. This OP was not the safest to occupy. The exact location of the OP was a tower built within the ruins of Café de L'Yser.

German officers at an open artillery battery in the dunes of Westende

A British 9-inch Howitzer with officers from the Royal Engineers, near Oostduinkerke

A German Battery in Middelkerke

The British also used other observation posts namely 'PP' – a building in Nieuwpoort-Bad near the front line; 'OV'- the top of a high dune not far from PP; 'VC' – a house south of Nieuwpoort on the road to St-Joris. Communication lines were laid to most of these observation posts. Many bombardments were co-ordinated from these OPs, often using cross-observation from several OPs with great success.

The Signallers had a very difficult time maintaining the communication lines. The line to Nieuwpoort-Bad was a particular problem with the number of shells falling in and around Nieuwpoort and its approaches causing endless difficulties by cutting the lines. On 19 August 1917, the shelling was particularly heavy, but the line was never out of use for very long. This was due to the hard work of the 'linesmen' (the maintenance team of the communications lines), Bombardier Allan and Gunners Ward and Carrington. A special report of their work was sent to headquarters, which led to Bombardier Allan being recommended for the 'Military Medal'.

The following incident is typical of the fearless way in which the Signallers carried out their work. One day, the Germans shelled the Battery Communication Post. Shells were exploding all around it and after a while one hit the telephone exchange. This was an elephant shelter of curved corrugated iron in the sand, protected by a 'shell breaker' of iron rails just above it. The Major feared the worst and immediately went to see whether there were any casualties. It was a hopeless mess. The shellbreaker had collapsed, the rails were badly twisted and part of the dugout had fallen in. On clearing away the debris, the Major found Gunner Mackay in the partially destroyed shelter, smoking his pipe and busy testing the communication lines to check how many of them were 'down'!

From the beginning both sides' guns were very active. The German artillery shelled British trenches, roads and battery positions almost continuously, whilst the British executed long-range shelling of hostile batteries or significant trench systems.

The Battery also supported other front line batteries in prearranged 'crashes' (collaborative shelling) on villages and houses in hostile areas. In this way, the Palace Hotel in Westende-Bad was 'crashed' several times causing significant destruction. In this fierce artillery duel, the German batteries had a great advantage over the British because their guns were well protected in concrete bunkers, making it very difficult to damage them.

The following extracts, taken randomly from the Battery Log Book, give an idea of the work done by the Battery:

2 September 1917: Forward Observation Officer ('FOO'), Lieutenant Wood, reported an enemy Trench Mortar ('TM') firing at a slow rate at our front line near Nieuwpoort. We were given permission to engage the TM at two o'clock and it ceased firing after our fourth round. Altogether we fired fifty rounds at the TM, obtaining several direct hits, setting fire to their ammunition and causing a small explosion at about 2.20pm and a very large one at 3.30pm.

15 September 1917: Shelling of bridge north of Nieuwendamme Fort with aeroplane observation. Bridge destroyed by No. 4 gun after thirty-three rounds.

17 September 1917: Lieutenant Wood (at PP) spotted a machine-gun firing from an emplacement in a shell hole. We fired thirty-three rounds at this, the last round dropping into the emplacement and destroying it.

29 September 1917: Corporal Mauchlin went up to 'Café de L'Yser' with the Major. They spotted an undestroyed concrete shelter in the German front line. No. 3 gun was turned on to this to show the Corporal how his gun fired. The Gunners performed well and in twenty-two rounds the side of the shelter was blown in.

24 October 1917: Fired on ammunition dump at Chapelle House. After sixty-third round the dump blew up.

Gunner Kenworthy, Royal Garrison Artillery, Koksijde Military Cemetery

Gunner T. Coates, Royal Garrison Artillery, Aged 25, Zuydcoote Military Cemetery

Gunner W. H. Burgess, Royal Garrison Artillery, Aged 29, Zuydcoote Military Cemetery

The enemy did not take long to locate the 135th Battery, which was then often heavily shelled. The Battery was deliberately targeted on many occasions causing a number of casualties, including Gunners Kenworthy, Coates and Burgess who were all killed. Once or twice some of the guns were so badly damaged that they had to be sent to the Ordnance Workshops for repairs.

Occasionally, a hostile attack with heavy shelling was 'answered in kind'. Some time in early October 1917 a hostile 5.9 battery began shelling British forward positions. The Forward Observation Officer, Lieutenant Wood, was immediately informed at the Beer Emma Observation Post. He observed the 'flashes' of the hostile battery in the dunes, north of Lombardsijde. The rear section of the Battery on the Blekker was immediately turned towards it. Salvos were fired and the hostile battery was silenced.

Some time later, the Battery was undertaking a counter-battery attack with aeroplane observation, when another hostile battery, very accurately, opened fire and the men of the Battery were forced to seek cover. The pilot, seeing the plight of the British Gunners, signalled for them to wait while he went off in search of the German battery. The pilot then informed another British battery of the position of the German guns and

Remains of the Decauville track in the dunes

soon thereafter the 135th Battery could resume shooting.

Early in October 1917 both sides began to settle down and life became somewhat more peaceful. This pleased the men and as this situation seemed likely to continue, the Major decided to build an elaborate concrete Brigade Command Post fitted with 'all modern conveniences' and containing rooms for the telephone exchange and wireless station. Second Lieutenant W. D. Hooper (who came to the Battery in July 1917) was placed in charge of this assignment and he had Bombardier Waghorn and Gunner Vernon as chief assistants. A site for the construction was chosen just south of the Rear Section, in the side of a sand dune that would provide some protection. The task of cutting away the side of the dune was no easy one and precautions had to be taken to prevent the sand falling into the hole as fast as they dug it out. Timber, cement, light and heavy arc-shaped metal trusses and corrugated iron were brought up on the Decauville railway whilst the digging was taking place.

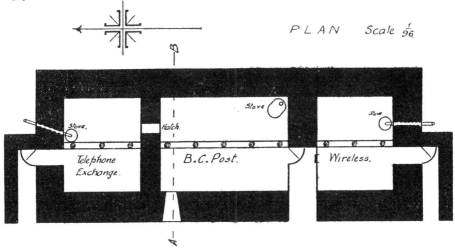

Ground Plan of the Brigade Command Post of the 135th Siege Battery

This track was specially extended to connect the main line to the building site. Once the 'hole' had been dug a raft of concrete nine inches thick, reinforced with expanded metal, was laid over the whole floor. The expanded metal sheets were turned up and short lengths of iron inserted to make a bond between the floor and the walls. Rod-iron dowels were also inserted to grip the three-inch planks on which the elephant irons were to rest. When the floor had hardened the cupolas were erected and strutted with heavy pit-props and the shuttering for the ends and walls fixed. After cutting an opening for a window and fitting the chimneys, the

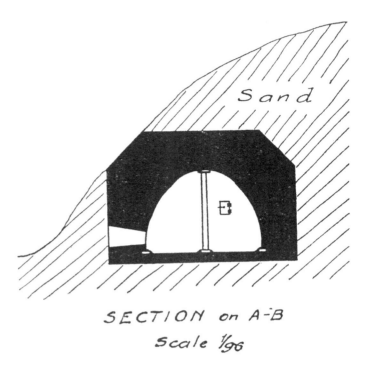

SECTION on A-B
Scale 1/96

Cross section of the Brigade Command Post of the 135th Siege Battery

structure was encased in three feet of concrete, reinforced by two layers of expanded metal. Sand to a depth of four to six feet was thrown over this as soon as the concrete had set. The sides were also covered with sand and grass planted for camouflage so that it would merged into the sand dune against which it was built.

Finally, woodwork, doors, tables and stoves were fitted into the rooms and the entire interior was painted white. This monumental work took six weeks to complete and 250 tons of concrete was consumed in the process. It was probably the finest Brigade Command Post on the Belgian and French coast. The men were therefore very pleased when they were allowed to move into the Post in November 1917.

Unfortunately, they could not enjoy the fruits of their labour for long. A few weeks later, the order was given to leave the post and an equally pleased French battery commander took over the position in early December 1917.

On 6 December, the Battery left Nieuwpoort sector and proceeded in stages to join the XIII Corps in front of Arras.

At times, the fighting had been severe and the Battery had suffered many casualties. They had done more than their share of good work and all sections of the Battery had acquitted themselves well. The Despatch Riders, Bombardier Purvis, Gunners Butcher and Chapman will always remember their time spent in the dunes. It required the highest courage and determination on their part to ride along the shell-swept roads, at all times and in all weathers.

Lieutenant Reid, Second-Lieutenants F. A. Stevens and H. Minns had joined the Battery while we were at Nieuwpoort and Battery Sergeant-Major Beaumont had come to take the place of Battery Sergeant-Major Falconbridge. Lieutenant Walters left the Battery at the end of November 1917 to join the 49th Heavy Artillery Brigade as Signal Officer.

The 135th Siege Battery was one of the many heavy artillery batteries that served in the dunes between Nieuwpoort and Koksijde. Another significant gun shelter was located near the 'Hoge Blekker' in Koksijde, which is now known as 'La Vigie'.

LA VIGIE

When General Rawlinson and the staff of the Fourth Army took control of the British sector on 8 July 1917, the French artillery had already left the area. At that time, only 176 of the 636 British artillery pieces Rawlinson needed for the offensive had arrived. The headquarters of Australian Siege Field Artillery was located in the Koksijde area. Their position was near the highest dune within the Hoge Blekker sector. Taking account of the constant hostility, both from the front line and from the air, they positioned their battery of two heavy guns just behind the Hoge Blekker summit, on the Koksijde side, to afford some protection.

The guns were each housed in a concrete bunker with the roof having a thickness of more than 2.5 metres of concrete. The guns were mounted on the chassis of train wagons and a single railtrack, protected by two concrete walls, on both sides of the track, went from the bunker almost to the top of the Hoge Blekker – today close to Fazantenparkstraat.

In view of the scarcity of artillery pieces and Rawlinson's planned offensive, which had to remain strictly secret, the existing batteries were instructed to limit their 'fire', so that the growing allied firepower was not betrayed. For these reasons, the guns on the Hoge Blekker were only taken from their concrete shelters to fire. Once outside the shelters, the guns were transported in between the concrete walls, which gave the guns protection against enemy lateral fire. Once the guns had fired their rounds on the German front near Lombardsijde, they were immediately driven back into the bunker. Because of the short rounds and the immediate movement of the guns, it was very difficult for the German observers to determine the position of the battery and to reply to the salvo.

It is not known what happened to the Battery after the departure of British and Australian troops from the sector in November 1917. The position was taken over by the French and there is no further information about the guns.

After the war, the two bunkers were stripped of all their equipment and rails. The two buildings were a tourist attraction for a while. In the early nineteen-twenties one of the two bunkers was demolished. Around 1923, contractor Remi Rys from Koksijde was commissioned to build a villa on top of the remaining bunker and to integrate the existing 'bunker construction' into the new project. The large opening, which provided access to the bunker for the gun, was adapted to a loggia with a double door and frame. By 1925 the villa was completed and because it had exceptional all-

Remains of a strong point from around the early 1920s

COXYDE. — Abris pour pièces d'artillerie.

Two bunkers of the heavy artillery battery near the Hoge Blekker.
The left bunker was demolished and the one on the right was converted to villa La Vigie

round views and the overall height of the villa, it was named 'La Vigie', which means 'The Watch'. Later, La Vigie served as an officers-mess for the Belgian Army. In this function, the building was subject to some minor changes. A garage was constructed at the left entrance to the former ammunition store and a tennis court was also installed. The ammunition storage rooms became a wine cellar and general storage room. The space where the gun once stood became a kitchen and general service space.

Coxyde-Bains La Vigie.

Villa 'La Vigie' in 1925

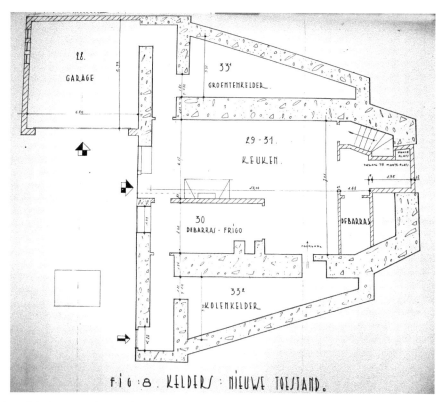

Ground Plan of the basement before the renovation of La Vigie into an officers-mess for the Belgian Army. Note the original shape of the bunker and the dimension of the concrete walls.

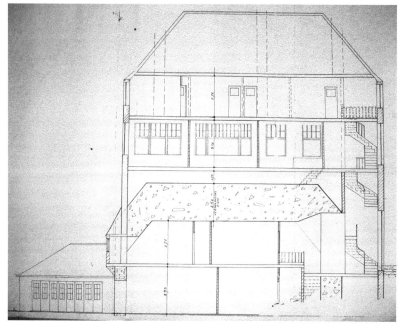

Cross section of La Vigie. Note the thickness of the concrete roof of the former bunker

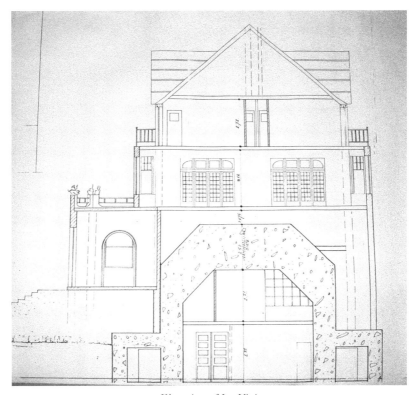

Elevation of La Vigie

La Vigie showing the original bunker

A story exists that in 1917 the Allies built a tunnel from somewhere near La Vigie to the Hoge Blekker. This tunnel would have been constructed of wood and if so, probably still exists today. In World War Two, the entrance was in a German bunker, close to the right of La Vigie (near the Overwinningslaan). In the 1980s the tunnel entrance, at that time used as a potato cellar, was sealed off by order of the person then responsible for the officers-mess because of a penetrating stench. Further research should provide more information.

La Vigie served as an officers-mess until 1993. The property then remained empty for years and has been increasingly affected by vandalism and decay. It was frequently used by the Koksijde police as a site for paintball fighting. After speculation about a possible real estate development on the site, the property was listed by the Flemish Heritage Department in 2003. In 2013, a project developer received the green light from the government to restore the villa to its former glory and integrate it into a complex of retirement flats. The project was finished in 2017.

Work in progress transforming La Vigie into a complex of retirement apartments

The transformation of La Vigie in 2017

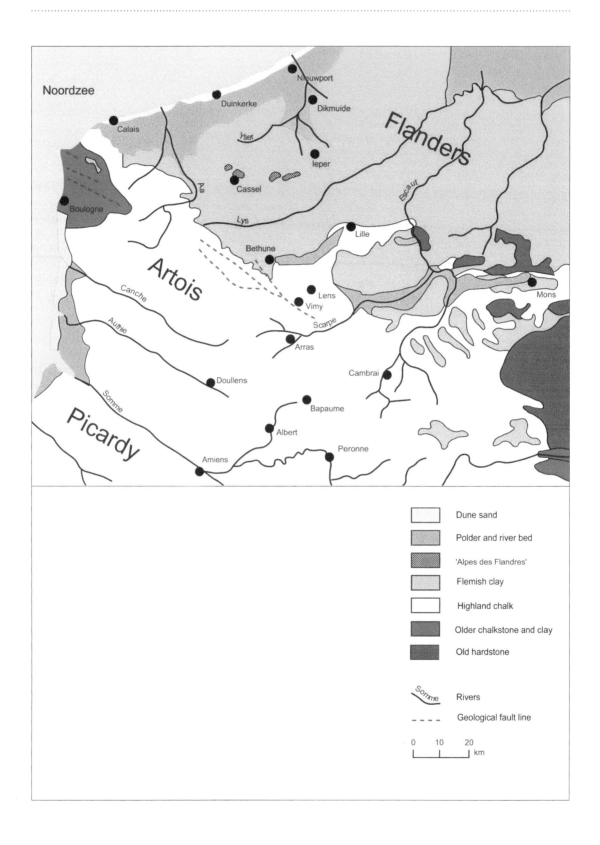

Noordzee

Calais
Duinkerke
Nieuwport
Dikmuide
Yser
Flanders
Ieper
Cassel
Aa
Boulogne
Lys
Lille
Escaut
Bethune
Artois
Canche
Lens
Vimy
Mons
Authie
Scarpe
Arras
Somme
Doullens
Cambrai
Picardy
Bapaume
Albert
Peronne
Amiens

Dune sand

Polder and river bed

'Alpes des Flandres'

Flemish clay

Highland chalk

Older chalkstone and clay

Old hardstone

Somme   Rivers

– – – –   Geological fault line

0   10   20
|___|___| km

CHAPTER SIX
TUNNELLING IN THE SAND DUNES OF THE BELGIAN COAST

This part of the book describes the work of the Tunnelling Companies in the Belgian coastal dunes, where the engineers had to cope with one the most difficult types of soil and therefore one of the most interesting on the whole Western Font.

In Nieuwpoort and the surrounding area there is a stretch of dunes 1 to 3 kilometres wide. The sea is relatively shallow at the coast and the surface of the beach climbs quickly to a ridge of sand dunes which are about 40 feet above the high water mark. These dunes offered excellent protection to the many dug-outs constructed in them. Usually there were some marshes on the land side with lines of small dunes running parallel to the coast. This was called the 'Brackpan', and most wells were built there.

The best illustration for this is the figure below. Olympus certainly stands out when it comes to size. This was a large dune, about 100 feet high, which offered an excellent position to the different observation posts built there.

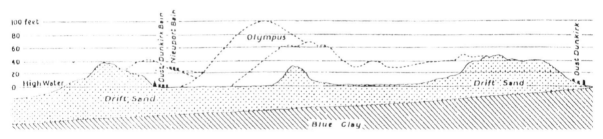

Profile of the dune area

The works in this area can easily be divided into three main categories:
1 Wells
2 Dugouts
3 Sunk Elephant Shelters.

1 WELLS

These were usually built in the 'Brackpan' as the ground water level was only between 6 inches to 1 foot below the surface. As the ground was running sand, it was necessary to use planking to shore up the sides from the top. The largest size available of the pre-made sheeting only had a diameter of 4 ft 6 in, and this was too small in view of the amount of water needed. It was decided to make

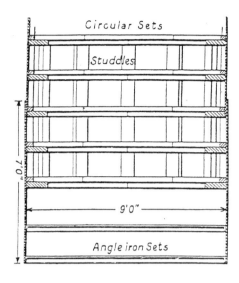

Circular Sets

Studdles

7'0"

9'0"

Angle iron Sets

PLAN OF COLLAR SETT.

7" X 4"

2'-6"

9" X 2"

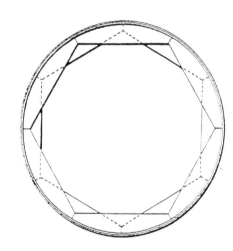

Above: Prefabricated wooden well segment

Top right: The way in which the prefabricated wooden segments for the wells were recessed is simultaneous to the system to sink segments of the shaft

Right: A variation on the system that was used for both the sinking of shafts and for the construction of wells

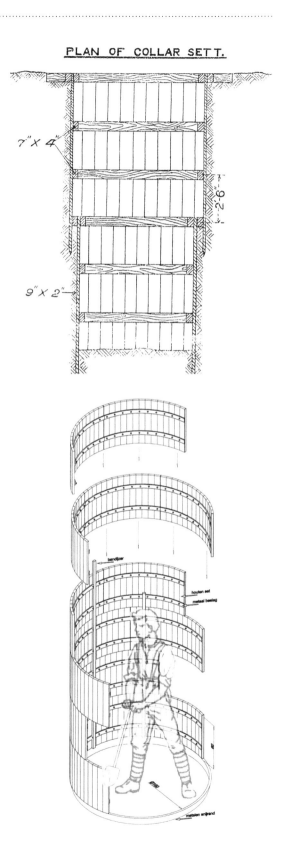

A British water well constructed from five-part wooden sections

Showing the detail of a section of a British well. Note the vertical iron band with which the different sections are kept together

A variation in the well system using steel segments

A Weekly Progress Report of the 256 Tunnelling Company Royal Engineers from the 22 August 1917, showing the different well constructions

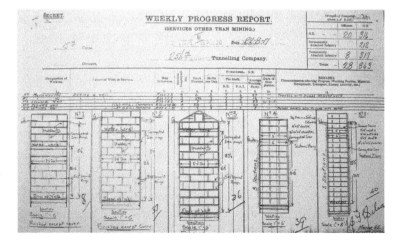

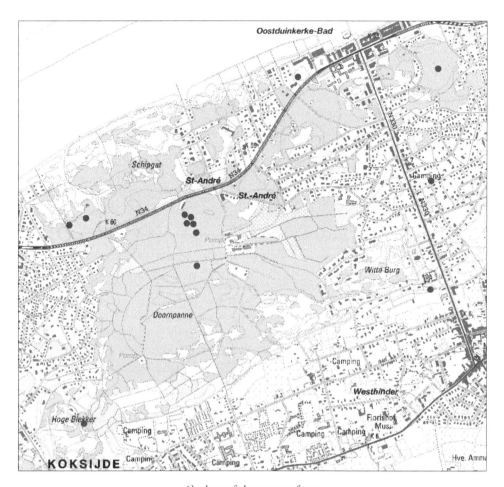

Geology of the western front

ready-to-install metal sheets. These consisted of a number of wooden circular segments (as in a cartwheel), propped up by wooden studs and covered on the outside with bent metal plates. The bottom or cutting edge was reinforced with two metal segments each fitted with two corner irons which were fixed to each other by means of bolts. The external diameter was 9 ft. Each section was 7 ft. high and fitted into the section below.

To sink the sections into the ground it had to be dug by hand. To help the sections sink they were filled with ballast, in the form of sandbags, until they were nearly full, apart from a central hole of about 2 ft in circumference. Extra weight was added using a large heavy superstructure of ground stakes and sandbags. The sand was brought up with buckets through the central opening.

The groundwater level was very high, and at first 'Dando' hand pumps were used to keep the pits dry. In some places twenty-four pumps were used in one pit, but they were defeated by the ground water at about 12 ft and the suction pipes nearly filled the central opening, making the removal of sand impossible.

Finally electric Pelepone pumps, connected to a central generator station, were used and the wells sunk to some 25 ft making about 20 ft water available.

Going deeper was impossible, as there were only two pumps available per shaft, each with a capacity of 2,000 gallons per hour, and at this depth they could only pump up water at low tide. The well pumped about 4,000 gallons per hour at high tide at a distance of some 450 metres from the sea.

When the wells had reached the appropriate depth a 3-inch thick wooden bottom plate was placed in the last wooden set in order to prevent the well silting up. About fifteen wells were sunk in this way.

A variation of this system was used for the sinking of shafts as well as for the construction of water wells. Wooden sections were prefabricated with a diameter of 160 cm and a height of 60 cm. One section consisted of five segments. These segments were conically sawed planks (the system for wooden barrels) and were kept together by metal fittings. The five loose segments were then fitted together

A similar dugout, partly emptied, in Boezinge. This 'Yorkshire Trench Dugout' construction was subsequently sprayed with foam concrete in haste and has now been completely destroyed.

with bolts and nuts until they formed a complete section. The various sections were connected to each other with vertically stretched steel strips. The lowest section had a metal cutting edge from under which sand could easily be removed. Because of the weight of the sections piled one on top of the other the construction sank into the soil until the necessary depth had been reached.

2 DUGOUTS (UNDERGROUND ACCOMMODATION)

Dugouts could only be made in dunes which stood 30 feet above the high water mark, because some 20 feet were needed for safety reasons. The galleries were 6 ft high and 3 ft wide.

Galleries and Inclines (entry points): The standard size of a gallery was 6 ft by 2 ft 6 in, widening to 4 ft for rooms. For safety reasons these could not made wider with the wood available at the time. The principle used for mining under the dunes was based on a system of piling boards and facia boards which was in use worldwide in unstable subsoil.

At first sets of 4½ and 6 inches wide were used, but later on, when the miners were more familiar with this system, sets of 11 inches wide were used in relatively wet sand. The dunes usually

The result of a partly collapsed gallery in sandy soil
(Mont Sorrel)

An example of an incline viewed from the bottom
looking up towards the exit

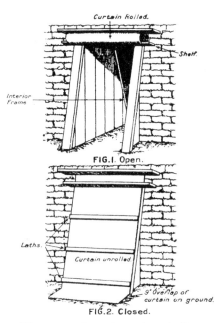

The gas-proof curtains set in an incline

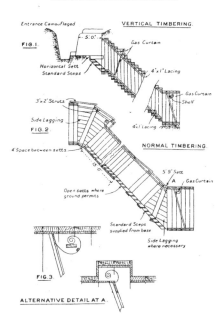

Various systems used to construct an incline to include
protection from gas

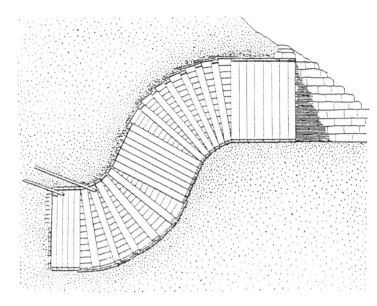

A cross-section of an incline in the side of a dune

consisted of perfectly dry sand (silver sand), which started to run from the moment it was no longer supported.

In some places it was so bad that the sand started to run like water from the smallest openings. A case was known of a man who was knocked out and whose head was covered in less than a minute by a stream of sand coming out of an opening, which could have been held closed if somebody had reached him in time. The man lay there for more than an hour, as boarding had to be built around him before it was possible to free him.

The entries were dug horizontally into the dunes until there was about 2 to 3 feet of sand above. Next the wooden boards were installed on the bottom, side walls and ceiling.

All inclines and access points to dug-outs were provided with a gas-proof curtain. This could be fitted within the construction at different points and using different methods.

The steepness of the inclined access points was kept at 60°. This was continued until the sand became damp, which was usually about 2 to 3 ft above the groundwater level. The gallery was then dug horizontally, resulting in the bottom of the gallery remaining some 6 inches above the groundwater level. That way the full height of the dune could be used.

The face boards had to be partly installed around the curve of the bottom, and then built out further. The spiling boards were placed across the first set and the edge of the previous set was lifted in order to make them more or less fit into each other. Next

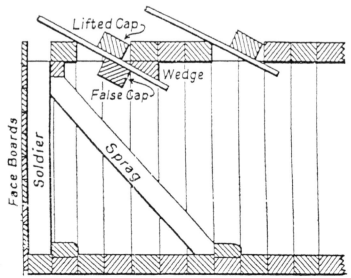

The principle of spiling

Sapper Tanner (left) and Sapper W. Bonar of the 2nd Australian Tunnelling Company during the spiling procedure under Nieuwpoort-Bad, 14 November 1917

A gallery undergoing the pinning process

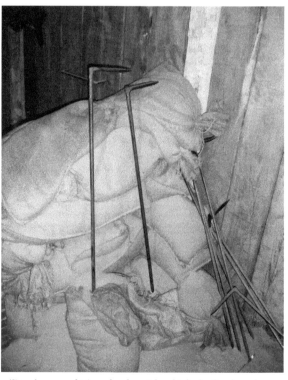

'Dogs': wrought iron hooks with which the faceboards are temporarily anchored to the side walls

SPILING

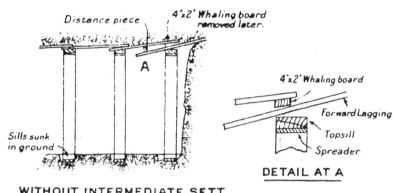

WITHOUT INTERMEDIATE SETT.

DETAIL AT A

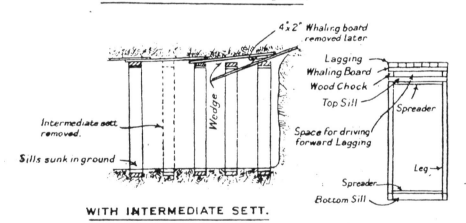

WITH INTERMEDIATE SETT.

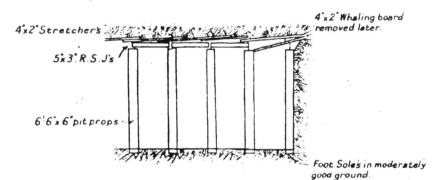

WITH PIT PROPS AND R.S.Js.

Different kinds of spiling used to adapt to the geological characteristics of the subsurface

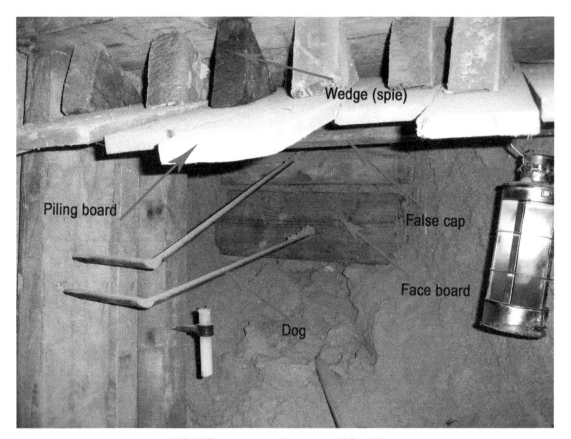

The different construction parts used for spiling

they were placed at an angle on a false cap (a temporary part of the ceiling). The latter was then fastened on a couple of planks which were temporarily nailed to the sides of the wooden structure. In this way the piling boards could be driven in further at a steep angle, until the false cap could be put under the next set and so on.

The face boards were handled one by one until there was one set width, and were then fastened with wedges. If a set was totally finished a 'soldier' (a strut) was installed against it to support the weight. Next all false caps were removed on one side and the legs quickly placed in between, kept in place by the wedges between the face boards. This operation was continuously repeated.

Most, if not all, tunnelled constructions under both Nieuwpoort Town and Nieuwpoort Bains were made in this way. The advance of the works with the spiling method was much slower than the traditional Clay-kicking, which was used in the clay subsoil around Ypres. Where the Clay-kicking could result in 15 to 20 metres of tunnel per day, spiling could only deliver 5 to 8 metres.

Shafts: In order to have observation posts or machine-gun posts it was necessary to have vertical shafts which were connected to dug-outs. Since good places to observe the enemy were also good places to be observed by the enemy, it was almost impossible to do any reconnaissance by daylight,

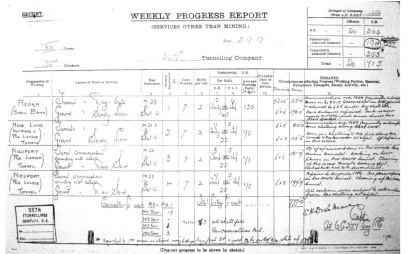

The Weekly Progress Report of the 267 Tunnelling Company Royal Engineers on 5 September 1917 records the progress of the works on the tunnel under the Rue Longue. The work continued for seven day in two shifts (spiling). In that time a distance of 999 feet 9 inches was reached, equivalent to 8.5 metres per day.

and very impractical by night, as no lamps could be used. Another consideration was the risk of an officer giving away his position during such reconnaissance. So the problem was: how to make a sound connection between the bottom, the man, the shaft and the dugout. Furthermore, it was impossible to work from the bottom up, as was usual in normal soil.

The problem was successfully solved by an officer who dug his gallery to a position, which he had calculated, had to be right below the place a shaft was needed. After dark he opened the ceiling of his gallery while at the same time wooden posts or beams were taken to the surface on the place where the shaft should be built, in order to construct a simple beamed shaft with posts and beams long enough to reach the gallery without filler pieces in between. The sand started falling into the gallery and was removed, and after a while a modest vertical opening appeared on the surface. A first set of bunding was laid over the opening, and the posts quickly placed around and pushed down, taking the set went down with them.

All rubble and surplus materials were removed through the gallery, giving the workers in the shaft plenty of space. In this way shafts of 18 to 20 ft deep were sunk in one night, and no traces of items such as wet sand, wood etc were left at dawn.

For machine-gun emplacements which were connected to a dugout, the method used was nearly always identical to the system used for inclines, the only main difference being that they dug outward from the existing underground construction. The emplacement for the machine-gun was usually camouflaged as a shell hole or was kept from enemy eyes by means of wooden frames covered in burlap and jute.

Surveying: In this part of the line one of the most difficult things was observation. The only instruments available were 4 inch prismatic compasses. Some of the British positions were in dangerous zones, and it occasionally happened that preset observation views made in the front of the line differed by up to 20° from the views taken from behind the line.

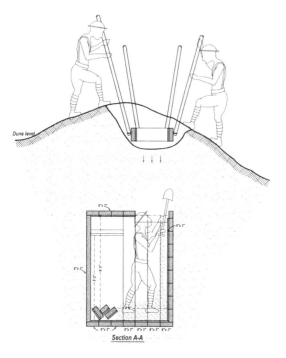

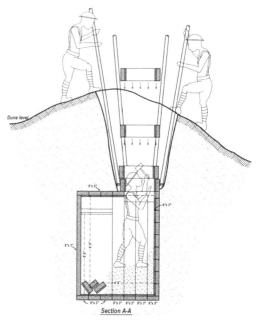

Method for sinking shafts

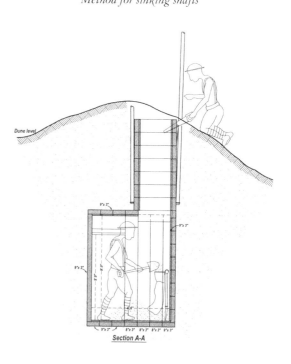

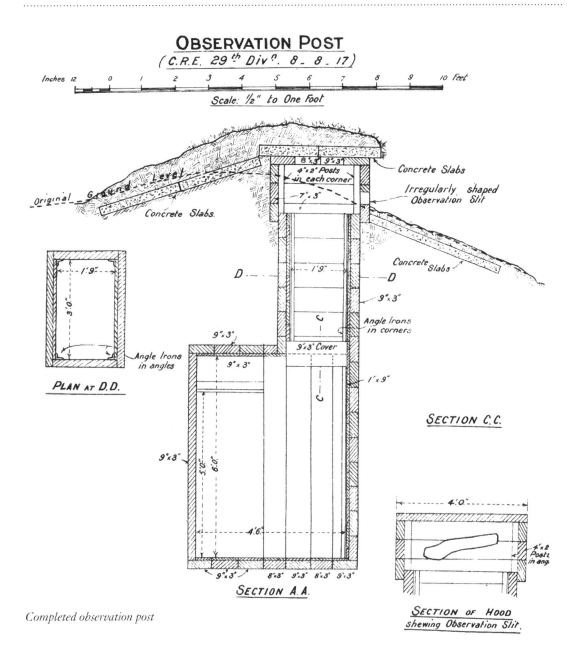

Completed observation post

It was later discovered that this was caused by the enormous amounts of metal, such as shells, cartridges, casings, shrapnel etc which lay just below the surface of the sand. When a hard wind blew, these were all exposed in such quantities that one could honestly not set a foot on the ground without standing on metal.

The greatest problems were usually caused by hidden munitions depots which were buried only a few centimetres below the sand in order to hide them from German airplanes and fearless scouts.

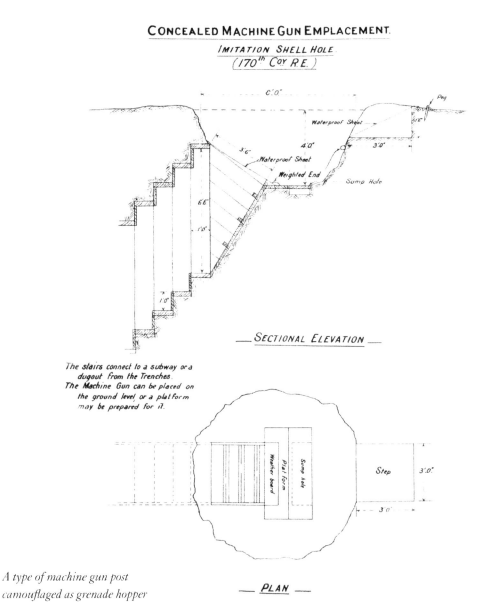

CONCEALED MACHINE GUN EMPLACEMENT.

IMITATION SHELL HOLE.
(170th Coy R.E.)

SECTIONAL ELEVATION

The stairs connect to a subway or a
dugout from the Trenches.
The Machine Gun can be placed on
the ground level or a platform
may be prepared for it.

PLAN

*A type of machine gun post
camouflaged as grenade hopper*

3 SINKING ELEPHANT SHELTERS (SINKING BENT CORRUGATED IRON SHEETS)

These were available in sections of two thirds of a circle with a radius of 4ft 6in. The centre was located 18in above the chord and was also the basis. They were built from 3ft wide sections (including the overlap) made from heavy steel corrugated plate in 6in channels. Each section was made by two bent steel plates, which were fixed at the top end with I-beams and bolts. The sections were fixed to the bottom pieces with angle irons and bolts.

A full-size Elephant was 18ft 3in long and this was the size that was usually sunk. During the sinking the pressures one had to deal with were nearly all from the side and ends. In order

View of machine-gun posts No 5 and No 4 and their firing range in Nieuwpoort-Bad. This place was called 'Broken Hill' by the 2nd Australian Tunnelling. On the left you can see the ruins of the St Bernarduskerk. At the bottom on the right we see Captain G. L. Smith MC, ATC and above right Major Webb, Australian Engineers

to cope with this pressure the whole structure was mounted on a wooden frame lengthwise and strengthened with stamped I-beams to distribute the pressure and to prevent any bending or breaking of the structure. The I-beams used were 11in x 5in, and all the wood in the frame was 9in x 3in (except the distance pieces between the stamps of the I- beams, which were 10in x 2in) as there was nothing heavier available. (See illustrations)

First the ground was dug out to an average depth of 6ft to offer the builders some protection. Next the frame and the corrugated sheets were assembled on the precise spot where they were needed. The sand was dug out further from below the frame. This was done from inside the construction, and at first the sand was thrown out through the open ends while the frame was left to rest on pillars of sand in the corners. When the sand had been removed to a depth of one foot under the frame, the four pillars were evenly dug away, letting the construction sink into the ground.

This procedure was repeated time after time.

After sinking the Elephant in this way to a depth of about 5ft, one of the ends was completely, and the other end partly, closed up with sand. It was usual that one end of the Elephant was connected with the feeder of a dugout which was opened to about a foot from the construction, and the other end was connected with an incline entrance, constructed after the Elephant had reached its ultimate depth.

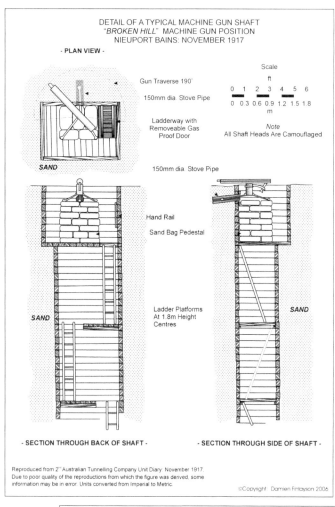

DETAIL OF A TYPICAL MACHINE GUN SHAFT
"BROKEN HILL" MACHINE GUN POSITION
NIEUPORT BAINS: NOVEMBER 1917

- PLAN VIEW -

Gun Traverse 190°

150mm dia. Stove Pipe

Ladderway with
Removeable Gas
Proof Door

SAND

150mm dia. Stove Pipe

Scale
ft
0 1 2 3 4 5 6
0 0.3 0.6 0.9 1.2 1.5 1.8
m

Note
All Shaft Heads Are Camouflaged

Hand Rail

Sand Bag Pedestal

Ladder Platforms
At 1.8m Height
Centres

SAND

SAND

- SECTION THROUGH BACK OF SHAFT -   - SECTION THROUGH SIDE OF SHAFT -

Reproduced from 2ⁿᵈ Australian Tunnelling Company Unit Diary: November 1917.
Due to poor quality of the reproductions from which the figure was derived, some
information may be in error. Units converted from Imperial to Metric.

©Copyright: Damien Finlayson 2006

Detail of a section of the shaft of a machine-gun post that was part of 'Broken Hill' in Nieuwpoort-Bad in 1917

The Weekly Mine Report of the 2nd Australian Tunnelling Company from 12 September 1917, which mentions the finishing of the machine-gun posts of 'Broken Hill', despite the heavy artillery bombardments

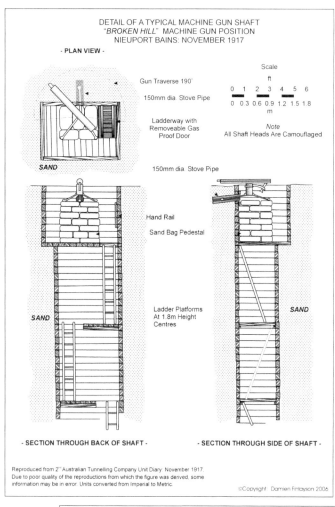

German aerial photograph of the dune area to the west of Nieuwpoort-Bad. We can clearly see that the location of 'Broken Hill' was crossed by the Germans. The white arrow marks the location of the machine-gun posts of the previous photo. 'Broken Hill' was located along the current Kinderlaan at 200 metres from the intersection with the Albert I-lane.

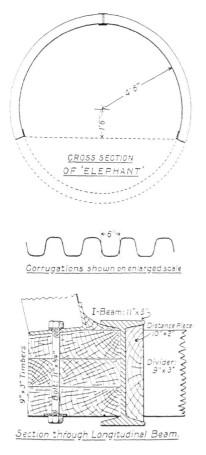

CROSS SECTION
OF 'ELEPHANT'

Corrugations shown on enlarged scale

Section through Longitudinal Beam.

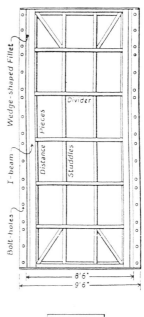

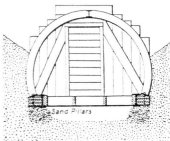

In order to save more time and effort the following method of sinking was developed. A set of 5ft 9in x 6in made out of 6in x 3in wooden beams was placed on each of the last distance pieces and the last corrugated portion of the Elephant. At each end of the construction a number of studdles were nailed to the distance pieces, and they were kept in place by diagonal planks nailed to them on the inside, keeping everything straight. The opening at the end of the construction was nailed shut from the outside, so it could be opened from the inside, once the construction was in its definitive location. The loosened planks were reused as sheeting. To prevent two sets collapsing at the ends due to the weight of the sand, a 9in by 3in stretcher was added, running the whole length of the construction from one set to the other. The stretcher was placed in the crown of the curvature of the corrugated plate. Pit props were placed between the stretcher and the bottom frame in order to support the roof and to keep the stretcher in place.

From that point on all excavated sand was evacuated through one end and placed, as much as possible, on the roof. In order to keep the end opening open while the construction

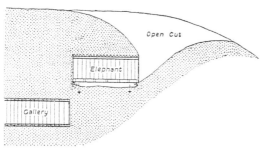

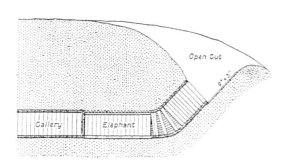

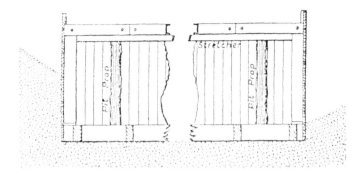

sank, Canadian mud shovels, driven by a couple of mules, were used to much success.

By the end of the operation, the incline entrance became too steep to be efficiently used and had to be given steps.

When the Elephant had reached the same level as the gallery, this was ascertained by pushing an iron bar through the sand at the end of the construction, the sinking was stopped and sufficient sand was place under the frame to prevent possible subsidence.

The previously closed opening at the end of the construction was then opened and attached to the gallery, after which the incline was finished, starting from the bottom. In order to move large quantities of sand the mud shovels were again used, drawn by donkeys, which were a great help during the digging works in the sand.

This and other similar methods only differed in the details. A large number of these Elephant shelters were sunk around Nieuwpoort, at depths varying from 5.5 metres to 8.5 metres below the surface. The problems concerning underground accommodation in sandy soil were solved.

Gunnerts T. C. R. Baker and Harrington of the 16th Battery, Field Artillery, AIF, rest in a dugout built out of elephant shelters in Nieuwpoort-Bad in 1917

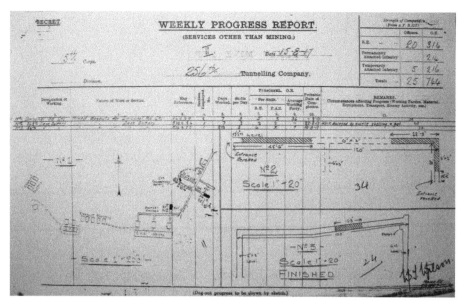

The Weekly Progress Report of the 266 Tunnelling Company Royal Engineers from 15 August 1917 describes the further development of the Headquarters Division in Oostduinkerke. Note the frequent use of elephant shelters. The construction was finished on 22 August 1917

After the war many of these constructions were partly or totally dismantled by the local population, which used the Elephant shelters as emergency housing and stabling for cattle. The last witnesses of this period can still be seen here and there. In the Victorlaan at Nieuwpoort there is still a former stable which was built out of Elephant shelters taken from the dunes of Nieuwpoort Bains.

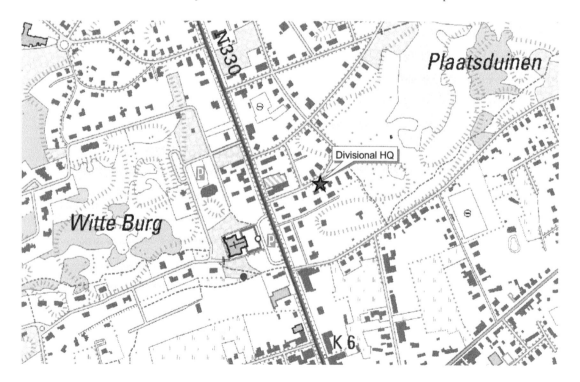

Above: An example of one of the elephant shelters after the war along the Victorlaan in Nieuwpoort

Right: The inside of a heavily battered construction. Note the U-profile at the top of the loose section. This was the way the sections were fastened together by means of nuts and bolts

Left: The current location of the underground division Headquarters in Oostduinkerke

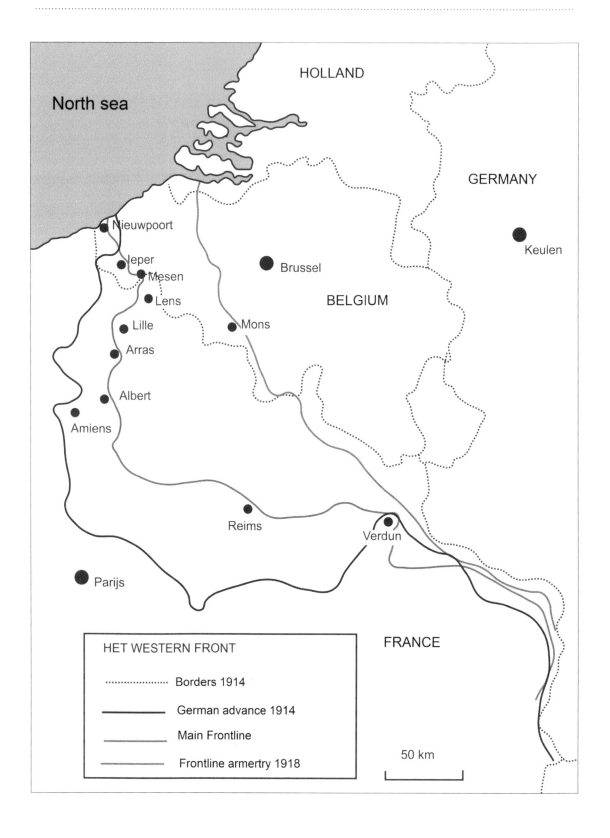

HOLLAND

North sea

GERMANY

Keulen

Nieuwpoort

Ieper

Mesen

Brussel

Lens

BELGIUM

Lille

Mons

Arras

Albert

Amiens

Reims

Verdun

Parijs

FRANCE

HET WESTERN FRONT

.... Borders 1914

German advance 1914

Main Frontline

Frontline armertry 1918

50 km

CHAPTER SEVEN

THE OPERATIONS OF THE 1ST DIVISION ON THE BELGIAN COAST IN 1917 'OPERATION HUSH'

GENERAL SITUATION

The year 1917 was a very moving year for the British Army and Navy. The failure of the French attack in Champagne in the spring and the setback that this failed attack had on the French troops, charged the British Army with the unfortunate task of keeping all the German units at the Western Front busy so that the French Army got the opportunity to recover without hostile interruptions. This commitment, grotesque as it was, was fully accepted and immediately transformed into several continuous battles along the coast from April to November 1917. Major operations succeeded one by one with astonishing speed. One attack followed another in Arras, Mesen, Ypres and Cambrai, with the result that all German divisions were pushed back and all the attention of the German military leaders was on the gaps forced in their lines by successive British attacks.

The French got the breathing space they desperately needed and managed to re-group their armies without being bothered. The Italians also gained from the British activity, as this prevented the Germans from sending a further six divisions to assist the Austrians in their attacks against the Italians. If the number of German divisions in Italy had doubled, the outcome of the war would have been completely different with horrendous consequences.

THE SITUATION AT SEA

The British Navy was also given a very difficult task. The German U-boat campaign became increasingly difficult to oppose which resulted in a constantly rising toll of ships which the British were fully dependent on for their food supply and power. The

German U-boats docked in Brugge

ships were sunk faster than the British could build them and it was just a matter of time before it became a very dire situation.

The German U-boats benefited greatly from the proximity of their bases on the Belgian coast, and it was the opinion of British admirals that the conditions would not improve if these bases were not eliminated.

Above: U-boats on the Brugge-Zeebrugge canal
Below: U-boat bunkers in the port of Zeebrugge

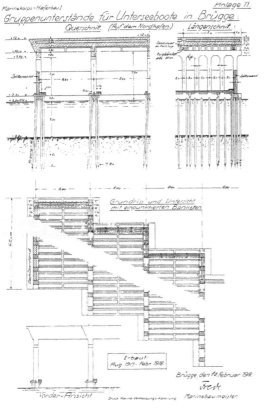

THE PROBLEM STATEMENT

The disabling of the U-boat bases could be accomplished either from the sea, the air or from land. Considering the strength of German coastal batteries, an operation from the sea would be extremely complicated. The entire Belgian coast, in the hands of the enemy, was strongly defended by up-to-date defences which include large calibre guns in great quantities.

The firing of these guns, when approaching ships at the coastline, was unpleasantly accurate and effective. An attack from the sea was therefore not an operation to take lightly.

An attack from the air was also not regarded as the ideal way to achieve the desired results. The German air defence was surprisingly complete and very efficiently organised.

Left: Construction plan of the U-boat bunkers at Zeebrugge
Below: Artillery diagram of the defences at the port of Oostende

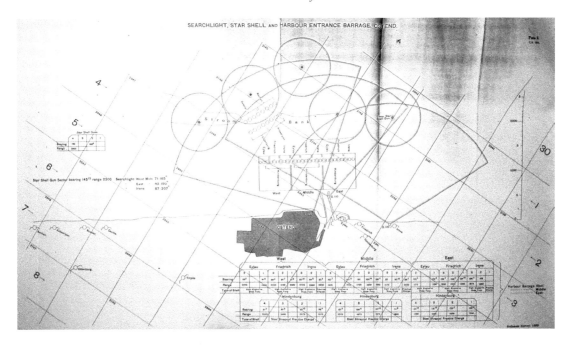

Coastal battery Hertha (4 x 21 cm) between Wenduine and Blankenberge

Inside view of the observation bunker of coastal battery Hertha

28 cm guns from Tirpitz battery

Therefore, it was decided that an attempt should be made to approach the U-boat bases from land. This was an important target for the British Army. It was believed the desired results could be achieved if the ground forces could conquer sufficient terrain along the coast, so the heavy railway cannons and the howitzers could be set up within range of the Zeebrugge U-boat base, so it would be continuously under attack. It was hoped that the activities of the U-boats would be so disrupted that the port would become worthless to the Germans. For this reason the northern operations of the British armies were given priority in 1917, but this prevented them from carrying out its two major missions, namely helping the French to stop or slow down the Germans and assist the 'British Navy' in threatening Zeebrugge.

THE OPERATION AT LAND IN 1917

The British attacks began in Arras and were later continued in the Ypres salient. The battle for Mesen was used as a preparatory operation for the more serious attacks further north. One of the goals of the third battle for Ypres was

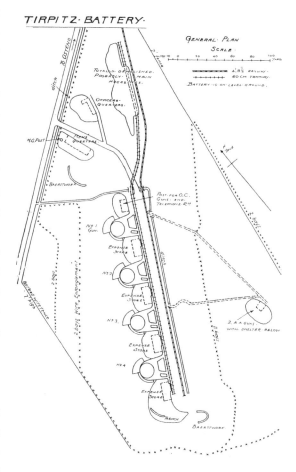

Plan of Tirpitz battery near Mariakerke

the neutralisation of Zeebrugge. With this goal in mind, 'the Fifth Army' was intended to move forward at the north-east of Ypres in the direction of Staden. Once that point was reached, the advance would be continued in north-east direction by 'the First Army', coupled with an attack on Oostende by British coastal units.

THE COASTAL SECTOR

Until the spring of 1917, the coastal sector was occupied by French units with the Belgian Army as the right hand. In view of the operation discussed above, it was necessary for British troops to take the place of the French on the coast. This was undertaken by the XV British Corps (1st and 32nd Divisions), who replaced the French in the second half of June 1917. The French were then taken back to their own areas. The '1st Division' occupied the sector along the coast, and the '32nd Division' the sector on the right side including the city of Nieuwpoort. The condition of the 1st Divisions was at that time as follows. The first line was about 550 to 750 metres east of the Yser

Above: German air photograph of coastal Kaiser Wilhelm II in the dunes of Duinbergen. Photo taken on 23 April 1917, from the observation balloon D. R. Lindberg

Below: Detailed plan of the canon well and the shelter for the crew

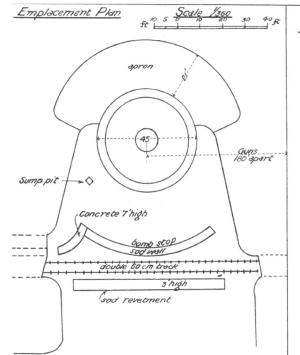

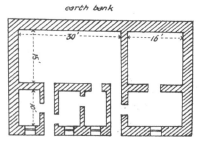

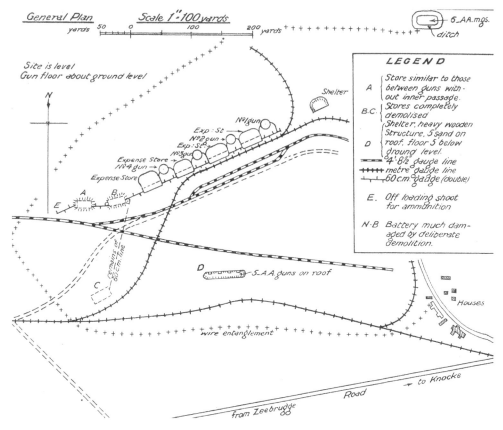

Above: General plan of the coastal battery Kaiser Wilhelm II

Below: German anti-aircraft battery near Middelkerke

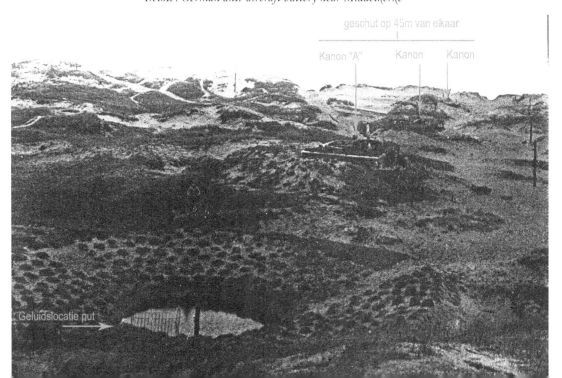

German 8.8 cm anti-aircraft gun at the battery near Middelkerke

river, which formed an excellent obstacle, flowing with a strong current, deep, wide and tidal. When the British replaced the French, there were only three floating bridges in the 1st Division Sector and these bridges were close to the mouth of the river.

No preparations were made to make any other bridges, and the insecurity of the two battalions that were defending east of the Yser river was obvious. During the period of French occupation apparently a 'live and let live' policy had been in place, and although the British were convinced that the sector was relatively quiet during the day, it was amazing that their presence to the east of the river was solely dependent on the goodwill of the enemy. The defence at the east of the Yser river was not resistant to bombing and the situation was far from satisfactory. However, immediate steps were taken to improve the situation. Materials were commissioned to construct additional bridges that could be raised in a very short time in case of emergencies. The digging of dug-outs started and the defensive work progressed very quickly. Raids were used for identification purposes only. Additional artillery was installed and air defence was placed on a more solid footing. It was fully recognised that until these improvements were made, the security of the advanced positions was largely dependent on the goodwill of the enemy, who realised that the redemption of the French by

Aerial photograph of the three floating bridges near the mouth of the Yser at Nieuwpoort-Bad, 14 June 1917

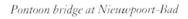

Pontoon bridge at Nieuwpoort-Bad

The end of a floating bridge on the side of Nieuwpoort-Bad

the British was no advantage to them. Nevertheless, it was decided that it was necessary to take the risks for reasons that will be further discussed.

THE GENERAL PLAN FOR THE ADVANCE OF THE XV CORPS

As already explained, British troops in the coastal sector had to work together with the 'Fifth Army' when they reached Staden (*Stade*). Because of this several of the German reserves on the coast became involved by attacking further southwards, which would make the march on the coast easier. This march was a difficult operation in every respect, the front was stretched out, extremely narrow and low, and on the right flank the land was under water, all of which made the operation extremely arduous. It was therefore of the utmost importance that the bridgehead at the east of the Yser river could be maintained to the east, because the loss of it would lead to an infinite delay, strongly impeding the passage over the Yser. In addition, it was decided that the march along the coast would coincide with an attack on German communication. The chosen division would go around the German right flank and be dropped in the rear of their defence. The '1st Division' was selected for this operation.

THE '1ST DIVISION' IN THE COASTAL SECTOR

The '1st Division' was chosen, presumably because no other division was available at that time, and it was probable they were only told later what role they were to play. But this role demanded special training in various areas, and taking into account the fact that the assignment was to be executed during the first half of August, it was decided to keep the division in line until July 16, and then retreat and to concentrate on a special camp west of Dunkirk, where communications had been left undisturbed. The fact that the French were being assisted by the British was not overlooked by the Germans. It was obvious to them that this meant the beginning of the loss of some strategic territory. It is doubtful whether the Germans fully realised at the time what the exchange of troops really meant, but nevertheless, they decided to make things as difficult as possible by attacking the bridgehead on the right bank of the Yser river. They succeeded on July 10 (Operation Srandfest), at a time when the improvements to the British defence system were still unfinished, and before they had managed to move all their heavy artillery in position. The German guns started bombing about 9.00 hours in the area occupied by two battalions of the '1st Division' east of the Yser, and on the bridges at the mouth of the river. These were soon destroyed and all attempts at repairs failed. The bombing increased in intensity and exceeded any other period of the war. The weak defences were destroyed, guns, 'Lewis Guns' and 'Vickers Guns' became unusable due the fact there was sand everywhere, and when eventually the German infantry came through, they could overpower the resistance without any difficulty. The two battalions that consisted of the 2nd King's Royal Rifle Corps (KRRC) and the '2nd Northants' were almost completely destroyed, only about one hundred men out of the two regiments escaped unscathed.

In the regimental diary, we read:

'10 July: Intense enemy shelling on all areas all day. Enemy attacked at 7.10pm, when about 70 per cent of the Battalion became casualties. Total loss 17 officers and 478 OR. This very terse statement was made after a disastrous day. The advance Companies of the KRRC and Northamptons had been moved into a network of trenches and posts on the east bank of the broad estuary of the River Yser. The only way of crossing was by one of a few narrow plank bridges. The enemy first cut off all communication with these exposed positions by laying down a very heavy curtain of artillery fire, then advancing in strength using bombs. The enemy action was completely successful and it virtually wiped out all British troops on that side of the river.

11 July: Capt. Smith, Capt. Butter, 2/Lt Gracie and about 20 men returned, having swum the Yser. Capt. Pallant MC RAMC, attached to the Royal North Lancs, managed to save several of these mens lives in the water.'

The army had to cope with the fact that a counter-attack was impossible due to lack of equipment, but it was vital to reoccupy the right bank of the Yser river as there was nothing left to prevent the same losses from happening again. Before this could happen, though, the entire supply of materials and reinforcement along the coast would need to be greatly increased.

WITHDRAWAL OF THE '1ST DIVISION' FOR SPECIAL TRAINING

The only advantage of the entire episode was that when the '1st Division' was withdrawn six days later, in line with the plan, the Germans undoubtedly relied on their recent successes and decided to take no further action. Meanwhile, preparations were made for setting up a camp for the division along the coast near Le Clipon, about 9 km west of Dunkirk. A large area was carefully defined, with a light rail network constructed to supply essential materials, food and water. These preparations were completed by 16 July, and the division marched westward after being relegated in line with the 66th Division towards the new camp. The British realised that the success of the planned operations was dependent on absolute secrecy. The hint of a rumour could seriously harm the success of the plan. Consequently, no one was told anything until the division was safely within the fences of the camp. Extensive security measures were taken to avoid leakage of information to the outside world. The people who stayed in the camp had no contact with anyone outside of the camp. Supplies were delivered through a system of locks, where the people bringing the supplies never met the people who received them. Special guards were constantly waiting at the camp's entrances, while the perimeter was constantly patrolled. All letters came via 'secure' staff at the base, and all leave was withdrawn. Last but not least, it was explained to the troops that the success of the operation, and for the safety of their own lives and that of their comrades, depended on their loyal cooperation in the complete confidentiality. The only people staying in the camp were those who would take part in the operation, even the horses of the division stayed outside the camp. Different units were kept apart for quite some time, and despite all the slander and inconvenience caused by the isolation, the men were to have no contact with the outside world. Due to the complete lack of transport in the camp, a light railway system was installed to manage the supplies.

THE PLAN OF THE OPERATION

Let's look at the plan of the operation in a bit more detail. The task of dropping a division into the rear of the enemy was not going to be easy. Various factors contributed to this difficulty. First of all, one should take into account the enemy itself. Since the early days of the war, when the first allied troops landed on the Belgian coast, the Germans were still nervous about their right flank. They had consistently focused on building defences along the coast and these defences were formidable in character, both in quality and quantity. These defence systems were provided with mobile units that could be extended to two navy divisions who were permanently stationed on the coast. Furthermore, as already mentioned, air defence was intact and effective. In addition to the formidable difficulties caused by the enemy, there were those caused by nature itself. The coastline was completely flat with no inlets or bays to provide shelter. The sea was not deep enough to allow large vessels to get close to the beach and there were several sandbanks that were constantly moving meaning the width of the beach at high tide changed regularly. The tides were very strong and the strong sea winds ensured that the water is frequently turbulent. These were just some of the difficulties they faced and they needed to find a way of solving them.

The difficulties caused by the enemy needed to be overcome by surprise. It was essential to camouflage the planned landing and at all costs keep the actual place and date a secret. The methods that would be used to ensure a complete surprise have already described, but they would be supplemented by other methods to blind and deceive the enemy when the time arrived.

Taking into account the shallow sea, the only Navy vessels able to support the attack were shallow monitors. These vessels, although they did have heavy guns, had little or no protection and a very low speed. They could not possibly bring the mission to a successful end with the powerful coastal batteries along the coast. It was therefore necessary for the safety of these boats to move to the landing site during the night, with the addition of smoke curtains from the accompanying tugs which would retreat once their task was completed. The necessity of the smoke curtain was another essential condition to the success of the operation. Ideally a wind should be blowing over the beach, but not be too severe as this would cause the sea to be rough, further complicating the situation. Then came the question of

Admiral Sir Reginald Bacon

ensuring a fast landing once the attack started and the alarm was given. A very fast landing was of the utmost importance.

This problem was resolved in a very ingenious way by Admiral Bacon, who had the command of the Dover Patrol, and who the soldiers had to work with during the operation.

He invented a building called pontoon which was 180 metres long and 9 metres wide. Three were built and they had to serve all vehicles, weapons, bikes, etc. belonging to the division, while a 3-metre walkway was left open over the entire length of the pontoon. This not only gave them access to the beach but offered accommodation for the troops as well. These pontoons had to be pushed by two warships, each of which was attached to the back of the pontoon.

These three pontoons, together with six ships formed three composite units each containing one brigade of infantry along with the necessary arsenal of heavy weapons. The plan was to use tugboats at night to push them to the planned landing at an appropriate time. The pontoons had to be grounded on the beach to allow the attacking troops to storm the beach, to continue beyond the beach defence and to strategically take up their positions before the enemy could gather enough troops to stop them.

A trial run of one of the three pontoons

THE SELECTION OF THE LANDING PLACE

Apart from the overall plan for landing, there were of course many other details that still had to be studied. It was of the utmost importance to see what impact the chosen landing site would have on the already planned operations. This presented itself as a bit of a dilemma. The further eastward the landing took place, the greater the effect would be on the success of the operation, but the greater the danger to the division due to its isolation. It was also important to know whether the landing would be affected if it was in the range of (a) the coastal batteries in Raversijde (*Raversyde*) and (b) the inland canons which covered the German line at the Yser river. Taking into account (a) it was necessary to disable the German guns in the Batteries at Raversijde. If this was not done, the Navy ships would be greatly hindered once the smoke curtain had been lifted and the sea, which had to serve as a supply line for the '1st Division', would be very insecure. Taking into account (b) the destruction of these guns was in favor of the 'XV Corps' troops attacking the coast. The range of these guns was close to Westende. After considering these various issues, it was decided that the landing should take place in

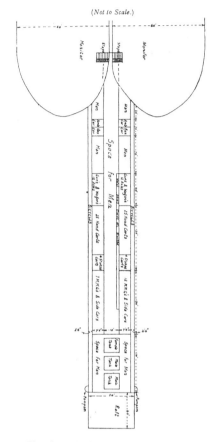

Sketch of the layout of the pontoons

Middelkerke (*Middelkerke*) and the other two between Middelkerke and Westende. It was hoped that it would be possible to send a column of planes from Middelkerke landing station to tackle the Batteries in Raversijde. Preparations had already been made for this action.

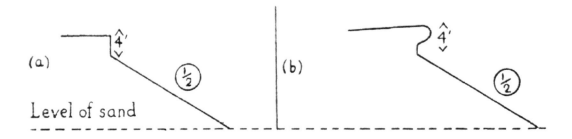

The two different types of dyke and the dyke edge positioned on the landing site

THE DYKE

In the area chosen for the landings, the coastline was protected by a concrete dyke of huge dimensions. The front of the dyke was at an angle of 45° and the pass of the top of the dike was three metres higher than the pass of the sand. The top of the dyke consisted of two different shapes. At one part of the front was a vertical uprising of about 1.20 metres to the level of the esplanade. The other consisted of a protruding part that was finished in a curve. The two different shapes are represented in the diagram at the bottom of page 150.

   The height above sand level varied depending on where it was and the weather conditions. In some places the sea at high tide hit the foot of the dyke, but usually there was always a strip of sand between the dyke and the sea. This dyke was considered a serious obstacle to the infantry, tanks, guns and vehicles that had to climb it. In order to find a solution to this problem, real-size models were made of both types of dykes in the camp in Le Clipon and in the 'Central Tank Workshops'. The tanks were tested on the various obstacles and notes were taken on whether they could drive over the type of dyke (a) without any tools, or they were stopped by type (b).

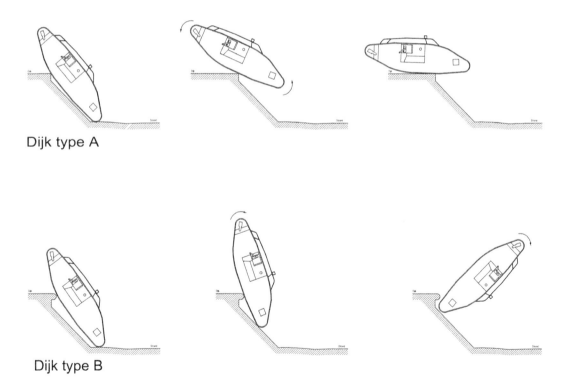

Dijk type A

Dijk type B

   The problem of the latter situation was solved in a very ingenious way. A spike-form extension or a shovel was made, specially designed to fit more or less into the cavity under the protrusion at the top of the dyke. This piece was carried on the end of a rag that was attached to the tank instead of the usual wooden beam, and could be detached by the crew inside the tank. It was intended that the tank took this extension on the dyke up to the cantilever. It would then be pushed into position just under the cantilever, and after the crew had completely disengaged it from the tank, they could ride over the dike.

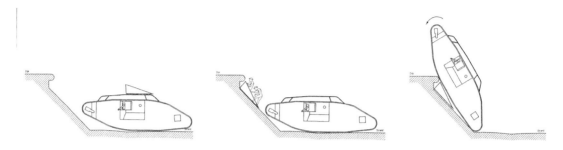

This theory was tested on a model dyke in the Tank Central Workshop, once with success, once without success, and this method of climbing over was later introduced into the schedule of the planned operations.

The model dyke in Le Clipon was used to practise infantry storms, which consisted of running over the dyke first without, and later with, full equipment. It was very interesting to experience how they made progress in this specific exercise. At first they were all at sea and could barely stand up on the slope of the dyke, not to mention running on it. It didn't take long for the majority of

The recreated model of the dyke in the dunes of Le Clipon during the training for the landing

the men to become accustomed to running up and down the dyke, even with heavy equipment such as bicycles, ammunition, etc. In order to help the men who were a little slower or had to carry exceptionally heavy or awkward charges, some of the men at the front had ropes with an anchor hook attached to them. The hook had to be fastened to the top edge of the dyke and the rope was then stretched over the slope of the dyke so that those who needed assistance could use the rope to pull themselves up. They still had the problem though of getting cannons and the like over the dyke. This was solved in the following manner. Of the three tanks planned at each landing point one was a 'female' tank fitted with a winch. This tank would follow the other two 'male' tanks, climb the dyke and position itself on top allowing the infantry could get itself to a place of safety on the beach. The tank would then focus on raising guns and other heavy material up the dyke. For this the tank was fitted with a wooden slope to make it easier for the wheels of the gun to pass over the edge of the dyke. So far the seawall and the problems surrounding that.

COMPOSITION OF THE LANDING FORCE

The following troops were available for landing: the complete '1st Division'; 2 Battalion Cyclists; 3 motor machining units; 9 tanks and the necessary mechanical vehicles.

When working out the landing power, the following factors should be taken into account:

a. Horses could not accompany the landing force.

b. The space provided by the Navy for the transport by sea of the units was severely limited.

c. The landing force had to be able to operate independently and for at least 48 hours.

Under these circumstances the following decisions were made:

a. All infantry, including trench mortar batteries ,were shipped without horse transport.

b. A composite manual artillery battery was taken with each infantry brigade, which consisted of:
    4 18-pdr guns and limbers.
    2 45in howitzers and limbers.
    5 ammunition cars and limbers.

c. One 'Field Company' together with one 'Pioneer Battalion', but without accompaniment of horse transport.

d. One engine machined battery assigned to each landing point.

e. The cyclists had to be divided over the different landings in this order:
    Landing left: 1 battalion
    Landing central: 1 battalion (minus one company)
    Landing right: 1 company

f. A small medical detention with two motorised ambulances for each landing place.

g. A set of handcarts for each unit to replace the horses and carts that had to be left behind. These were used to transport ammunition, grenades, tools, water, spare parts, etc.

h. Special signalling agreements should be developed. These are discussed later.

i. Three tanks were placed on the front of each pontoon in one line. The two 'male' tanks were the first and second, the one 'female' tank last.

PREPARATIONS FOR THE LANDING FORCE, ON THE NAVAL SHIPS

Now that the general composition of the landing force was established, it was decided to find the best possible method for getting the troops on the pontoons and boats in order to land them as quickly as possible and without any confusion. It was of course of utmost importance that the landing troops could settle on land as quickly as possible as the surprise was the prime condition of success. It was also important that the remaining troops and equipment could be landed without delay, and the ships released as they would come under fire as soon as the smoke curtain was pulled up. Experiments were performed on the beach in the camp near Le Clipon to find out how these objectives could best be achieved. The ground plans of the boats were made to scale on the beach with the various obstacles on the deck, such as guns, fans, chimney pipes, etc. This meant that the available deck space had been recorded and the actual practice run provided valuable information about the number of people who could be transported by the ships. A model of a pontoon was also deployed in which the loading of the various vehicles and equipment was practised. After much thought it was decided that the schedule as shown on the figure of the pontoon would be used.

It was also decided that the central corridor of the pontoon was to be taken by the two first battalions side by side, so that the moment the tanks started moving the first two battalions could simultaneously ascend the beach and push forward to form an ever-expanding bridgehead. The troops were trained to hit the beach as quickly as possible by actually repeating this manoeuvre on the model inside the camp. The manner by which the operation was improved by these exercises was amazing. Competitions were held between the 3 Brigades, with the result that the measured time needed to clear the pontoons and associated boats was reduced to about ten minutes.

At one point they considered using chariots for the transport of guns, ammunition and supplies, but this created so many difficulties trying to push it through the soft sand that it was decided to switch over to manpower for transporting the guns and ammunition.

FORSEEN SUPPLIES FOR THE ARMY

The question of what supplies the army should take was one that had to be carefully considered. The space provided for stock was strictly limited, as well as the means for transporting them. It was therefore important that everything that was not deemed essential was left behind. Ammunition for guns and machine guns was of course one of the primary necessities.

Once the division had landed, there was the possibility they would have to defend themselves against counter-attacks, so the ammunition had to be within reach. Another essential thing was water.

There had to be a sufficient reserve of fresh water, as it was uncertain if there would be a local stock of water on land. Tools, spare parts, sandbags etc. all had to be available. The tools to be taken were also of great importance to the field units who needed to be independent for some time. Intensive selection was made and consulted on what to do and what had to be left behind. Explosives also formed a very important item, as they were of vital importance in the battle against Raversijde's coastal batteries. A supply of water and pumps was also provided.

After deciding what had to be left behind and what did not, it was concluded that the available amount of chariots was insufficient to transport everything that had to be taken. It was therefore decided that certain stocks such as spare parts, water and ammunition, which were not immediately required at landing, would be loaded onto rafts and pushed onto the beach the moment all the troops had embarked.

INFORMATION ABOUT THE LANDING PLACE

The next necessary point was giving instructions to the troops before landing. For this purpose, a very precise model of the coast was laid out in a specially designed barrack in the training camp. On this model, every house could be seen, the colour and shape were displayed as accurately as possible.

The gathering of information needed to work out the model was a very difficult task, but the details were collected from many different sources and by the end they had reached a very high degree of accuracy. Some of the information came from direct observation, powerful telescopes were drawn to points within the British lines from which the coastline could be seen from Westende and Middelkerke.

The reinforcements in the villas on the dyke of Middelkerke

Above: German artillery on the seawall in Westende

Below: German trench between the villas in Westende

Above: Aerial photo of the Westende and Middelkerke litter
Below: Aerial view of the dyke with the hotel Belle-Vue in Westende

Above: Hotel Belle-Vue

Below: The Ten Bogaerde farm in Koksijde served as an airport and was the departure point for many observation flights

One of the canvas aircraft tents near Bogaerde farm

Other information came from pictures and postcards dating from just before the German occupation. Information also came from aerial photographs taken during an unpleasant flight of No. 34 Squadron RAF, delivering lateral photos taken at an altitude of less than 50 metres, from the coast between the Yser river and Middelkerke, together with other vertical images taken from a greater height.

These aerial photos were mainly responsible for information about the positions of hostile batteries. The aircraft left from Koksijde where they were stationed near the farm Ten Bogaerde. The surrounding fields of the farm served as an airport and the aircraft stood in large canvas tents near the farm.

The lateral photos were taken in three flights. During the first flight, the plane flew at full speed along the coast from the British positions, and after reaching Middelkerke, it turned towards the sea to fly back to the airport. The Germans were completely taken by surprise and the plane remained undamaged. Another risky flight was necessary as there were some gaps in the line of aerial photographs. This was done in the opposite direction and the plane approached Middelkerke from the sea and flew along the coast towards British lines. It came under heavy fire and was eventually taken down on the beach at about 200 metres east of the Yser river.

The pilot and observer, who were unharmed, managed to free themselves and ran to the Yser,

The wreck of the crashed aircraft on the beach

chased by the Germans. They threw off their clothes and swam across the river (one of them had to leave his last piece of clothing on some barbed wire in the river) and were then helped by a suspicious British soldier who immediately took them to his Commanding Officer. In this manner they were eventually saved.

Because the scale model was limited to the planned landing location, it was very important for it to be carefully monitored so that this vital information could not be leaked in any way. The barracks were therefore strictly controlled by guards who denied access to anyone who did not hold a special pass from the Divisional Headquarters. Initially, only senior officers had permission to study the scale model, and it was decided that it would only be shown to the men participating in the operation at the last moment. It was intended that every section would go to the barracks and that their role in the operation would be explained on the scale model. They trusted by doing this each man understood clearly what was expected of him and that misunderstandings and confusion could be avoided.

THE TACTICAL TRAINING OF THE TROOPS

The troops had to be trained for open warfare. The vast majority of them had only experience in construction and trench war; a dynamic moving war was a completely new concept for them. Nevertheless, they took full advantage of this new form of training and significant improvements were soon noticeable. The landscape around Le Clipon was very similar to the place where the soldiers would be operating which was a great help in the training. Schedules were drawn up for the various 'Brigades' and Battalions who performed the tasks expected of them with a high degree of effectiveness.

It was already explained that it was important to eliminate the coastal batteries in Raversijde as early as possible. These consisted of four units each with four 6-inch ship canons which were situated between Middelkerke and Oostende.

Above: Battery Aachen with its 4 × 15 cm artillery at Raversijde
Below: Observation bunker at the Aachen Battery

4. - MIDDELKERKE. — Batterie « Amterwpen ».

Above: Battery Antwerp with 4 × 10.5 cm fortress cannons that were captured during the conquest of Antwerp.
This battery had no real strategic function but served more to deceive the hostile air observation (Raversijde)
Below: Battery Aachen and the barracks for the crew

Above: Battery Aachen, the place where the royal chalet used to be

It was decided to send a flying column to these batteries as soon as possible after the landing, to eliminate them. Those columns would contain a battalion cyclist, a 'motor-machine gun battery', and a 'field company' detachment placed on bicycles. These troops had the opportunity to practise a manoeuvre in the environment of Le Clipon, which was very similar to the landscape at the landing point. It was intended they would attack the coastal batteries from Middelkerke, eliminate the guns and then retreat. As far as one could see, the batteries were unprotected from the land side.

Because it would be a surprise attack these sides could be taken on the condition that the entire operation could proceed without delay.

They needed to think carefully about the method used for destroying the guns. It was decided to experiment with 'thermite' (a mixture of aluminium powder and

The unprotected rear of battery Aachen

Above: Back of Aachen battery

Below: An example of the effect of thermite for disabling cannons

iron oxide powder which combined creates an extreme heat up to 2500°C). They used captured German cannons, supplied by GHQ, to give the Divisional Engineers the chance to run tests. The product was found to be efficient enough to justify its use. Its weight was noticeably less than that of gun cotton, it was quick to use and safe when ignited. It was decided to use it, if time allowed, in combination with gun cotton to increase the amount of damage caused.

FRAMEWORK OF THE ORDERS

As the men would be very close to each other on board the ships, it would be impossible to eat a good meal during the trip. It was therefore necessary to give them a meal just before they left the camp and the Navy agreed to serve hot chocolate whilst sailing. This was the only thing they could have besides the small food supplies that the men carried themselves.

The Divisional Headquarters had to be transferred by a small vessel (M25, which was plundered on 16 September 1919), and remained completely detached from the rest of the fleet. It was designed to leave a short time after the departure of the other vessels.

THE SEA JOURNEY

The trip itself was scheduled to begin in the early evening. The ships (monitors) and the pontoons were preceded by a number of small vessels commissioned to make a smoke curtain to camouflage the landing. To mislead the Germans, added to the smoke curtains, they planned to carry out fake attacks at Zeebrugge some days prior to the date of the actual landing. On that day,

The M26, a similar ship to the M25, on which the Divisional Headquarters would be transferred

there would be intense activity along the entire coast, as far as the German lines ran. It was hoped that the Germans would be confused and remain in ignorance of the actual landing plan.

During the surveillance, a telephone cable had to be rolled out by the M25 so that the headquarters of the 1st Division could be in constant contact with the 'Fourth Army HQ' near Dunkirk. Preparations were made to allow each monitor in each group to roll a cable from a central point marked with a buoy. These cables, together with the one that was rolled out by the M25, had to be brought together in a junction box and hopefully could be brought ashore. This meant the Divisional Headquarters would continuously be in contact with the three brigades through a cable running below sea level, both before and after the landing. Additional means of communication were provided in the form of wireless broadcasting facilities for the three brigades and the Fourth Army, and pigeon post for the remainder. Visual signalling would also play a major role as soon as the smoke curtain had been cleared.

THE LANDING

The landing itself was planned to take place at dawn. It also needed to be at more or less high tide so as to minimise the distance between the landing and the dyke to be crossed by the troops. These two conditions limited the number of available dates at which the landing could take place. As already discussed, the weather and the wind also played an important role, as there needed to be a light breeze coming off the sea so the smoke curtain stayed in front of the vessels. With too much wind the waves hitting the beach would be too strong making the landing difficult. Finally, it should be remembered that the whole company could only begin when the Fifth and Second armies in Ypres had made sufficient progress and reached Staden. The chances of getting all these conditions together in one day was not very high, and in the end the operation was never executed because the last condition was never reached. Nevertheless, a date was set in advance on which the first two conditions would be fulfilled, namely, high tide at sunrise. Everything was put in place pending a favourable course of the proposed actions. Given the weather conditions played a very big part in the success of the operation, it was of course impossible to count on it in advance. Frequent weather forecasts were forwarded, but none of the predicted dates at which time and tides were favorable were consistent with favourable weather conditions. Most of the scheduled dates were virtually impossible.

However, the plan of the final landing was simple. The tugboats first made a telephone connection with the communication stations as discussed before, after which they subsequently took their positions behind the pontoons. These were pushed immediately towards the beach. As soon as they were at a distance of about 300 metres from the beach, using 12-in, 6-in, 12pdr, etc., they opened rapid fire on the houses and the defences in the immediate area of the coastline. One should take into account that the moving of the fleet towards the beach had to be camouflaged with a smoke curtain along the entire coastline, so firing guns on the pontoons was done more or less blindly. The scope of the gun was also very limited, but they were convinced that the bombings would be effective. They relied mainly on the moral effect of the bombardment on the enemy rather than the material damage they would inflict. The moral effect of such action was indeed terrible. The number and weight of the guns used (four 12 in and 6 in in each group), the smoke, the time of day, would all contribute to this, and it was hoped that the morale of the German machine gunners would already be seriously affected before the infantry attack commenced. The bombings at sea were timed to last only a few minutes, no more than five, after which the infantry and the tanks stormed the beach. The two 'male' tanks followed by the 'female' tank would ascend the dyke and deal with any resistance in that vicinity, while the infantry firmly strengthened their footing om shore.

One should not forget that each infantry section had its own assigned task, and knew exactly what was expected of them, thanks to the model in the camp at Le Clipon.

Units of 'The Royal Engineers' were included in the first wave of attacks with the task of tackling all unexpected obstacles on or across the dyke.

It was already known that the barbed wire barriers were electrified on the dyke, and the Royal Engineers and some of the first infantrymen were equipped with rubber handled grips to cut through the barriers. Preparations had already been made to take care of the German ammunition warehouse which had been located just before landing. This would happen using heavy shot from the XV Corps area, a day or two before the chosen date of landing.

The 'Pioneer Company' was ordered to remove the pontoons as quickly as possible from all vehicles and supplies, so that the Navy units could retreat before the smoke curtain cleared. The first goal was to get as quickly as possible on land, there was no time for even the slightest pause. The troops were forced to pull up as quickly as possible to be able to achieve the next goal.

THE ATTACK OF THE XV CORPS

At the same time that the landing of the 1st Division would take place, or shortly thereafter, the XV Corps would attack north-east from Nieuwpoort and Nieuwpoort-Bad. The attack of the XV Corps and the '1st Division' would mean great mutual assistance. The XV Corps had the hard task of crossing the Yser on its own part of the front, but the '1st Division' landing, and especially the right and central landing force, were supposed to be capable of neutralising all shots coming from the German batteries that hit the Yser Front, as they were located in the immediate environment of landing. The Germans had made a weak choice in deciding where they could build their batteries. They were practically driven back on a narrow strip of high-level, shallow ground on the coast, because the underlying polders were very flat and under water. It was hoped that the '1st Division' could take advantage of this weakness in the German defences, making the whole attack a total success.

THE OPERATION

The left brigade of the 1st Division, as discussed earlier, would send a command unit as soon as possible after the landing to deal with the batteries at Raversijde, between Middelkerke and Oostende. It was very important that these batteries were eliminated so that the Navy vessels had free play at sea and could ensure communication with the '1st Division'.

The command unit consisted of one battalion cyclist, a set of engine machine guns and a detention of the Royal Engineers on bicycles.

The Royal Engeneers had thermite and gun cotton with them with the aim of eliminating the 6-in coastal defence guns. As already mentioned, they had practised using this type of explosive. The Command Unit had to return as quickly as possible as they wanted to avoid any shortcoming of armed forces, as well as a possible counter-attack by hostile elite groups. There was no reason why the command unit would remain in Raversijde, as the batteries would remain unusable after they had withdrawn. This unit would still be needed for operations, which would take place in the eastern or north-eastern direction in order to threaten a retracted line of German divisions further south. There was no intent to push to Oostende immediately, the intention was to isolate the area by advancing south of the city. This was the reason why the immediate withdrawal of the command unit was ordered. The withdrawal was meant to support a battalion move from Middelkerke to Raversijde.

As soon as the second goal was reached, strong patrols of cyclists would ride with engine guns to Leffingen and Slype with the aim of occupying the bridges across the Plassendale Canal and blocking the various crossroads. The landscape was of such a nature that they had to depend fully on the existing roads. Hopefully, by occupying key points it would yield good results. However, the '1st Division' was unable to get far enough inland, due to the total absence of any horse transport. For this reason it was necessary to work out how to advance using the transport available to them. It was hoped this would be possible during the first night after landing, as it was intended that the transport would cross the Yser near the mouth and move along the beach until they could accompany the division.

Of course it was impossible to count on this, and for those reasons the division had to be prepared to continue without transport. They soon realised that without any form of transportation the division's mobility would be greatly reduced, making any exploration of the area impossible. They also had very poor artillery support, only twelve 18-pdr and six 4.5-in howitzers, added to which the stock of ammunition was strictly limited.

Supplement of stocks by sea could not be counted on as long as the batteries at Raversijde were still in operation, although the Navy opted to bring sloops ashore with different stocks.

However, in view of the importance of success without the hindrance of further delay, it was decided to get the horse transport across the beach to the division, the first night after landing. All horse transport was first collected in the quiet neighborhood of De Panne, and from there departed as quickly as possible for Nieuwpoort-Bad where they would cross the river Yser.

DIVISION MANAGEMENT OF OPERATIONS

The manner in which the division would lead the operations would not be easy. As discussed earlier, the 'Divisional Headquarters' on the M25 were connected by a cable below sea-level to the three infantry brigades both before and after landing. It was calculated that during and shortly after the landing there would be a collision of men and materials on the beach and that would make it difficult to control the operation. It was therefore decided that 'Divisional Headquarters' should not be landed before a wider strip of land was taken from the enemy, which would allow more time to concentrate on the brigade itself. This decision resulted in a certain amount of delay. It was assessed that the transfer of Divisional Headquarters to land could not take place as long as the smoke curtain was still restricting vision.

The division reserve consisted first of a battalion of the right-wing brigade, and it was hoped that, due to the progress of the XV Corps, it would be possible to supplement and forward this brigade, which would then form the bulk of the division reserve.

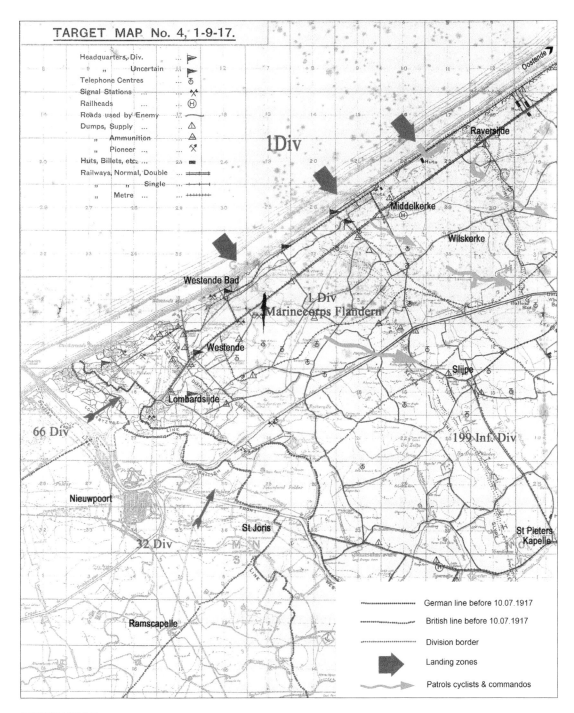

CONCLUSION

This was the complete schedule of the operation and the manner in which the preparations were to be made.

It was, however, never carried out, given the progress of the Second and Fifth Army east of Ypres was never sufficient to justify such action. One can only guess what would happen if the operation had taken place. It is clear that the chances of success were largely dependent on surprise. It was assumed that they could take the enemy completely by surprise if it had taken place on the first of the predicted dates. The longer it went on, the more chance the Germans would start to suspect an attack was imminent, but they would still remain in the dark regarding the terms of location and time. Even if they had attempted a landing at a later date, the surprise would probably still have played its role. It was never felt the division would fail to get a firm footing on shore, and once this had happened, one could only hope they would keep what they had won. Of course a possible hostile counter-attack could have been greatly hampered by the swampy ground, and that mobile artillery would already be out of use at landing times. Subsequently, the attack of the XV Corps would result in a large number of casulaties among the German troops. The results of the success would be far-reaching. It was not exaggerating to assume that the confusion on the coast caused by the landing would be in the hands of the Second and Fifth armies. Oostende would most likely have fallen into British hands and Zeebrugge would, if not taken, be neutralised. A large part of Belgium would therefore be recaptured. The consequences for shipping in the canal would upset the morals of the Allies and severely affect the Germans. The effect in Germany of such results could have resulted in fifteen months recovering from the damage. But these are only assumptions. The fact remains that the landing never took place and the war lasted for another year.

CHAPTER EIGHT
THE DIARY OF MAJOR W. E. BUCKINGHAM, INSPECTOR OF MINES, ROYAL ENGINEERS

Major William Edward Buckingham was Assistant Inspector of Mines for the 4th Army. He worked for the Controller of Mines of the 4e Army, who, in turn worked for Brigadier-General and Mine Inspector, Robert Napier Harvey, the lead figure with respect to mines and tunnels.

W. E. Buckingham advised the tunnellers about the best working methods and reported back about the quality of their work and their efficiency. He was also responsible for the apportioning of the necessary materials, depending on the type of construction that was being built. Part of his work was passing on new ideas, experiences or tools across the various units.

Major W. E. Buckingham was a recipient of the Military Cross and the Croix De Guerre. He was born on 16 October 1887 and died having taken his own life on 8 June 1931.

MAJOR BUCKINGHAM'S VISIT TO NIEUWPOORT ON 8 JULY 1917

Inspection of the work by the 2nd Australian Tunnelling Company XV Corps.

This company is tasked with the construction of:

a) 2 offensive mine galleries

b) 2 subways

c) dug-outs

d) the sinking of wells (almost completed)

The works were started at the end of June 1917 when the area was taken over by the French. The ground at the front line consists of dunes with valleys and hollows lying between the dunes. The front line trenches lie parallel to and about 700 feet (200 metres) north east of the River Yser where they follow the same course towards the sea. The Yser is around 30 metres wide here. Near its mouth are three floating bridges.

No mines or mined dug-outs had been made by the French owing to the difficulty of mining in sand. They had installed 'cut and cover' shelters (covered trenches) with varying thickness of cover

The start of one of the three floating bridges at the mouth of the Yser (eastern bank)

Right: Soldier humour. A French covered trench, also called 'cut and cover', bears the name of Café-restaurant. This is the covered trench in the St-Jacobsstraat. In the background you can see the brewery in the Ieperstraat

Below: Inside view of a French 'cut and cover' construction in Nieuwpoort

Nieuport. — *Abris souterrains.*
Subterranean shelter.

UN LONG COULOIR SOUTERRAIN A NIEUPORT

The remaining wooden structure of a French covered trench in 1918

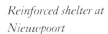

Reinforced shelter at Nieuwpoort

French concrete bunkers in the dunes of Nieuwpoort-Bad

between 30 cm and 1.5 metres, as well as concrete shelters which tended to be used as observation posts or machine gun positions.

MINE GALLERIES

Mining is impossible in the valleys and hollows between the dunes, owing to the water being so close to the surface.

The groundwater level is so high in many places that 'valleys' between the dune hills in the winter spontaneously come under water and form a 'panne'

There are two points, however, where the lines are only 70 and 50 metres apart and where dunes exist through which galleries could be driven with a view to blowing up German posts and trenches at these points.

Both mines were subjected to an inspection. The timber had been carefully put in the dug-out spaces.

No. 1 mine gallery had water lying on the floor in places and sand was very watery at the face where the sill was being installed. This showed that the gallery was being driven at the right depth. (The position of mine gallery No. 1 is just outside the Lombardsijde 14A Quarter, close to the beach 250 metres northeast of the lighthouse.)

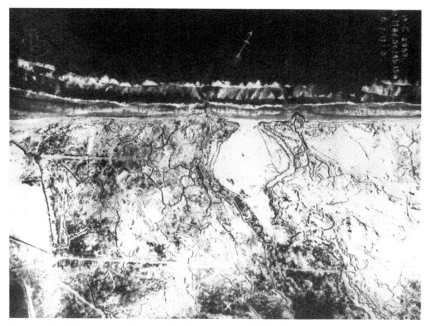

An aerial photograph of the western front endpoint, taken on 6 July 1917, four days before the great German attack. The piece of no man's land is clearly visible. It was there that the 2nd Australian Tunnelling Company was digging two offensive mine galleries beneath the no man's land with the aim of blowing up the German positions

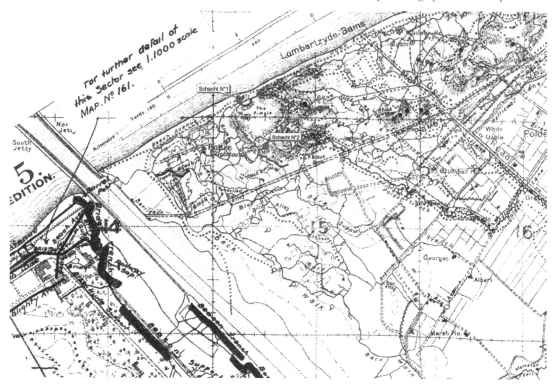

Location of the two mine shafts in early July 1917

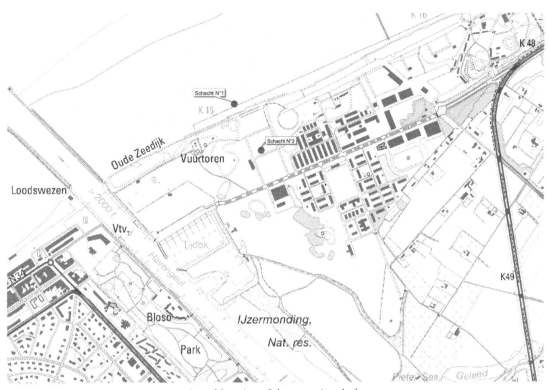

Actual location of the two mine shafts

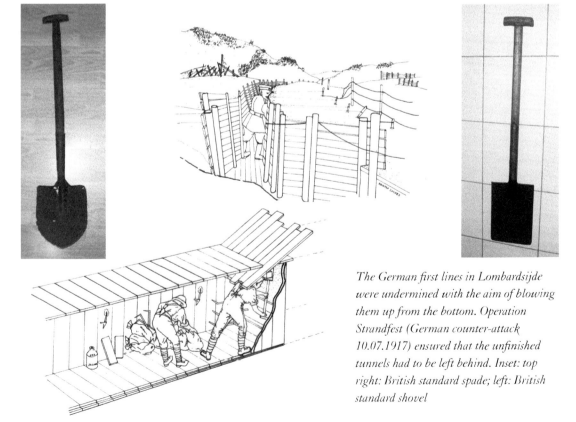

The German first lines in Lombardsijde were undermined with the aim of blowing them up from the bottom. Operation Strandfest (German counter-attack 10.07.1917) ensured that the unfinished tunnels had to be left behind. Inset: top right: British standard spade; left: British standard shovel

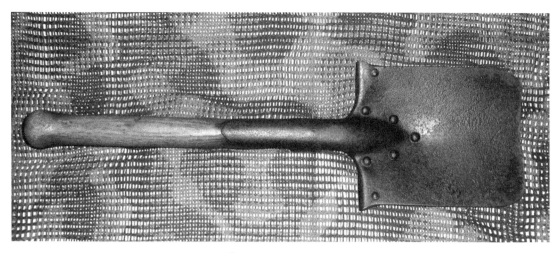

German infantry shovel

No water was lying in mine gallery No. 2 and a front sill at the face head has just been put in so water could not be seen. (The position of mine gallery No. 2 is also within Lombardsijde 14A Quarter, 200 metres to the southeast of No. 1 and 50 metres northwest of the depot of Quarter 14A.)

TOOLS: The tools in use at the face at the time of inspection were G. S. iron shovels and German Infantry shovels (which formed part of the basic equipment carried by the Infantry). Both appeared suitable.

Larger wooden shovels were seen in the gallery. These would be used as soon as the gallery was more advanced. It avoided the metallic scrape made with the iron shovels. Pieces of wood for scraping the sand from the face by hand were also made.

SPOIL (DUG OUT SAND): A certain number of 'spoil bags' (jute bags with dug out sand) were found in the trench near No. 1 mine which could not be emptied on the previous night owing to shelling. An adjacent trench that ran in the direction of the sea, was used to store the 'soil bags' with sand taken from the mine. Major Buckingham emphasised that it was important that the repairs and extensions of the tunnels were carried out with care and should not be regarded as a way to get rid of the excavated sand. He also mentioned this to company superiors.

The sand bags from mine gallery No. 2 could easily be emptied in a hollow between two dunes in daytime. The work was being done satisfactorily.

IN GENERAL: Major Buckingham inspected German lines from the British front line and posts. Nothing special was noted. German barbed wire fences had been installed extremely well and were double in places. Several British trenches had been heavily damaged by German shell fire.

The German barbed wire barriers and positions as Major Buckingham saw them

SUBWAYS (TUNNELS)

It was proposed to drive two subways, each about 1,400 feet (450 metres) long, for front to rear communication. The first was planned some 60 metres in front of the beach and was to run under the dune along the Boyau Michel (this boyau ran underneath the dunes of Lombardsijde to the southwest of the lighthouse), with thirteen entrances.

On the date of the inspection ten entrances had been started, about five of which were finished. From the rear end 90 metres of gallery had been driven. By following the dune about 4.5 to 6 metres of cover could be obtained, with the exception of a few places. The galleries were started at a height of 6 feet (1.8 metres) and a width of 4 feet (1.2 gallery metres). After a while the width was reduced to 3 feet (0.9 metres). This greatly simplified working in the sand as the face was not so liable to run in. The gallery was extremely close cased and the 'Spilling' method was used to prevent the top of the face from running in.

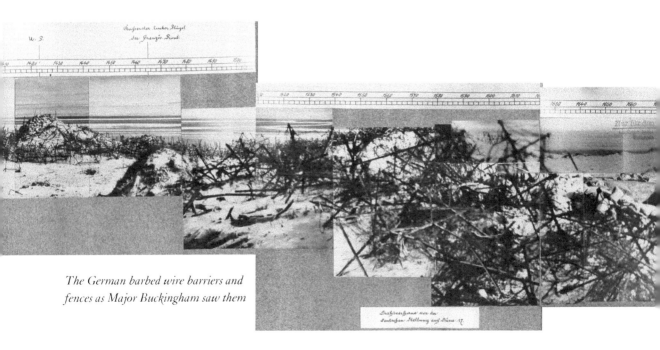

The German barbed wire barriers and fences as Major Buckingham saw them

The second subway was to run under a dune close to the sea (alongside Boyau Colonel Volet). On the date of the inspection a start had been made with the two entrances. The timbering at the entrances was unfinished and was apparently receiving further attention.

DUG-OUTS

A dug-out for 'Brigade Battle HQ' and the 'Battalion HQ' was being constructed under a horseshoe-shaped dune close to the Boyau Leclerc (location: former naval base in Lombardsijde, now a nature reserve). This tunnel was being driven using the dimensions 6 by 4 feet throughout. The width of 4 feet at the face of the tunnel created a great deal of problems with running sand which is why the 'face boards' (see 'Spilling') had to be lagged constantly while being worked.

WELLS

A short way forward of Koksijde Bath a well 1.80 metres in diameter using steel tubing was being sunk to a depth of 4.5 metres. Water was reached just below ground level and could be managed using four-hand Lilt and Force Hand Pumps. These works were nearly completed.

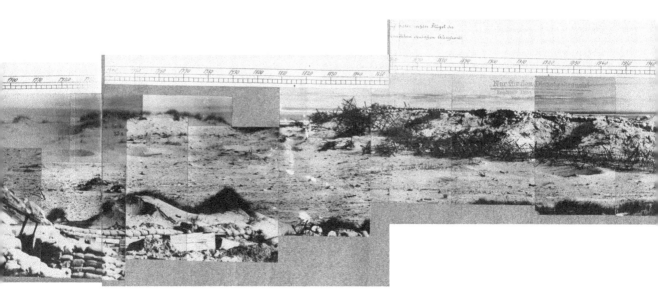

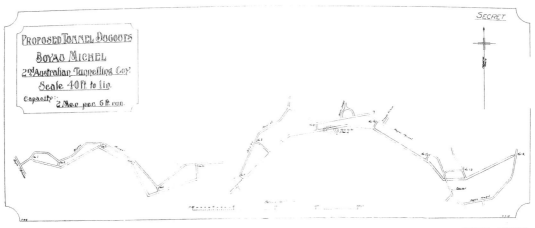

Plan of the Boyau Michel Tunnel Dugouts situation, 4 June 1917

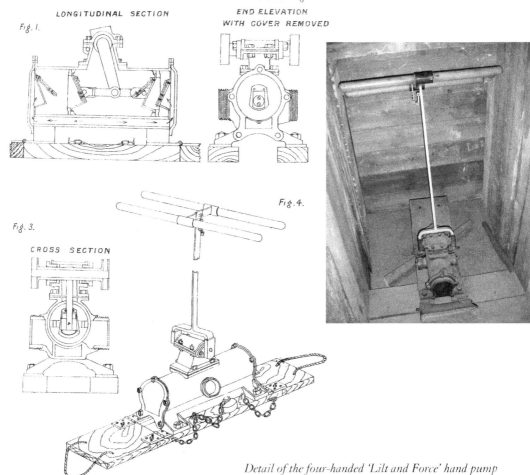

Detail of the four-handed 'Lilt and Force' hand pump

Another well with wooden frames and lagged sides with a diameter of 2.40 metres and a depth of 5 metres had been driven at the same place.

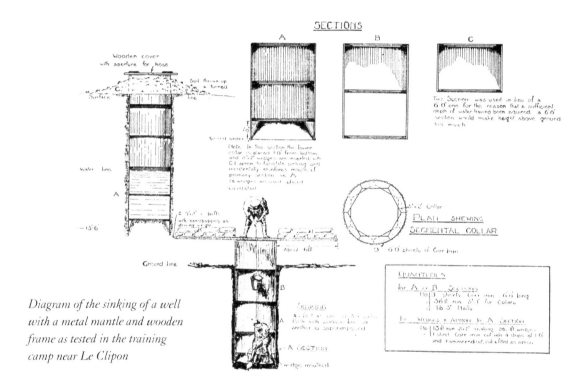

Diagram of the sinking of a well with a metal mantle and wooden frame as tested in the training camp near Le Clipon

The visit to Nieuwpoort and Major Mullingan 30 August 1917:

Left G.H.Q. at 8 am together with Major David and went to the Controller of Mines 4th Army's Office. Left Major David there and continued on to 257 Company Royal Engineers at De Panne, where I picked up Captain De la Mare and continued on in car to the Pelican Bridge in Nieuwpoort. From the bridge continued on foot to the city of Nieuwpoort.

At the southern end of Nieuwpoort we got into RUE HAUTE Subway (subway under the High Street). The cover over this varies from 2 to 15 feet (0.6 to 4.5 metres) approximately under street level. The maximum cover being obtained in the centre of the town where the ground rises.

There was about 6 inches (15 cm) of water lying on the floor of the subway. Captain De la Mare was afraid it would not drain away.

The Pelican bridge before the devastation

The prodigious Pelican bridge

The pontoon bridge to replace the destroyed Pelican bridge

Above: To this day, the original concrete of the destroyed original Pelican bridge is still visible

Below: The Hoogstraat as Major Buckingham saw it

RUINES DE NIEUPORT   La Rue Haute, a gauche les ruines de l'Eglise
1914 - 1918   The High Street, the ruins of the church on the left
RUINS OF NIEUPORT

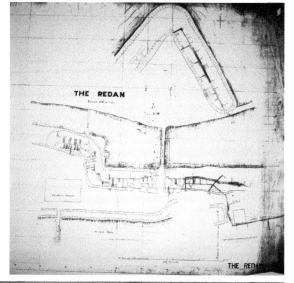

Above: The Weekly Progress Report of the 257 Tunnelling Company Royal Engineers of 1 August 1917 mentions that the Rue Haute tunnel has been finished

Right: The plan of the 257 Tunnelling Company Royal Engineers of the dug-outs near the Redan

Below: The plan of the 257 Tunnelling Company Royal Engineers with the route of the tunnel under the Hoogstraat

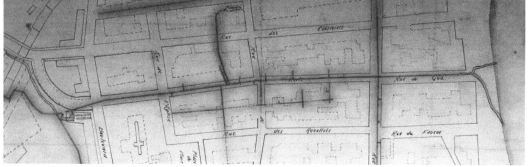

The subway was made with 6 foot legs (1.8 metres posts). An extra 3 inches (8 cm) in height would have considerably improved the subway, especially where beach boards had been put down to keep men out of the water lying on the floor.

The ground through which this subway runs was all sand. At the northern end, in RUE du QUAI (Kaaistraat), it runs into an old French covered boyau which is partly sunk into the ground and partly built up above ground level.

A branch of this subway along the RUE LONGUE (Langestraat) had been badly blown in for 50 foot (15 metres) by shell fire. This was being repaired. We then continued on to the REDAN, but had to wait about an hour before we were able to cross the river (Yser) on account of the heavy shelling.

The series of dug-outs in the Redan nearest the River Yser were dry and had been recently cleaned out by the Infantry. The electric lights were not on at the time of the inspection.

We then continued on to the series of dug-outs furthest from the river in the Grand Redan. These consisted of a single wide gallery with a number of entrances. There was a considerable amount of water on the floor of some of this gallery and for that reason a new floor was being put in above the original one. This dug-out was still being worked. The size of gallery is 7 foot 6 x 6 foot (2.30 m x 1.8 m). The ground is clayey sand, very good for working in.

Aerial photo of the big and small Redan

WEEKLY PROGRESS REPORT.

(SERVICES OTHER THAN MINING.)

SECRET

XV Corps.

35th Division.

257th Tunnelling Company.

Strength of Company (From A.F. B.213.)	Officers.	O.R.
R.E.	17	234
Permanently Attached Infantry	–	153
Temporarily Attached Infantry	–	160
Total	17	550

The Weekly Progress Report of the 257 Tunnelling Company Royal Engineers of 8 August 1917 with the mention of the works on the Redan tunnel

We continued to NOSE LANE dug-out. This dug-out also consists of a single gallery. In this case a little narrower 6 foot 3 (1.8 m x 0.9 m). This gallery also has some water at one point where the gallery is rather low.

With reference to the water in these galleries, Captain De la Mare stated that he hoped to get the sluices operated better so that at low tide more water is drained off this ground into the Yser. After seeing the NOSE LANE dug-out we returned across the Yser via the lowest bridge (the floating bridge off the Kaaistraat).

At this point the bank on the Nieuwpoort is built up vertically to form a wharf. On the north side the bank slopes up at about 1 in 1, finished with paving stones, above which there is a grass-covered mud wall.

On the Nieuwpoort side, the ground goes back almost level from the wharf-edge. The level of the water here is said to be generally 8 foot 9 (3 metres) below ground level.

For this reason it would be best to select some old building for the site of the shaft and only dig down about 6 feet (1.8 metres) for the chamber at the top of the shaft and obtain protection for the top of the shaft by means of concrete.

About 60 foot (18 metres) from the edge of the wharf there are the remains of isolated buildings which might just give the necessary protection from enemy view. By going back another 90 feet (30 metres) back from the river one comes to the main buildings of Nieuwpoort.

A concrete shaft could very well be built in one of these buildings without being seen. What's more, the

Above: Dam near the Oesterput 'La Huitrière'

Below: The plan of the 257 Tunnelling Company Royal Engineers of Nose Lane dugout

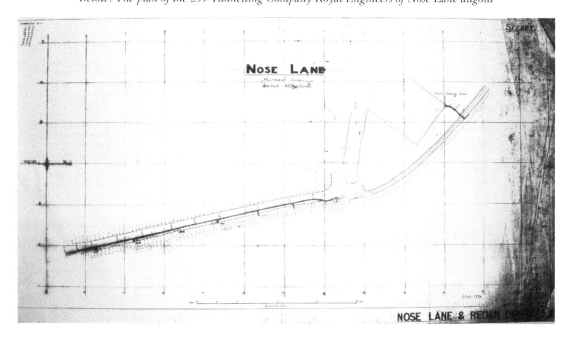

Above: The pontoon bridge along which Major Buckingham and captain De la Mare leave Nose Lane

Below: The finished of the banks of the Yser as described by Major Buckingham

The quay with the start of the Nieuwpoort roofing. In one of these buildings the construction of a shaft meant the construction of a tunnel under the Yser was possible

walls of this building will offer protection while the concrete is setting. There are also cellars which could be of use.

This position about 150 feet (45 metres) from the edge of the river is more suitable than one closer to it as it is less likely to get concentrated shell fire on it.

On the north side of the River Yser at this point there is one building, marked 'dressing station' on office plan. This building about is 24 feet long and 12 feet wide (3.5 x 7 metres) as paced outside, but because of the thickness of the walls, brickwork strengthened with concrete, the width inside is only 18 feet (5.5 metres). The roof consists of concrete 3.6 feet (1 metre) thick.

The structure on the Redan that served as a dressing station and was selected by Major Buckingham to sink a shaft for the construction of the Tunnel under the Yser

This building would be a very good one from which to sink a shaft, as the house already gives great protection. The span of concrete is at present too large. Additional concrete columns in the middle of the room would considerably strengthen it.

The great disadvantage of sinking a shaft in this house is that this is a point which would probably attract very heavy shelling from the enemy in the event of an operation by either side. The water level on this side is thought to be about 5 feet (1.5 metres) below the floor level of this building.

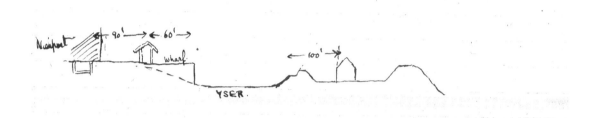

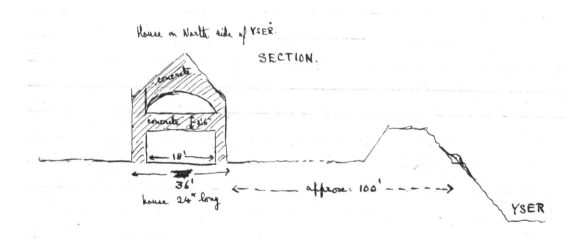

As regards the different methods adopted in sinking a shaft, Major Mullingham is in favour of the 'Freezing Method'.

After the ground where the shaft needs to be sunk is frozen there is no danger of the air bubbling out and sand rushing in. If anything goes wrong with the refrigeration plant, the ground will stay frozen long enough for the plant to be repaired.

The work required for the Freezing Method is:

1) Installation of refrigeration plant and the pouring of concrete bed and roof for protection of shaft head.
2) Boring of holes for freezing ground round shaft.
3) Freezing ground (which would take about one month).
4) Sinking shafts (about one month).
5) Driving the gallery (say one month).

This would mean about four months for all the work.

THE FREEZING PROCESS

The freezing process consists of boring a number of holes about 4 foot (1.2 metres) apart, around a circle radius approximately 4 foot (1.2 metres) greater than the radius of the shaft to be sunk. These holes are lined with a pipe of about 4 tot 6 inch diameter.

The holes are sunk to such a depth as to pass completely through the quicksand and into the impervious (clay) strata below. The freezing mixture is then circulated through these pipes and a cylinder of frozen ground is formed around the columns of sand through which it is desired to sink the shaft.

In the case of Nieuwpoort fifteen such bores would be required.

The freezing plant is not considered to be very large consisting of cylinders of liquid carbon dioxide and other chemicals. A small pumping plant is therefore required to circulate the freezing mixture at sufficient pressure.

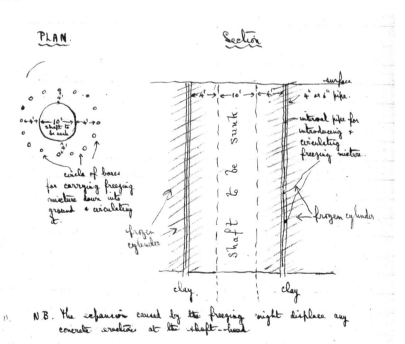

The principle of 'Freezing', outlined in the diary of Major Buckingham

MAJOR BUCKINGHAM'S VISIT TO THE 257TH COMPANY ROYAL ENGINEERS XV CORPS OP 8 NOVEMBER 1917

Left the GHQ (headquarters) at 7.30 am and arrived at the 257th company H. in De Panne at 11.00 am. Picked up guide here to take me to the Plaetsburg Dune. On arrival at the Plaetsburg Dune I met Lieutenant Colonel Preedy, Major Cropper and Major Guinylther.

Visited some of the faces of dug-outs here with Lieutenant Colonel Preedy, Major Cropper. The work was going on well and the ground 'under control' in all places that had been driven. The 'Faces' (ends of a gallery that are being driven) were carefully boarded up while being worked. This boarding was being held in place with specially made 'Dogs' about 2 foot 6 to 3 foot (75 to 90 cm) long (long hooked iron bar with sharp points at both ends).

Major Cropper informed me that the men of the two sections who have been working the longest had got into the way of the work and got from 6 to 10 feet (1.8 to 3 metres) driven a day. The men of the third section which had made the tunnelled drain from the Redan to the Yser were beginning to get used to working in the sand and were getting on all right.

There is a certain amount of work to be done in correlation with the removal of the 'spiling boards'. Otherwise the galleries look very nice and have been well driven.

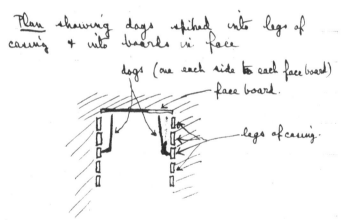

Major Buckingham's comment on the
'Spiling' principle

Continued from here with Major Cropper to Nieuwpoort and picked up Captain Tempelton in officer dug-out in Nieuwpoort. Continued along the Rue Haute subway, which was dry and in good condition. We crossed the Yser and arrived at the drainage tunnel which was designed to drain the water from the Redan into the Yser. The construction of this tunnel was a very neat job. The tide was low so we went down the shaft into the drainage tunnel to have a look at the sluice doors. These are just strong wooden doors hanging down so as to open towards the Yser only. An emergency sluice lifted vertically up or down is also provided.

Captain Tempelton said that the water in the Redan had gone down somewhere about 2 foot (60 cm). A certain amount of water was running out of the sluice while we were there. We then went on to have a

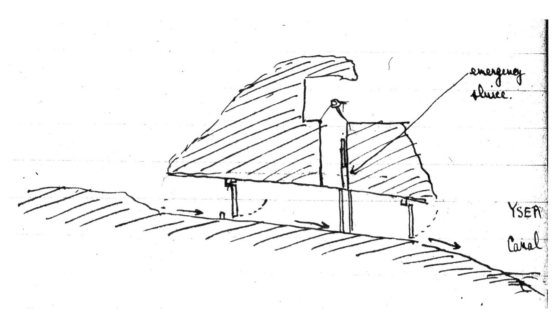

Sketch of the emergency lock that was to ensure the drainage of the Redan (Buckingham diary)

look at the entrance to the drainage system. The water was held up here by a bank of mud, which Major Cropper said he was getting removed. This will lower the water another 1 foot (50 cm).

This is a good piece of engineering work which will make a lot of difference in the drainage of the dug-outs and the ground generally.

From there we continued along the Redan dug-outs. A good deal of extra flooring had been put in to raise the floors from the water. All the floors seen were dry and the dug-outs were in pretty good condition. Infantrymen were cleaning the galleries in places.

We continued along into the 'Vauxhall – 5 Bridges Subway'. The spoil is being got out through a vertical shaft slightly to the west of Vauxhall Bridge. On the surface the spoil is run away in a trolley and tipped into an old basin (the oyster pond). The trolley line is camouflaged against enemy airborne surveillance.

We continued along the subway with a dimension of 6 foot 3 (1.80 x 0.90 m). This has been quite well driven and setts put in evenly.

The work in the subway has been stopped for the present because of other work at the dressing station and making some sumps (wells) and pumping recesses in the Nieuwpoort subways, which needed to be completed. After reaching the 'face' (end of the tunnel) we turned back and got out by an entrance at Vauxhall Bridge. We crossed this bridge over the Yser and continued to the 'Rue Longue Tunnel' where sumps and recesses for pumps are being put in at all the low places.

Except at one point this subway was on the date of inspection free of water. Major Cropper said that the water had been about one foot deep in it.

The narrow-gauge railway that was used to transfer the excavated earth to the oyster pit

Plan of The Australian Electrical and Mechanical Mining and Boring Company (EMM&B Co.) with indication of the dug-outs under the Redan and Vauxhall bridge (No. 13) where Major Buckingham crossed the Yser through the 'covered boyaux' in the Sint-Jacobstraat to descend in the 'Rue Longue tunnel' under the Langestraat

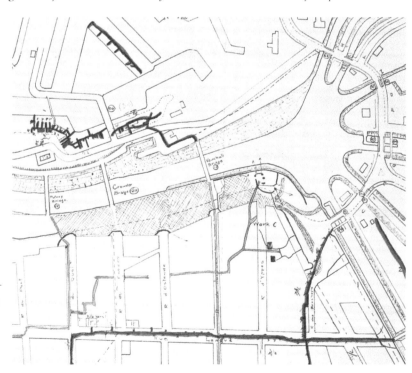

Britons and Belgians in the Langestraat near the City Hall, 1917. Under their feet is where they worked at the 'Rue Longue tunnel'

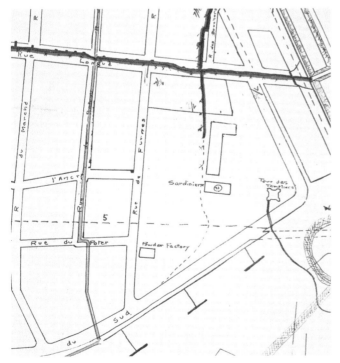

On the plan of EMM&B Co. we see the onset and the progress of the works on the connection tunnel between the tunnel under the Langestraat and the Bombproof ('the Power House')

We continued along the Rue Longue Tunnel to the Power House. Here men under the command of Major Cropper were putting in a corrugated iron screen and were going to build it up behind with sandbags to form an isolation barricade in case of fire.

The Devil's Tower and the Bombproof as Major Buckingham saw them. An underground connection was provided between the Langestraat and the Bombproof

From here we went to inspect the connection between the 'Rue Haute Subway' and the Dressing Station (underground first aid station). Work was being pushed ahead in three faces here, in order to get the connection finished within about seven to ten days. The gallery was being driven from the Dressing Station end and both directions from intermediate cellars of ruined houses. The spoil was being disposed of inside ruined houses.

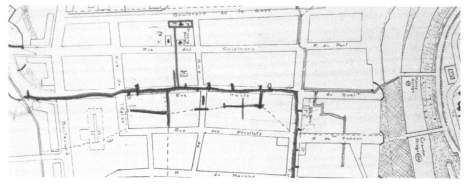

The EMM & B Co. map shows the 'Dressing Station tunnel' that runs from the Hoogstraat to the Astridlaan

At the Dressing Station end, spoil had been previously disposed of on the surface. When the place had been shelled subsequent to a German aeroplane flying low over the dressing station, complaints had been made that it was the spoil that was showing up.

The spoil had been very well camouflaged when I saw the place. Near the dressing station were two small bunkers. Only one of these bunkers still remains. They served as temporary accommodation for the injured who had already been given first aid in the underground dressing station and were awaiting transport to 'Ambulance de l'Ocean' in De Panne. This transport was usually by night in a horse and cart or in an ambulance.

The hospital 'Ambulance de l'Océan' in De Panne where most of the wounded from Nieuwpoort were brought

One of the many wards in the wooden barracks of the hospital

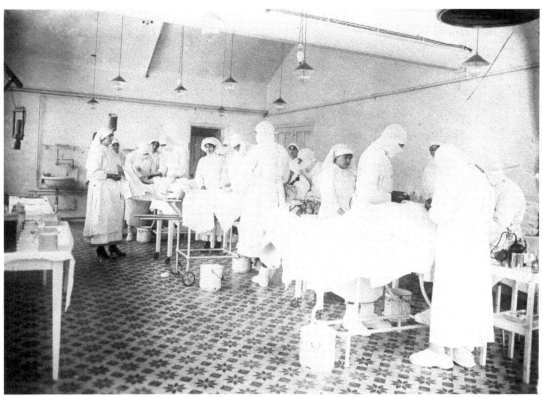

Above: The operating theatre in the 'Ambulance de l'Océan' in De Panne

Below: The supply of injured from the Nieuwpoort sector was largely by ambulances or horse and cart

Above: The dressing station tunnel pillbox that is still there.

Below: Two members of the 2nd Australian Tunnelling Company are putting sleeping bones in a dugout under Nieuwpoort-Bad, 13 November 1917

On my way back I called at 'Controller of Mines 4th Army's office'. Colonel Preedy informed me that he was arranging his work so that it would be in a suitable position ten days from then, i.e. mid-November 1917, to hand over.

Handing over is supposed to start on the 17th of November 1917. He stated that Plaetsburg Dune dugouts will just be finished, apart from the bunking (construction of bunks).

Once the bunking is completed there will be accommodation for	*300 men*
Kent Camp will be completed with accommodation for	*300 men*
Norfolk Camp will be completed with accommodation for	*100 men*
West Surrey Camp will be completed with accommodation for	*200 men*
East Surrey Camp will not be quite completed yet accommodation for	*300 men*
Brisbane Camp, 184 Company hopes to complete this with assistance from 257 Company, accommodation for	*300 men*
This makes a total accommodation of	*1,500 men*

Colonel Preedy hopes that he will be able to have the same Companies under him after the change.

V. E. Buckingham
Major. RE
10/4/17

CHAPTER NINE

THE DORSET REGIMENT IN NIEUWPOORT 1917

In mid-May 1917 the 32nd Division received orders to move north. At that time, the battalion was based in Saint Quentin, near Hazebrouck in the Pas-de-Calais region. The move to Belgium was made on 15 May. The following day Major L. C. Hope joined the battalion and assumed command. From Teteghem the battalion marched to Dunkirk and on to Koksijde. From there they moved to Nieuwpoort where the battalion was to relieve 3rd French Regiment.

The following day, 17 June, they relieved another battalion of 3rd French Regiment.

Captain W.A. Smellie writes about this period:

Unexpectedly, we were ordered to relieve the French on the Belgian coast sector, near Nieuwpoort. We moved quickly to the coast, transported in buses to Oostduinkerke. After a short journey, we arrived at our billets in a hutted camp within the dunes. The camp was also close to the sea and very pleasant. The sector was very quiet so the men were able to enjoy any opportunity to swim, but later this had to be limited to specific areas because the Germans started to shell bathing parties. The next day most of the officers were busy reconnoitring our new sector. We were ordered to take over the Nieuwpoort sector. The 1st Division was deployed in the dunes northwest of the Geleide Creek.

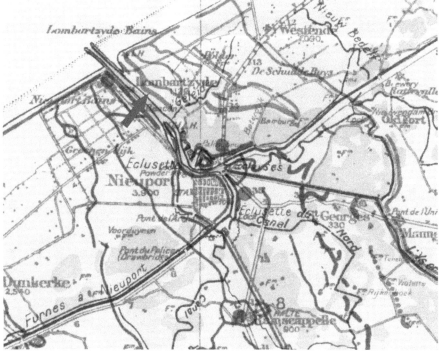

Trench map showing Lombardsijde and Nieuwpoort

Above: View of the German front line in Lombardsijde. These consisted of large barbed wire barriers and sandbags
Bottom: Triangle Wood, today known as the 'Littobos'

One of the bunkers in Triangle Wood

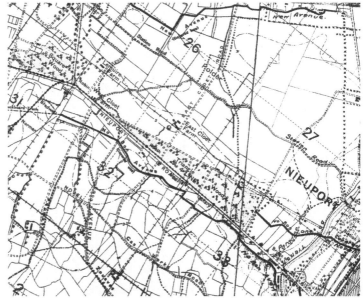

1917 Trench Map showing location of Triangle Wood west of Nieuwpoort

The communication post in Triangle Wood

The coastal landscape and front were very different. Instead of trenches there were large barricades ('breastworks') everywhere, criss-crossing each other without any obvious structure. Occasionally, a summer house or shelter was to be found with a table and chairs. It was just like a holiday resort – because nobody fired, one could feel safe and get a good view of the surrounding terrain from above the parapet. The lines were not very clear and about 100 yards (90 metres) apart, connected by communication trenches constructed above ground. There were some concrete bunkers, but few dug-outs.

Behind us, about a half mile (800 metres) from the front line, ran the Yser. The only protection against artillery fire in our sector was in Triangle Wood (now known as 'Littobos'), a wood west of Nieuwpoort. Hostile batteries were just 300 yards (250 metres) in front of us, manned by German Matrosen troops.

It was an unusual and delicate situation. The breastworks of the trenches were in a poor condition and not bullet proof. In the first four lines of the Lombardsijde sector, there was little shelter from shell fire and being located close to flooded areas, the water came right up to the breastworks.

In those days Nieuwpoort was very quiet. The French saw this sector as a 'rest area' and it was therefore poorly maintained.

Inside the communication post in Triangle Wood

Access to all the sub-sectors held by the Dorsets ran through the streets of Nieuwpoort and then onto pontoon bridges over the Yser. The bridges were frequently destroyed by German shell fire. Front line relief, shift changes and evacuations were always very tense. During the night Nieuwpoort was bombarded with gas and every other type of shell.

Battalion headquarters was housed in a concrete reinforced bunker called the 'Rubber House'. It was a very solid building and could withstand a direct hit from a 5.9 in shell. The biggest annoyance within range were the German 'Minenwerfers' and apparently there were plenty of these available. Direct hits caused considerable damage to the trenches and completely destroyed breastworks.

Right: German Matrosen in the trenches at Lombardsijde
Below: German Matrosen in the lines at Lombardsijde

Above: German Matrosen in the lines at Lombardsijde

Below: Belgian-French trenches similar to those taken over by the Dorsets

Ruines de Nieuport   1914-18   Tranchée belge à Nieuport.
The ruins of Nieuport   Belgian trench in Nieuport.

RUINES DE NIEUPORT - RUINS OF NIEUPORT   Abris le long de la route de Nieuport Bains
1914-1918   Shelter beside the road from Nieuport-Bains

Above: The type of shelters that the Dorsets encountered when arriving at Nieuwpoort
Below: French soldiers in a quiet period near the Ganzepoot (Five Bridges), Nieuwpoort

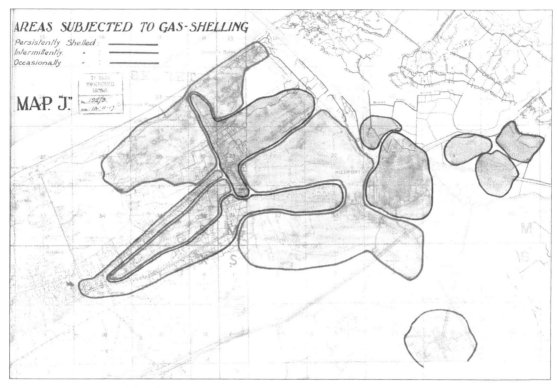

Map showing intensity of gas bombardments around Nieuwpoort

Above: View of the front on the right bank of the Yser

Left: Men of 2nd Australian Tunnelling Company near a camp in the dunes of Koksijde. They are (from left to right) Captain Garnett J. Adcock, Adjutant 2/ATC; Major E.W. Webb MC, 7th Field Company; Regimental Serjeant Major McGain, 2/ATC; on the far right are three unknown men of the South African Scottish Labour Company attached to the 2nd Australian Tunnelling Company

Top left: Germans bring a 'minenwerfer' into position in the line

Bottom left: German aircraft on their way to Dunkirk

Top right: British movements are closely monitored from the German lines with a trench periscope

Bottom right: The Dorset's dreaded minenwerfer

Behind the lines, the camps near Koksijde were constantly bombarded and when the Battalion were resting at Dunkirk, German air raids harassed the men.

Preparations for the 3rd Battle of Ypres (Passchendaele) were already well underway. This initial offensive was to be followed by a British Naval amphibious landing behind the German lines in conjunction with an attack by the XV Corps, on a two-Division front, along the coast from Nieuwpoort. Our position north of the Yser was about 1,000 yards (900 metres) deep and it was vital that none of this was lost.

The problems encountered in constructing additional defences in Nieuwpoort were almost insurmountable. When we were digging we encountered water at a depth of only 1 foot (30 cm) below the surface. This meant that sandbags had to be brought over a long distance to thicken the breastworks. At that time, the enemy had superiority both in air power and artillery. As a result, the enemy observation was excellent and consequently our newly strengthened positions were almost immediately destroyed.

The result of German artillery on the British strengthened positions

GERMAN ATTACK ON NIEUWPOORT 10TH & 11TH JULY 1917
Operation Strandfest (Beach Party)

On 10 July 1917, the enemy commenced a massive bombardment on the Lombardsijde sector. By 10.30 it became apparent that the bombing was much more violent and persistent than usual, and the 14th Brigade, then in Ghyvelde, was prepared to leave within thirty minutes. A little while later they left for Koksijde. The situation was bad. At 19.30 the 1st Division reported that the enemy had reached the Yser river bank. The enemy also attacked on the front of the 32nd Division, but was eventually pushed back, until only a small piece of the British 'Nose/Nasal trench system' remained in German hands.

The battle lasted three more days. On 12 July, the Battalion took over the Defences of Nieuwpoort, held by the 16th Northumberland Fusiliers. On 15 July, the Battalion relieved the 15th Highland Light Infantry and 5/6th Royal Scots in the Defences, to the left of the Nieuwpoort-Lombardsijde Road. It was in this part of the line that we had lost a section of trenches. In this German attack, there were remarkably few casualties on both sides. Some of our casualties were recorded as 'KIA' (Killed in Action) or became 'Prisoners of War'. The number of British Prisoners of War in this action was high.

On 17 July 1917, Lieutenants F. C. Dice and W. V. Richards, each with eight men, attempted to attack the enemy down Nose Alley and Nose Support trenches. The Germans saw the men and sent up an emergency rocket. Almost immediately the German artillery responded with very heavy shell fire, machine-gun and rifle fire. The two attacking parties immediately retired without success.

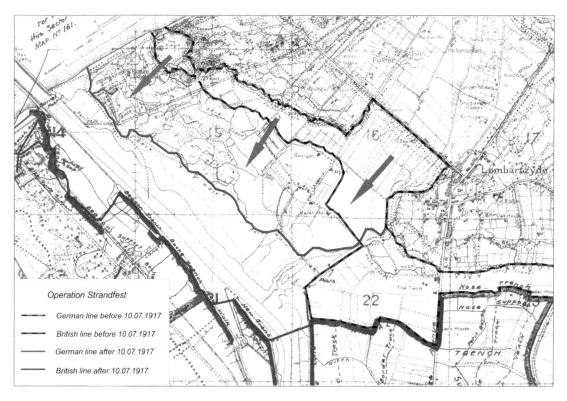

Operation Strandfest

——— German line before 10.07.1917

——— British line before 10.07.1917

——— German line after 10.07.1917

——— British line after 10.07.1917

The German attack on 10 July 1917, called Operation Strandfest, caused the loss of British territory north of the Yser, causing the British to retreat behind the river

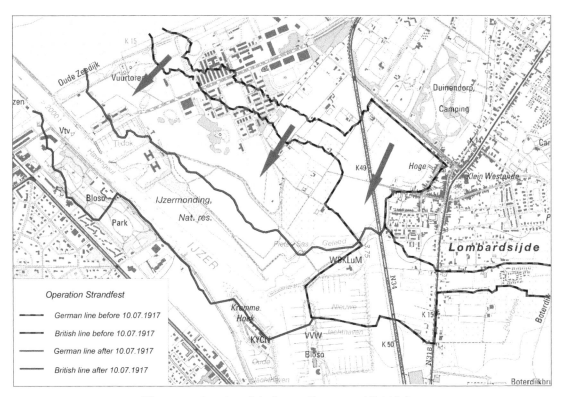

The current location of the former German and British lines

Germans of the Marine Korps Flandern firing a Trench Mortar during the attack on the British lines 10 July 1917

Three men were killed; 2/Lieutenant Dice and nineteen men were wounded and one man was missing. This action took place just before the Battalion was relieved by the 5th Kings Own Yorkshire Light Infantry and during the relief the enemy struck a heavy blow, killing one man and wounding Lieutenant T. C. Coates and five other men.

After a gas bombardment and a smoke barrage, the Germans attack from their trenches in the dunes of Lombardsijde

On the right side of the line, the water was chest high. Captain Smellie writes: We are almost surrounded by water in a Polder landscape. There is a river running through the front line, which has separated my company from the company on our right side.

Our sector front line trench was a breastwork barricade made from sandbags, called 'Nun Trench'. At the end of the trench, there was a forwarded listening post ('Nun Post') that ran to within 25 yards (22 metres) of a German listening post. The listening posts were very similar with both having a small raised platform at the end. To the right of this was the river (the old Yser) with a duckboard walkway.

The walkway was one of the few routes to the other company between the Boterdijk ('Butter Dyke') and the inundated areas. Battalion Headquarter was in an old brickworks behind 'Nun Support' trench, on the other side of the river.

Above: British artillery answers the German attack (photo courtesy of Eddy Lambrecht)

Below: German Matrosen in a newly captured British post near the mouth of the Yser, Nieuwpoort 12 July 1917. Note the hole in the pier on the Lombardsijde side, which was the result of the explosion of a German 'Fernlenkboot' (radio-controlled boat) in March 1917

A German 'Fernlenkboot' is being prepared. This was a radio-controlled motorboat filled with explosives for destructive purposes. It was the forerunner of the guided torpedo

In this part of the sector, a German did something remarkable every morning. From the raised platform, straight across from us, he raised his head, smiled, bowed and then disappeared. We waited for him on several occasions, but it turned out that the head was made from papier-mâché. Every now and then a real head would pop-up.

A German 'Fernlenkboot' is stored in a concrete bunker

Above: Several German casualties of Operation Strandfest were buried in the first instance near the dug-outs of the Grand Dune (the Apfenberg) in Lombardsijde

Below: The grave of a German soldier buried in a hurry in the dunes of Lombardsijde.

Above: Immediately after the Germans' captured new ground, the trench orientation was changed
Below: View of the German lines near the Great Hemme farm.

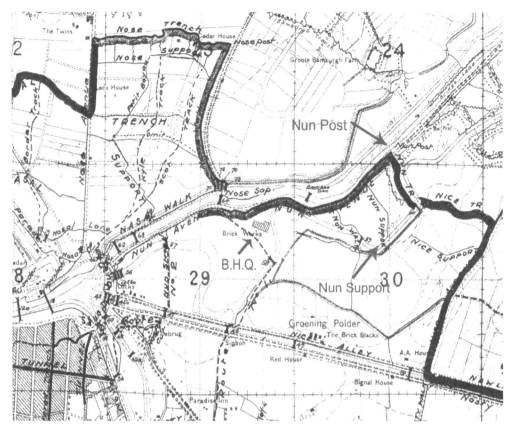

Trench Map showing location of Nun Post, Nun Support and Battalion Headquarters

*An example of the papier-mâché heads
used to fool the enemy*

Major H. C. Lloyd had assumed command on 5 July and he paid a great deal of attention to field training when the Battalion was out of the line. When the Battalion was at 'rest' they trained regularly, but the atmosphere was relaxed and there were also opportunities to swim. Billets and shops were generally good, if sometimes scattered around. When billeted in De Panne there was also a fine hotel, De Terlinck, where one could get a good meal. Later billets were in Coudekerque-Branche and St Pol, which were effectively suburbs of Dunkirk, which was accessible on foot.

The battalion ended its last tour in this sector on 3 October 1917 and then went out of line until December. The 32nd Division was resting and training in readiness for the final attack on Passchendaele's terrible battlefield.

Above: The German front line, just yards away, near the Plassendale Channel in Nieuwpoort

Below: Hotel Terlinck, by the sea, De Panne

CHAPTER TEN
THE SECOND AUSTRALIAN TUNNELLING COMPANY IN NIEUWPOORT-BAINS (JUNE–NOVEMBER 1917)

In preparation of 'Operation Hush', at the end of June 1917 the British XV Corps took over the Belgian coastal sector from the French. The aim of the operation was to capture the ports of Zeebrugge and Oostende. This operation was planned to coincide with the 3rd Battle of Ypres.

The 2nd Australian Tunnelling Company was sent to Nieuwpoort-Bains to help the XV Corps with the preparations for the operation. They arrived on 16 June 1917.

The Company had 28 officers and about 660 other ranks, all under the command of Major Edric Mullingan. The Company was divided into four sections:

No. 1 Section, under the command of Captain Leslie de Jersey Grut
No. 2 Section, under the command of Captain George Smith
No. 3 Section, under the command of Captain Frederick Phippart
No. 4 Section, under the command of Captain Arthur Cohlen.

Major Edric Mullingan (standing), CO of the 2nd Australian Tunnelling Company with Captain Malcolm Ross next to the sand bags used to camouflage the entrance of a tunnel in the dunes at Nieuwpoort-Bad, 12 August 1917. Given the pipes for the pump and the bags spoil (excavated sand) at the entrance, we assume that this tunnel is still was not finished

Each of these Section Commanders had so far survived the war, and had been awarded the Military Cross. Edric Mullingan had been awarded the Distinguished Service Order, the Belgian War Cross and was three times mentioned in dispatches.

In the front line it was normal to detonate mines under enemy strong posts at the start of larger offensives. The aim of this was to cause confusion, and to delay enemy digging towards the British positions. Shortly before, the technique had been applied with overwhelming success in the case of the nineteen heavy mines which had been detonated at the start of the Battle near Messines on 7 June.

Captain Grut's No. 1 Section immediately started with offensive tunnelling from the British lines to two fortified German positions, where the German line crossed a couple of large dunes, known as 'Black Dune' and 'Grande Dune', some 600 metres east of the Yser. The access to the front was via three pontoon bridges across the Yser, called Richmond Bridge, Kew Bridge and Mortlake Bridge.

The other sections of the Company began building observation posts (a total of six by No. 2 Section under Captain Smith), dug-outs and machine-gun emplacements in the dunes in Nieuwpoort-Bains,

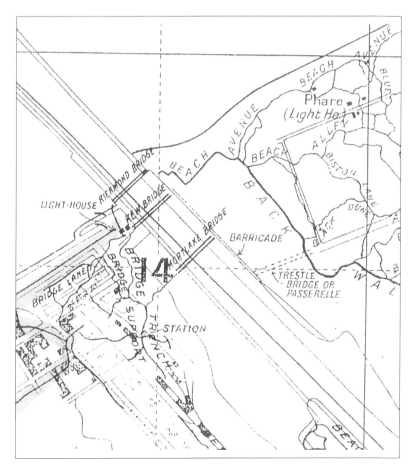

Left: The position of the three floating pontoon bridges in the sector of the 2nd Australian Tunnelling Company

dug-outs at places further away (a Divisional HQ in Oostduinkerke Bains and a XV Corps HQ called 'Kursaal Dug-outs' in La Panne), as well as wells for drinking water in Oostduinkerke Bains.

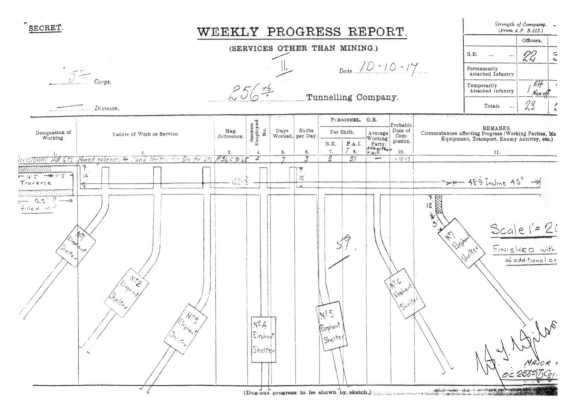

The Weekly Progress Report with a sketch of the division headquarters in Oostduinkerke-Bad

The Company Headquarters (CHQ) was at first sited in Koksijde Bains, but was later moved to La Panne, after heavy German bombardments made the position untenable. The Company Camp was in the dunes of St-Idesbald. The No. 3 section's CHQ was in the basement of a villa on the promenade at Nieuwpoort-Bains.

On 10 July the Germans, who suspected a British attack in the near future, launched a counter attack (Operation Strandfest) against the British Division occupying the lines in the Belgian coastal sector. The British had not anticipated the attack and were not prepared for it.

The mining work east of the Yser was carried out that day by a squad of No. 1 section of the 2nd Australian Tunnelling Company. The squad had two officers (2nd Lt. Walter Mortenson and 2nd Lt. Ernest Hargraves) and 47 other ranks, of whom most were subscripted labourers who had to assist the tunnelling men. The Infantry troops were from the 1st Battalion Black Watch Regiment and the 1st Battalion South Wales Borderers (both part of the British 1st Division).

The seawall of Nieuwpoort-Bad near the villa where No. 3 Section of the 2nd Australian Tunnelling Company had its headquarters in the basement

Officers of the No. 3 Section of the 2nd Australian Tunnelling Company at their headquarters in Nieuwpoort-Bad, 12 August 1917. (From left to right: Captain Frederick Phippart, Lieutenant (Lt.) C. H. Blumer, Lt. L. S. Lambert and Lt J. Malcomsen)

The entrance to the basement of the ruin where No. 3 Section had its headquarters

*Members of the 2nd
Australian Tunnelling
Company at the entrance of a
dugout in Nieuwpoort-Bad*

Two other battalions of
the 1st Division, the 2nd
King's Royal Rifle Corps
and the 1st Northampton
defended the front at
Nieuwpoort Bains when
the German attack broke loose. All troops in the dunes to the north of the Yser were completely
cut off from their rear guard. The three pontoon bridges were completely destroyed during the
late morning of 10 July by the firestorm which preceded the attack by the German infantry which
had been equipped with flamethrowers. By eight o'clock that evening all British defences had been
overrun, and the Germans had control of the eastern bank of the Yser.

Next day, at dawn, one officer (2nd Lt Hargraves) and five other ranks of the tunnelling group
had managed to swim across the Yser. None of the advance Infantry troops managed to escape, and
only three officers and 60 other ranks, out of more than 1,300 officers and men of the 2nd King's
Royal Rifle Corps and the 1st Northampton, managed to swim across the canal, thereby avoiding
capture or certain death.

*View from an
observation
post on the new
German front
line after 10
July 1917*

Sgt. Charles H. Angus was one of those who did not manage to cross the Yser that day, because he could not swim. During the retreat he and some other members of the No.1 Section remained on the bank of the Yser, and were taken prisoner. In the report of the Court-Martial on 16 September 1918 in Switzerland he testified how the commanding officers fled across the Yser in a boat, and left him and the remainder of the Section behind.

C O N F I D E N T I A L.

(COPY).

Statement by a Prisoner of War interned in Switzerland.

Statement forwarded by Captain Charles Mills, 51st Battalion, Official Representative of the A.I.F. in Switzerland.

Original Manuscript filed with Records.

Administrative Headquarters,
Australian Imperial Force,
London,
S.W.1.

14th November 1918.

Re .No.   478.

Rank.   Sergeant.

Name.   Angus, Charles Henry.

Unit.   2nd Australian Tunnelling Company.

Circumstances of Capture.

(a)   Date.   July 10,1917.

(b)   Place.   Nieuport(on Belgian Coast)

(c)   What happened immediately before Capture.

After about 12 hours bombardment by the enemy, starting about 8 a.m. the British resistance was broken.

Officers seen during engagement.

Lieut. Morten,Lieut.Hargraves(2nd Aust.Tunn.Coy.,) the latter Officer escaped across the canal by boat,leaving myself and L/Cpl. Window on the canal bank.   Lieut.Morten. was captured with his men in the front line.

What happened immediately after Capture.

We were marched to Dendumond in Belgium, about 35 miles from the place of capture. I stayed two months in Dendumond being starved, and then two weeks in Dulmen,where we received medical attention and were subjected to vaccination and five innoculations.   Then I was taken to Lechfeld in Southern Bavaria where I remained for about 12 months. I was then exchanged into Switzerland.   I did no work in Germany. Twenty-two of my shift were also captured but I am unable to give names as the Germans took all my correspondence.

(Signed)   C.H.Angus, Sgt.
2nd Aust.Tunn.Coy.,
16.9.18.

The interrogation report of the Martial Council in Switzerland of 16 September 1918 m.b.t. Sgt Charles H. Agnus. This document was made available by a Sgt Agnus' niece who plans to visit the site where her grandmother was captured in 2006

Of the forty sappers and the one officer of the 2nd Australian Tunnelling Company who were captured, five sappers died as Prisoners of War in Germany. At least one man, 3988 Sapper Patrick Minogue, who was seriously wounded during the attack, returned to Australia before the end of the war. After having been shot in the foot, and wounded in the leg by a steel grenade, he was saved by a German machine-gun team, who kept him in their dugout for two days before managing to take him to a dressing post at Middelkerke. From there he was taken to a hospital in Brugge, and then to a POW hospital in Hamburg. His wounds resulted in the shortening of one leg, which was why he was declared a POW non-combatant. He was sent back to England under a POW exchange programme, and with some fellow partners in misfortune taken back to Australia. His fellow tunnelling troops waited for the end of the war in their POW camp deep in Germany. Five of the Australian POWs died in Germany before they could be repatriated to Australia. Most died of Spanish influenza.

The prisoners of war of Operation Strandfest were led through Oostende under great German interest

Notwithstanding the substantial losses of 10 July, the British plans and preparations for 'Operation Hush' continued unchanged. The 1st Division was pulled back from the front on 16 July 1917. Preparations for the planned coastal attack would continue with far less troops than the previous three weeks. The 66th (2/ East Lancashire) Division took their place on the front at Nieuwpoort.

The 3rd Battle of Ypres, which started on 31 July, did not conform to the expectations of the British GHQ and the anticipated quick gains of terrain were foiled because the troops got bogged down in the mud. The planned date for 'Operation Hush' was continuously delayed until, halfway through October the decision was taken to abandon the operation. Prior to that, the 2nd Australian Tunnelling Company had carried on its construction activities, mainly around Nieuwpoort-Bains. The most ambitious of these

Above: The British captured at Operation Strandfest were transported to Oostende where they were temporarily accommodated in a school in the Hazegras district

Centre: The captured British were taken to Brugge via the Desmet-Denaeyer bridge

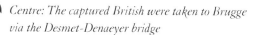

Left: The British–Australian prisoners of Operation Strandfest were shown in Brugge in a parade to Admiral Ludwig von Schröder who was visiting the city. From Brugge they were put on transport to Germany

constructions was the 'Infantry Subway' which was constructed through the basements of the buildings on the promenade to the ruins of the pilot's building and the lighthouse at the mouth of the Yser.

Above: The dyke in Nieuwpoort-Bad, August 1917, looking in the direction of Oostduinkerke

Below: The dyke in Nieuwpoort-Bad, August 1917, looking in the direction of Lombardsijde

Above: The esplanade at Nieuwpoort-Bad, which ran along the 'Infantry Subway'

Below: The pilot building and the lighthouse. The end point of the 'Infantry Subway'

Behind the ruins of the villa Hurle Bise, the tunnel split into a number of other tunnels, the two most important of which were known as Beach Tunnel (from Hurle Bise to the old pilot's building) and Bedford Tunnel, which ran southward to the Regina Trench behind the Hotel Regina and the old brewery.

Above: The Hotel Hurle Bise in May 1917

Right: The current villa Hurle Bise

Above: Hotel Regina just before the outbreak of war

The former, post-war, Hotel Regina

There were thirteen inclines into the tunnel, at intervals of about 50 metres. Two other tunnels, Bexhill Tunnel and Bristol Tunnel, ran from the tunnel under the Promenade to Bath Avenue, a trench which ran besides the promenade on the beach side. Work on the Infantry Subway was mainly carried out by Captain Leslie De Jersey Grut's No. 1 Section.

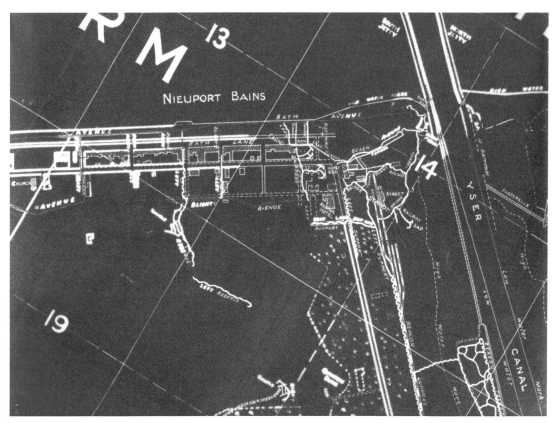

Trench map of the 2nd Australian Tunnelling Company with situation September 1, 1917, shows all trenches and
tunnels under Nieuwpoort-Bad

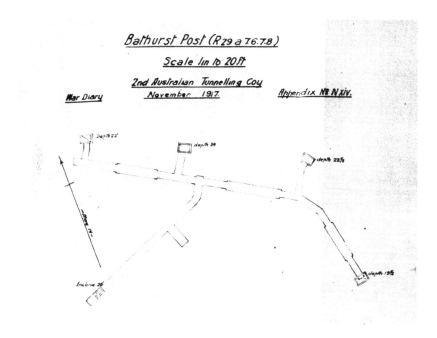

Plan of the Bathurst Posts

A large number of dug-outs were built in the dunes behind Nieuwpoort-Bains. Some were needed for the accommodation of the machine-gun emplacements, other were purely for human accommodation. Most were called after the Australian towns where the miners originated; Cobar, Ballarat, Broken Hill, Bathurst and Bendigo posts were all named for mining towns, while Melbourne, Sydney Ridge and Adelaide were named after large cities.

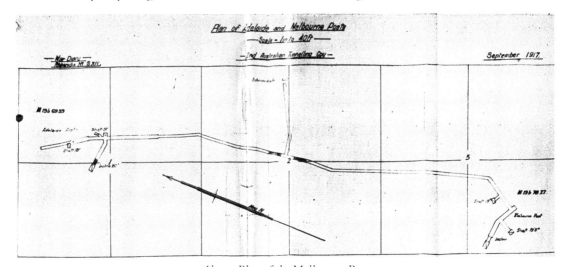

Above: Plan of the Melbourne Posts

Below: Weekly Progress Report of the 2nd Australian Tunnelling Company from Bathurst Posts,
14 November 1917

Manly Post got its name from a famous surfing beach in Sydney. Boppy Mountain was called after a large mining site near Cobar in far western New South Wales. It is clear where Kangaroo Post got its name. Other dug-outs, Left Reserve, Right Reserve and Dune 18 were simply called after their location.

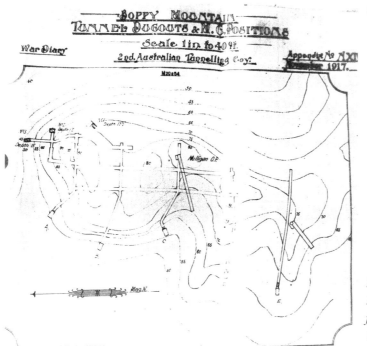

Left: Plan of Boppy Mountain

Below: Weekly Progress Report of the 2nd Australian Tunnelling Company from Boppy Mountain, 14 November 1917

Left Reserve Dugout was the largest in Nieuwpoort Bains. It could accommodate an infantry company of some 240 men. Broken Hill Post was the most complex machinegun emplacement, with its accommodation for the gunners and spaces for repairs and ammunition storage. Also, six observation posts were built. All these constructions were built in the very fine dune sand!

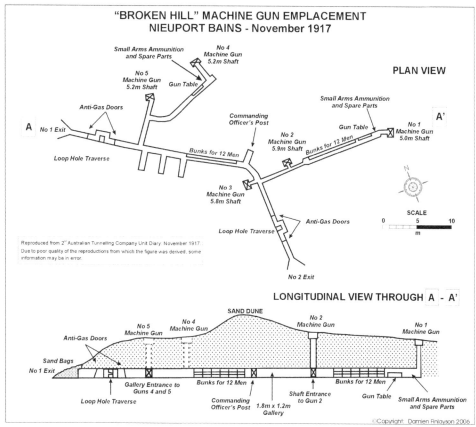

Above: Floor plan and cross-section of the machine-gun emplacement Broken Hill, Nieuwpoort Bains, November 1917

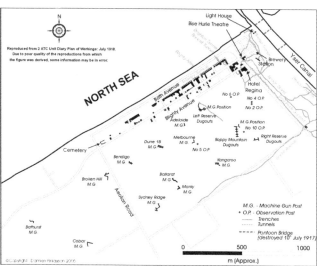

Right: Situation of the main dug-outs at Nieuwpoort-Bad, 1917–1918

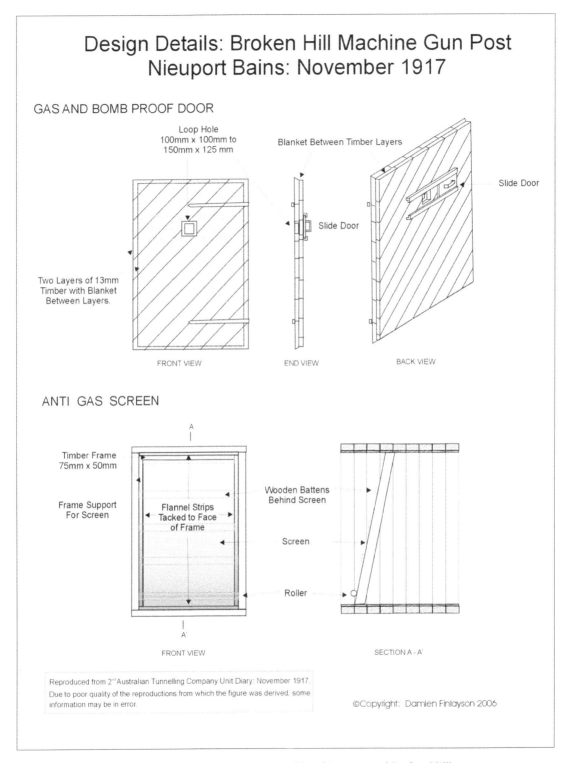

Design Details: Broken Hill Machine Gun Post
Nieuport Bains: November 1917

GAS AND BOMB PROOF DOOR

Loop Hole
100mm x 100mm to
150mm x 125 mm

Blanket Between Timber Layers

Slide Door

Slide Door

Two Layers of 13mm
Timber with Blanket
Between Layers.

FRONT VIEW   END VIEW   BACK VIEW

ANTI GAS SCREEN

A

Timber Frame
75mm x 50mm

Frame Support
For Screen

Flannel Strips
Tacked to Face
of Frame

Wooden Battens
Behind Screen

Screen

Roller

A'

FRONT VIEW   SECTION A - A'

Reproduced from 2ⁿᵈ Australian Tunnelling Company Unit Diary: November 1917.
Due to poor quality of the reproductions from which the figure was derived, some
information may be in error.

©Copyright: Damien Finlayson 2006

Detail of the existing gas protection of 'machine-gun yard Broken Hill'

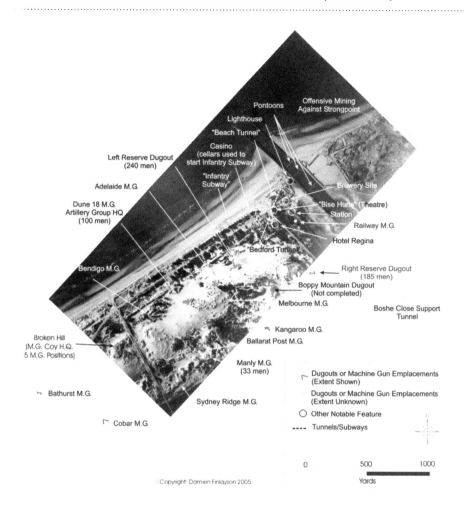

Pontoons
Offensive Mining Against Strongpoint
Lighthouse
"Beach Tunnel"
Casino (cellars used to start Infantry Subway)
Left Reserve Dugout (240 men)
Adelaide M.G.
"Infantry Subway"
Brewery Site
Dune 18 M.G. Artillery Group HQ (100 men)
"Bise Hurle" (Theatre)
Station
Railway M.G.
Hotel Regina
"Bedford Tunnel"
Bendigo M.G.
Right Reserve Dugout (185 men)
Boppy Mountain Dugout (Not completed)
Melbourne M.G.
Boshe Close Support Tunnel
Kangaroo M.G.
Ballarat Post M.G.
Broken Hill (M.G. Coy H.Q. 5 M.G. Positions)
Manly M.G. (33 men)
Dugouts or Machine Gun Emplacements (Extent Shown)
Dugouts or Machine Gun Emplacements (Extent Unknown)
Bathurst M.G.
O Other Notable Feature
Sydney Ridge M.G.
- - - - Tunnels/Subways
Cobar M.G.

0   500   1000
Copyright: Damien Finlayson 2005
Yards

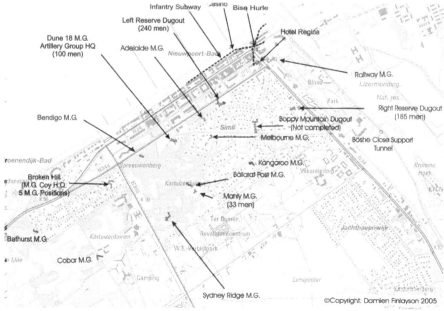

The actual location of the various underground constructions under the current Nieuwpoort-Bad

Infantry Subway
Casino
Bise Hurle
Left Reserve Dugout (240 men)
Hotel Regina
Dune 18 M.G. Artillery Group HQ (100 men)
Adelaide M.G.
Railway M.G.
Bendigo M.G.
Right Reserve Dugout (185 men)
Boppy Mountain Dugout (Not completed)
Melbourne M.G.
Boshe Close Support Tunnel
Kangaroo M.G.
Ballarat Post M.G.
Broken Hill (M.G. Coy H.Q. 5 M.G. Positions)
Manly M.G. (33 men)
Bathurst M.G.
Cobar M.G.
Sydney Ridge M.G.
©Copyright: Damien Finlayson 2005

GALLERY SETTS

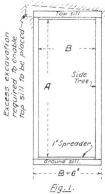

Excess excavation required to enable Top sill to be placed

Top sill.

B

A

Side Tree

1" Spreader

Ground sill.

B + 6"

Fig. 1.

Cases, 7 to 11ins. wide

Suitable Dimensions.

Purpose	A	B
Main subways	6'6"	3'6" or 4'0"
Dug-out passages	6'4"	2'9"
Inclines — 1/1 Vertical Timbering	8'4"	2'9" to
Normal Timbering	4'10"	4'6"
Mine galleries Normal size	4'10"	2'9"
Minimum	4'3"	2'3"
For Demolitions	4'3	2'3"

Above: The metal frame of the winter garden of 'Villa Crombez' in Nieuwpoort-Bad, 14 November 1917. Notice the men of the 2nd Australian Tunnelling Company had a tunnel under the building. The wood in the foreground of the photograph are tailor-made 'mining frames' that are ready for the further expansion of the 'Bath Lane Tunnel'. Despite the fact that this is a picture of the Villa Crombez, this ruin was called the Casino

1" Spreader   Top sill

Frame of 4"x4" or 5"x5" timber

A

B

Fig. 2.

Side trees

Ground sill

Frame of Pit-props 4 to 6 ins. dia.

A

B

Fig. 3.

Frames.

Left: Diagram of the sections of the used mining frames

In order to execute test drilling in Nieuwpoort (map ref.: M.28.c 9.5), a special squad was formed of men who had drilling experience. A drill with a small diameter was used. The squad was led by Lt. Daniel Mackenzie and Lt. Lionel Lambert. Drilling formed a very important part of a plan to dig a tunnel under the Yser. The work was dangerous and difficult. The drilling had to be stopped five times due to all sorts of obstacles before the first borehole was ready. At the sixth test drilling the top of a layer of blue Ypres clay was discovered. The blue clay was perfect for tunnelling, but was found at a depth of 27 metres. On the other bank of the canal test drilling was carried out, with the same outcome. An Australian geologist, Lt. Loftus Hills of GHQ, received the results and processed the data. The plans for the tunnel under the Yser were cancelled when it became clear that the planned British operation on the Nieuwpoort front would not take place.

The 2nd Australian Tunnelling Company

The 2nd Australian Tunnelling Company executed the following during the time they were based at Nieuwpoort Bains. The construction of the various structures was carried out by:

No. 1 Section – Captain Leslie de Jersey Grut

- Offensive Mining towards 'Grande' at 'Black' Dunes – Nieuwpoort Bains
- Infantry Subway – Nieuwpoort Bains
- Bexhill & Brighton Tunnels – Nieuwpoort Bains
- (supposed) Railway Machine Gun Post – Nieuwpoort Bains

No. 2 Section – Captain George Smith

- Water wells – Oost Dunkerke Bains
- Station Tunnel Dugouts – Nieuwpoort Bains
- Advanced Divisional HQ – Oost Dunkerke Bains
- Boppy Mountain Dugouts – Nieuwpoort Bains
- 6 x Observation Post – Nieuwpoort Bains

No. 3 Section – Captain Frederick Phippard

- Kursaal Dugouts (XV Corps HQ) – Le Panne
- Broken Hill Machine Gun Post – Nieuwpoort Bains
- Sydney Ridge Machine Gun Post – Nieuwpoort Bains
- Bendigo Machine Gun Post – Nieuwpoort Bains
- Bathurst Machine Gun Post – Nieuwpoort Bains
- Cobar Machine Gun Post – Nieuwpoort Bains

No. 4 Section – Captain Arthur Cohen

- Boyau Michael Dugouts – Nieuwpoort Bains
- (supposed) Boyau Col Vaulet Dugouts – Nieuwpoort Bains
- (supposed) Boyau Leclere Dugouts – Nieuwpoort Bains
- Hurle Bise Subway – Nieuwpoort Bains
- Left Reserve Dugouts and Machine Gun Post – Nieuwpoort Bains
- Dune 18 Artillery Dugouts – Nieuwpoort Bains
- Boche Close Support Tunnel – Nieuwpoort Bains
- Adelaide Machine Gun Post – Nieuwpoort Bains
- Melbourne Machine Gun Post – Nieuwpoort Bains
- Kangaroo Machine Gun Post – Nieuwpoort Bains
- Ballarat Machine Gun Post – Nieuwpoort Bains
- Manly Machine Gun Post – Nieuwpoort Bains
- Boppy Mountain Machine Gun Post – Nieuwpoort Bains
- (supposed) Right Reserve Dugouts and Machine Gun Post – Nieuwpoort Bains
- (supposed) Right Reserve Dugouts and Machine Gun Post – Nieuwpoort Bains

When the 2nd Australian Tunnelling Company left Nieuwpoort Bains on 18 November 1917, they had built a total of 4,834 metres of underground constructions, without counting the geological test drilling.

WAR DIARY.

APPENDIX N No. (1X).
NOVEMBER 1917.

SUMMARY OD FOOTAGE DRIVEN IN WORKINGS IN COAST SECTOR.

Workings.	Adits.	Inclines	5'x3' Shafts	6'x4' Shfts.	6'x3' Galleries	6'x4' Galleries	4'3"x 2'3" Glrs	TOTAL
Nieuport Bains. (Mining Offensive	7'		16'				633	656
Boyau Micheal. E (Dugouts)	50½	92½			54½	480½		687½
Boyau Col Vaulet. (Dugouts)	6	20½				36		62½
Boyau Leclerc. (Dugouts)						354		354
Cost Dunkerke-Bains (Wells)								125
Nieuport Bains Infantry Subway.	76	322			3,512			3,910
Tunnel under Road.			20		52			72
Railway Mach.Gun.					209			209
Station Tnl Dugouts	14		20			88		122
Hurle Bise.					22	55		77
Left Reserve Dugouts	59½	106			85½	806		1,057
" " Mach.Gun.			36		111	60		207
Right Reserve (Dugouts)				47		470½		517½
" "(Mach Gun)			23		29			52
Advanced Divisional Head-Qrts Dugouts.	176½	261			570	376		1,385½
Bexhill & Brighton Tunnels.	17	29				416		462
Dune 19. Artillery Dugouts.	24				41	322		387
Kursaal Dugouts.				6	316	100		422
Boppy Mountain. (Dugouts)	40	65			552	432		1,089
Boche Close Support			6		303	6		315
Machine Gun Posts. Broken Hill.			90		283½	234		537½
" Bendigo.			35		88	77		200
" Sydney Ridge.			97½		128	128		421½
" Adelaide.		20	37		200	76		333
" Melbourne.		20	38½		77	36		171½
" Kangaroo.			38		10	114		162
" Ballarat.			38		61	80		172
" Manly.	6	15	56		108	188		373
" Bathurst.		20	60		100	60		247
" Cobar.			104½		385	106		575½
" Mt Boppy.			46		80	53		179
Observation Posts			272		45½			317½
	478½	971	1,931½	53	7,408	5,101	633	15,801½

18/11/17.

. . . .

Report of the total number of metres excavated by the 2nd Australian Tunnelling Company

Nine men of the 2nd Australian Tunnelling Company died during the fighting or because of the wounds they had suffered during their time at Nieuwpoort Bains:

27 June: Sapper 5622 George Smith; KIA – Unknown circumstances

George Thomas Smith

George Smith was conscripted as 40-year-old farmhand from Oatlands, Tasmania, to serve with the 2ATC. He was enlisted on 18.04.1916 and left for France on the ship 'Ulysses' A38 from Melbourne on 25.10.1916. On 29.01.17 he arrived in France where he was hospitalised in the St. Omer due to illness. He rejoined his unit on 06.04.1917. On 11.05.1917 he was re-hospitalised in St. Omer. On 01.06.1917 he rejoined his unit and was sent to Nieuwpoort. On 27.06.1917 he was listed as KIA. He was buried in Nieuwpoort Bains Military Cemetery No.3. In 1924 this cemetery was exhumed and the remains were reburied in Ramscappelle Road Military Cemetery at Nieuwpoort. No remains of George Smith were found. Together with some other victims of whom the graves could not be found he was given a tombstone and special memorial in the Ramscappelle Road Military Cemetery at Nieuwpoort. George Thomas Smith left a wife and 6 children.

The widow of George Smith (middle), Katherine May pearce and his youngest son Reginald Smith (top 5th from the right) together with farm workers in 1935

Grave of George Thomas Smith at Ramscappelle Road Military Cemetery, Nieuwpoort

Grave of Frank Ward at Koksijde Military Cemetery

10 July: Sapper 571 William Coleman; KIA – During Operation Strandfest

William Coleman's name is listed on panel 7 of the Menin Gate at Ypres. His body was never found. He enlisted as a 42-year-old labourer from Norton's Summit in South Australia on 09.10.1915 and was 44 when he died at Nieuwpoort. He left a wife (Emily) and two children.

10 July: Sapper 4141 Alfred Fitzgerald; KIA – During Operation Strandfest

Alfred Fitzgerald was killed on 10.07.1917 at the age of 45 at Nieuwpoort, son of Thomas and Catherine Fitzgerald from Queensland. He was a native of Newcastle-on-Tyne, England. His body was never found. His name is listed on panel 29 of the Menin Gate at Ypres.

20 July: 2nd Corporal 4007 Frank Ward; KIA – Hit by a shell.

2nd Corporal Frank Ward was a 27-year-old miner from Long Gully, Bendigo, Victoria, who enlisted in February 1916 with the 2ATC. He emerged from a tunnel in Nieuwpoort Bains between 10:00 and 12:00, when a shell hit. The official report notes: 'He was practically blown to pieces' which gives an impression of his wounds. Sapper Geake, who witnessed this, collected the remains. 2nd Corporal Ward was buried at the Koksijde Military Cemetery along the B. Vandammestraat at Koksijde on 21.07.1917.

1 September: Sapper 671 Joseph Pinal: KIA – Unknown circumstances.

Joseph Pinal was a 20-year-old miner from Bendigo, Victoria. No further details about his death are known. He is buried at the Koksijde Military Cemetery along the B. Vandammestraat at Koksijde.

21 September: Sapper 6635 Patrick McKee: Died of wounds – Unknown circumstances.

The graves of Joseph Pinal (Koksijde Military Cemetery), Patrick McKee (Zuydcoote Military Cemetery) and Frank Cooper (Koksijde Military Cemetery)

Patrick McKee was a 37-year-old bookkeeper from Brisbane, Queensland. He was heavily wounded at Nieuwpoort and was transported to a hospital (probably Cabour) where he succumbed to his wounds. He was buried at the Zuydcoote Military Cemetery.

15 October: Sapper 7145 Frank Cooper: KIA – Hit by a shell.

Frank Cooper was a 38-year-old plumber and bicycle seller from Broadarrow, Western Australia. He had only spent a few days with the 2nd Australian Tunnelling Company when, during working on the

machinegun post Broken Hill, a heavy shell came through the entry to the construction and exploded. This happened on 15.01.1917 between 11:00 and 12:00. Part of the construction collapsed. Some men, including Sapper G. Grainger, needed 4 hours to dig the victims out. Frank Cooper was dug out with a broken neck, which was the cause of his death. He was buried at the Koksijde Military Cemetery along the de B. Vandammestraat at Koksijde.

15 October: Sapper 5768 John Lawson: KIA – Hit by a shell.

John Lawson was also working in the machinegun post Broken Hill when the shell hit and exploded. He was instantly killed and was dug out together with Sapper Frank Cooper. John Lawson and Frank Cooper are buried next to each other at the Koksijde Military Cemetery along the B. Vandammestraat at Koksijde.

Left: Grave of John Lawson at Koksijde Military Cemetery

Above: Frank Cooper and John Lawson were buried next to each other

18 October: Sapper 2467 Percy Hocking: – Died of wounds.

Percy Hocking suffered a serious shot wound at Nieuwpoort Bains. Although he was transported to a Field Ambulance Advanced Dressing Station he died of his wounds. (His father-in-law, Sapper 3921 Joseph Smith was part of the same company.) Percy Hocking is buried at Ramscappelle Road Military Cemetery.

Right: The grave of Percy Hocking at Koksijde Military Cemetery

There was even time for humour in the German trenches at Westende. Look at the helmets of these soldiers

CHAPTER ELEVEN
THE REPAYMENT

SITUATION REPORT BY HANDLING OVER THE COMMAND TO THE FRENCH ON 17 NOVEMBER 1917

Mid-way through November 1917 the sector Nieuwpoort was handed over to the French upper command. All British and Australian forces left their positions and the trenches were taken over by French forces who were very keen on the new and well-constructed British infrastructure and billets. The French upper command received a detailed report of all the actions during the British and Australian occupation of the sector.

LIST OF BATTLES AND RELIEF

On 14 July 1917 the sector holding an area on the coast report that Schoorbakke (a small village on the Yser river bank between Middelkerke and Diksmuide) was completely held by German Naval units. On 14 July the 3rd Marine Regiment of the 3rd Naval Division was relieved by forces of the 199th Division in the Lombardsijde- sector who were held in reserve during the successful German attack on July 10th north-east of the Yser river brook (Operation Strandfest).

The Lombardsijde sector was occupied by fragments of the 199th German Imperial Division and the 3rd Naval Division. The latter were partially relocated to the Ypres battle front starting from 16 October. The last men left on 17 October. The 199th German Imperial Division stayed in their lines until 20 October, when they were relieved by the 16th Bavarian Division. After this they headed to Brugge for a rest. At the start of November they were also transported to the Ypres sector. In the southern sector (from Boterdijk near Lombardsijde to Schoorbakke) the lines were permanently occupied by three Matrosen Regiments who switched watches continuously.

OVERVIEW OF OCCUPATION OF THE FRONTLINE (BETWEEN 15 JULY AND 14 NOVEMBER 1917)

Sector	Unit		Division
DUNES Sector	11th Bav.I.R.	)	
POLSER Sector	21st Bav.R.I.R.	)	16th Bav.Div.
LOMBARDSIJDE Sector	14th Bav.I.R.	)	
BAMBURGH Sector	4th Matrosen Regt.	)	
RATTEVALLE Sector	1th Matrosen Regt.	)	2nd Naval Div.
MANNEKENSVERE Sector	2nd Matrosen Regt.	)	

During the period of British occupation of the Nieuwpoort Sector, the German moral was very good.

Above: These photos typify the relaxed atmosphere in the German trenches at Lombardsijde

Left: Quiet moments at Lombardsijde

First of all the German troops were very reluctant to be taken prisoner and the majority of the British raids on the enemy strongholds could count on a very strong resistance.

ENEMY INTENTIONS

Several German prisoners of war that were taken during raids on the forward battle posts declared that the enemy planned an attack south of Lombardsijde with the British positions east of the Yser River as their objective. The most recent message came from an deserter of the 60th Artillery Battalion that was send to the Ypres area and decelerated om November 13th that he had heard rumors about a planned German attack south of Lombardsijde. The Germans would attack the area between the sea shore and the village of Schoore to relieve the bog pressure more to the south on the Passchendaele Ridge. Men told that the declaration of the deserter was unreliable, but it is possible that the man picked up the story later during his fleet end stay near Gistel in enemy territory.

REPORT OF ENEMY ACTIVITY IN THE AIR FROM 1 JULY UP TO 12 NOVEMBER 1917

The meteorological circumstances during the major part of July were very unfavourable for air battles. These bad circumstances put a stop to nearly all aerial photography. During this period the sky was mainly protected by fighter patrols. During September and October, with the exception of some bad weather in the first fourteen days of the month, the weather was advantageous for air battles.

The enemy tactics in the air were distinguished by their defensive nature. When the wind blew from the south, the skies were heavily patrolled while there were very heavy battles going on behind their own lines particularly they had the wind to their advantage. In the early morning some enemy planes were spotted flying very low over our trenches, observing if they were heavily

A German Albatross DIII 2296/16 of the 1st Navy Feldjasta is ready for a reconnaissance flight over the Belgian coast

defended or not. Enemy photography reconnaissance flights were mainly made by planes flying at high altitudes. Mostly they used the same flying methods for this type of work. Planes came across the sea until they reached their targets and left again with the nose of the aircraft pointing down. During the British occupation of the sector there was a constant registration of German artillery positions from the air.

This resulted in the destroying of several machine-gun posts and a large number of explosions in nearby battery positions. The German aircraft which were out on aerial observation were continuously intercepted by British air patrols. In return the enemy left no opportunity to bombard Dunkirk and the surrounding area. These attacks were usually made by airplanes that took off at dusk from their airfields and preferably when weather conditions were favorable.

German aircraft of the type Albatros DV at the airport of Snellegem, which was also used as a base for flights above the coast

The aerial bombardments were particularly violent between 16–31 October. This was due to the bright full moon and the favourable atmospheric conditions. Dunkirk was bombed on eleven out of the fifteen days, this time with a load of fifty bombs. Delayed and immediate detonation were applied to bombs that ranged in weight between 5 and 75 kg. There was also mention of the use of incendiary bombs. Apart from the considerable amount of material harm that was inflicted, the number of victims were remarkably low compared to the large number of bombs that were dropped. There were one or two unfortunate cases, one when a number of victims were killed when a particularly large bomb penetrated a basement where several people sought shelter. In another case, an enemy plane flew very low to the ground and blasted a street in Malo with machine-gun fire.

The Royal Naval Air Service dropped a total of about 230 tons of munition on enemy airfields, docks and so on.

*Allied aerial photograph of the German airfield at Uitkerke, which was located between the current Brugse
Steenweg and the Schaapstraat (where the company Legrand is now located)*

In this case we count over 1,320 twenty-pound bombs dropped on the forward German sectors and about 100,000 artillery pieces were fired into their trenches and battery positions.

The 4th Brigade Royal Flying Corps was involved in 940 battles with these results:

	July	Aug.	Sept.	Oct.	Nov.	Total
Destroyed enemy aeroplanes or went down in flames	16	24	23	9	4	76
Enemy aeroplanes put out of action but not destroyed	16	21	31	6	6	80

Report of enemy artillery activity on the XC Corps front between 20 June and 15 November 1917.

Two things were striking during this entire period. First was the relationship between guns and howitzers that was constantly high (howitzers compared to cannons by about 3 by 2), especially in the beginning of this period. Firstly, this prevented the German troops from a planned number of artillery attacks on the disadvantaged positions. Secondly, most of the German shelling was focused on the British battery positions. From 20 June, when the XV Corps took over the front line, there was a growing hostile artillery activity. These ranged in severity from day to day and were contained until 10 July, when there was a successfully attack deployed on the British positions to the East of the Yser river, between the river and the sea. On the day of the attack the shelling was extremely violent and reached far over the disadvantaged areas in Koksijde and Veurne. The German artillery remained extremely active until three days after the attack. There was no question of a big withdrawal of any artillery The target was the network of trenches and connections behind the front lines.

During the rest of the month of July and the beginning of August the activity was remarkably low. The front was quiet. There was no mention of a large withdrawal or any artillery. In the second half of August the German shelling reduced and given the poor weather conditions, it was assumed that it had withdrawn a few cannons. The use of just one gun per position was striking for this period.

Around the second week of September the German artillery activity increased again, the target area now Nieuwpoort and the various bridges. This was most probably due to the statement made by a prisoner of war after his capture on 17 September following the German attack between the 'Nieuwland Polder' and the Nieuwpoort–Lombardsijde road. Towards the end of September the activity got lower in intensity. The gradual decrease was especially noticeable from mid-October to mid-November. It is highly likely that a withdrawal of artillery took place in this period. By mid-November it was relatively quiet, but counter-battery work was systematically supplied from the German side, whenever the weather conditions allowed it. The bridges around Nieuwpoort were the target of shelling day and night. A lot of use was made of alternative positions during the entire

period following the 10 July attack, after which the number of displacements of battery decreased, especially during the last weeks of October.

GAS ATTACKS

On the German side there was intensive use of gas shells, especially in favourable weather conditions and from time to time on a large scale, when the wind had a speed of 15 to 30 miles/hour. The following is a list of the number of days by month that gas attacks were carried out:

July	9
August	8

September	7
October	20
November (until 12th)	9

TARGETS

The main targets of the shelling with gas grenades were the centres of Nieuwpoort, Nieuwpoort-Bad, the Redan battery positions in the dunes and on both sides of 'the AEOLIAN ROAD' (current Kinderlaan), 'TRIANGLE WOOD' (Litto bos) and roads in the front positions. Aeolian Road or Route Eolienne as it was called, received its name from Greek mythology. Aeolus was the son of Hippotes that is mentioned in Homer's *Odyssey* as the Keeper of the Winds. The Aeolian Road lays in a gap between two dune formations and runs straight to the seashore; there is always wind on that spot. The defence line called 'Aeolinie' was situated along the road of that name. This line consisted of a line of fortifications mainly built up by the Belgian Army.

The intention was to create a second line in case the Germans managed to cross the Yser river. If this should happen, all units would be ordered to retreat behind the Aeolinie and the area between the line and the Yser river would be completely shelled out of existence, after which the area would be recaptured again. Today there are still some remains of this line visible.

Remains of the Aeolinie near 'Square Wood' in Oostduinkerke

Remains of the Aeolinie near 'Square Wood' in Oostduinkerke

Ramscapelle and almost all battery positions within 5000 yards of the front line were regularly shelled with gas shells. Many times 'Minenwerfer' grenades filled with gas were reported in the trenches to the West and South of Lombardsijde.

TYPES OF SHELLS

Different types have already been identified, some were even noticed for the first time. At the end of July was 'the sneezing mixture', which later turned out to be a German 'Blue Cross' was widely used and on 21 July Nieuwpoort and its surroundings was heavily shelled with grenades of the type 'Yellow Cross'. This was the most commonly used type of gas shell by the Germans during all attacks. Variants on the type of 'Green Cross' were also used.

These shells were first noticed at this part of the front:

> 15 cm How. Gas shell, consisting of Phenyl Carbylamine Cloride.
> 15 cm. How. Green Cross, consisting of Phosgene, Di- phosgene en Dipheyl Arenious Chloride.

The firing of gas projectiles at Westende 1917

METHODS OF USE

The use of gas shells by the German troops went as follows:

a. 'Blue Cross' or diphenyl chlorosine is also called Clarck: it falls into the category of irritators. These were used both at day and night against open positions as Oostduinkerke, battery positions, and roads that were used by enemy troops and transport. It became increasingly used together with 'Green Cross' and 'High Explosive' (HE) shrapnel grenades. Blue Cross work by suffocation and is lethal at high concentrations. The gas was so thin it could not be filtered by the customary gas masks. If inhaled it induced a suffocating feeling or queasiness, causing many soldiers to take their gas masks off. At that time men were exposed to the effects of 'Green Cross' which was fired simultaneously. The percentage of 'Blue Cross' used in a shell was not high and its detonation and destructive effect was very similar to the type 'High Explosive'. The exact concentration that was used is hard to assess.

b. 'Yellow Cross' or dichloroethyl sulfide is also called Yperite or mustard gas: falls into the category of blister tractors. It was primarily used against Nieuwpoort and battery positions, and was always combined with the shelling of High Explosive calibres. The usual way of working was to start the artillery barrrage with a concentration of gas for ten minutes followed

Left: a 7.7 cm grenade, found on the former battlefields. This was one of the most used carriers for Blue Cross and Yellow Cross

Right: diameter of a 7.7 cm grenade. The glass bottle was the recipient for the desired type of gas

by HE for the next 20 to 30 minutes. This was repeated daily with intervals of approximately 30 minutes. In many cases the total operation lasted more than three hours. It was usually 7.7 cm guns used for this type of gas attack.

c.   'Green Cross' or chlorpyrcin. Falls into the category of suffocation. This was seldom used and always in combination with other gases and H. or Shrapnel.

A Livens projector. It was frequently used at Nieuwpoort on both the British and the German side. It was fired electrically in series of twenty-five

A Livens projectile containing gas

The Germans used gas in a defensive way, for the neutralisation of British artillery and to shell the advanced communication posts.

BRITISH GAS ATTACKS

From 23 July to 30 September the British executed eleven gas attacks against the German positions in the dunes at Lombardsijde, Nieuwdamme fort, 'Groote Bamburgh Farm' and 'Rat Trench'. During these operations 5,505 deadly poisonous gas loads were fired and 14,431 carcinogenic shells (together with more than 100 tons of gas). Gas shells were additional to the regular artillery used to neutralise hostile batteries. The only information about the consequences was obtained from prisoners who were victims of the gas themselves. Most of those men belonged to the German Reserve-Infanterie Regiment No. 273 and Infanterie-Regiment 'Kaiser Friedrich III' No. 114, both belonging to the 199th German Division.

When their regiment fought in the Coastal Sector in July 1917, they suffered 200 dead and 130–140 of whom were victims of gas. Later reports of this regiment wrote about very heavy losses. The period between October and mid-November 1917 was much quieter without any significant incidents.

This report was handed over to the French high command on 17 November 1917 but somehow got lost. It was first discovered again in British archives in 1999 when making inquiries for this book.

CHAPTER TWELVE
OPERATION STRANDFEST
THE ORIGINS OF CLOSE AIR SUPPORT AND FIRST USE OF YELLOW CROSS

This was to become the first operation in which artillery, aviation and infantry were working together, an operation coordinated from the air. Today the Operation Strandfest is still known but it's historic importance has been completely forgotten. This is the story of a small scale operation, with major results in new warfare and aerial warfare.

So, starting half October 1914, the biggest part of the coastline of Belgium became occupied by the German Marine division, the future Marinekorps Flandern. From the Dutch border to Lombardsijde was now in German naval hands, including the important harbours of Zeebrugge, Oostende and Brugge. The Germans had originally also hoped to gain possession of Dunkirk and Calais, but this had been nothing more than wishful thinking. Nieuwpoort played a crucial role because there the lock and sluice system provided the Belgian Army with a last defence weapon against the strong German advance that they hadn't been able to stop since the crossing of the Belgian border on 4 August 1914. They knew about the water system around Nieuwpoort from Karel Cogge of Veurne and the expertise on the practical side of how to handle the lock system from local shipper Hendrik Geeraert, stopping the Germans permanently in their advance on the Yser.

The importance of the Belgian harbours was quickly discovered by a number of officers in the German admiralty who were looking at the possibilities of using the ports. The harbours of Zeebrugge and Oostende each had a canal leading to the port of Brugge in the hinterland, making Brugge an ideal base for submarines, torpedo boats, destroyers, motorboats, etc.

On 15 November a second German Marine Division was added to the first one and the Marinekorps Flandern was established under the command of Admiral Ludwig von Schröder, also called the 'Löwe von Flandern' or the Lion of Flanders, who was sixty years old.

On the 3 June 1917 a third Division was added. Most of the coastal area was now in hands of the 1st Division, while the 2nd and 3rd were in charge of the areas nearer the front. The Lombardsijde area was next to the 3rd Division sector.

Brugge, Zeebrugge and Oostende were soon to become U-boat bases from where the feared U-Flottille Flandern I and II were to operate. The UB and UC coastal U-boat types (small, manoeuvrable submarines with shallow draft, well suited to navigation of coastal channels and harbours) sank no less than 2,554 ships, excluding the military vessels, while operating from Flanders, something which was not halted by the 'blockade' of Zeebrugge and Oostende during April and May 1918.

Not only were the U-boats dangerous, but from time to time there were raids by German torpedo boats and destroyers operating from the same harbours on all Allied shipping in the channel, a few

Admiral Ludwig von Schröder entered the newly established Kaiserliche Marine in May of 1871. Prior to World War One, he served on several different ships and commanded the Blitz, as well as the training vessel the Moltke. Von Schröder retired from active duty in 1913. He was reactivated and named commanding Admiral in Flanders, where he was in charge of both the sea-going forces and most of the naval infantry, which by mid-December 1915 became officially known as the Marinekorps Flandern. After transfer to the Baltic and near War's end, von Schröder was ordered by the Kaiser to take action against mutineering German sailors in Kiel. He advised Reichskanzler von Baden that the proposed measures were to harsh, and the orders were thus not carried out. Ludwig von Schröder died in Berlin-Halensee on 23 July 1933 and was buried at the Invalidenfriedhof. His son Ludwig was a general in the Wehrmacht during World War Two.

times with serious consequences. The strategically important significance of this was recognised by both sides and soon after the Marinekorps had control of the coastal area, the British started shelling the harbours with monitors and other vessels. This resulted in a fist 'Atlantikwall', a network of trenches, bunkers and batteries along the Belgian coastline to defend the harbours and prevent the Allied troops from landing on the coast and weakening the Western Front.

About forty-two batteries can be named, added to which are a number of Flakbatteries etc., calibres from 5, 8.8 and 10.5 cm to the average 15, 17, 21 and 28 cm, to the enormous 30.52 and 38 cm guns. Some of these batteries were railway guns such as Battery Deutschland (four x 38 cm guns) at Bredene.

The coast was secured but now the air also had to be secured. This was done with a large number of naval air units such as the Marine Feldflieger Abteilungen, the Marine Jagdgeschwader, the Kustenflieger Abteilungen, the Seeflugstatione, Seefrontstaffel(s) and Marine Schustas.

Soon the coastline became a difficult place to penetrate for Allied troops. Allied commanders had been playing with the idea to land on the Belgian coastline and get their hands on the strategically important harbours, and perhaps even end the war this way by attacking the German Army in the rear. It has to be said that the German High Command also seriously feared a landing on the mouth of the Schelde at Zeeuws Vlaanderen, Dutch territory, from where they could easily attack and occupy Brugge and Zeebrugge.

Right and below: Battery Deutschland at Bredene was clear for action on 3/6/1917 with 3 heavy guns of 38 cm. In 1918 more than 220 guns (of 8.8 cm to 38 cm) were placed between Knokke and Lombardsijde.

During the night of the 6 on the 7 June 1917, Haig started another of his campaigns, another bloody one, for which he was well known, as were most of the other commanders on either side. It resulted in the capture of Messines and Wijtschate – the Third Battle of Ypres – it's real target is most of the time forgotten and has even been removed from its historic goals and context. The idea was to force an opening in the German front lines and fight a way to the Belgian coast in order to capture the harbours of Zeebrugge and Oostende. The big offensive really started on the 31 July 1917 and would result in not even 10 kilometres of terrain taken from the enemy. Passchendaele was captured finally on 6 November. Capturing Oostende and Zeebrugge had already been completely forgotten by that time.

On the 20 June 1917, the French Army handed over the Nieuwpoort sector to the British, something Admiral von Schröder became aware of the next day. He suspected now that an Allied, read British, landing was imminent. Indeed such plans existed on the Allied side for a landing at Westende and Middelkerke under the code name 'Hutch'. But one day before the handover by the French to the British, on the 19th, a patrol of the 3rd Marine Infanterie Division captured eleven prisoners of the 32nd British Division. This confirmed the fears of von Schröder that a British attack or landing on the Belgian coast was imminent.

Immediately von Schröder started planning Operation Strandfest, which was to take the last allied strongholds on the eastern side of the Yser near Nieuwpoort. This was an area of a depth of 1200 m over 3 km. He asked permission to do a pre-emptive operation to seize the bridgehead on the eastern bank. For this he got the 199th Infantry Division in reserve while the attack would mainly be done by the 3rd Marine Division. The operation was to be led by General der Infanterie von Quast, commander of the Garde Korps. During the last two weeks of June more units of the 3rd Marine Division were taken from the lines to rehearse the forthcoming operation and this probably happened partially at Bredene.

General der Infanterie von Quast (1850–1939) was in January 1917 assigned to lead the prestigious Guards Corps, a command he held until September when he was named commander of the 6th Army.

On 6 July the final preparations started as the coastal and other batteries started shelling this part of the front. It would go on like this till the operation itself had started. Originally the operation was to happen on the 8th but had to be postponed due to the weather conditions, which were extremely bad for the time of year. However, this seems to be a point of discussion and many sources contradict it by saying that it was to happen on the 9th at 20.00 hours. It seems that orders arrived early that day to say the operation was to be delayed by twenty-four hours due to the heavy storm and heavy rain.

So the actual Operation Strandfest happened on the 10 July 1917. That day was dry but stormy. At 6 a.m. the first batteries started opening fire on the British lines. About two hours later many of the British telephone lines were down and signal lamps were used to try to get in contact with the artillery.

At 10 a.m. Feldflieger Abteilung 231, who operated from the airbase of Jabbeke, Marine Feldflieger Abteilung I that operated from Vlissegen and Marine Feldflieger Abteilung II that operated from Jabbeke-Snellegem aerodrome, attacked British lines and destroyed the bridges over the Yser river. Due to the weather conditions the planned gun support from the destroyers and torpedo boats of the Flandern Flottille had to be cancelled.

By this time the shelling became worse and worse and all communications between the two banks of the Yser mouth were destroyed. The trenches were still in rather good condition. With the bridges over the Yser destroyed there was no possibility for reinforcements, and even worse the roads leading towards the front were also under gunfire. The British feared that something was going to happen and started bringing in reinforcements including trucks and lorries from Dunkirk, but this was too late.

At 11.30 a.m. only one bridge remained in good condition, Putney, the others were already out of use.

At 13.05 p.m. they discovered the first use of gas. Indeed a new kind of gas shell was used, and it caused sneezing, affecting the eyes, throat, and in some cases led to violent sickness.

At 15.30 more gas shells. About this use of gas there can be found also a few lines in the *Australian Official History*, Volume 4, p. 962:

Some batteries suffered through the enemy's use, for the first time, of what was to become his most dreaded gas shell, which smells, like new mixed mustard according to the diary of the 36th H.A.G.

Weekly Progress Report – 36th Heavy Artillery, 10 July 1917

The 1st division were holding the part of the front that the enemy took and suffered hard. A few men came back across the Yser by swimming. Enemy isolated troops in this area by destroying bridges across the Yser. It is also reported that there were over 1000 gas casualties in Nieuwpoort with the new gas, which smells like newly mixed mustard.

View of the narrow dunes strip just for the 'Seekessel'. Left, in the background we see the buildings of Nieuwpoort-Bad. Right, on the beach, just in front of the 'Seekessel', barbed wire defences were made (type: 'chevaux de frise'). This formed the most northern limit of the Western Front.
(Photo E. Mahieu)

The barbed wire defences on the beach beacon the 'no man's land' in front of the 'Seekessel'. A group of German soldiers, secure in their position, pose for a group photo. The photo was taken from the enemy (British) lines. (Photo E. Mahieu)

The same diary says : The enemy were using a new gas shell freely. Shell bursts like a small H.E. Gas makes you sneeze and causes your nose and eyes to run. Smell is like cayenne pepper. This actually was the Blaukreuz shell, a different type from the mustard – *gelbkreuz* – shell. Both these new shells were used in this action.

By 16.50 the front line was severely damaged, the whole right side was completely wiped out, the second line was also in very bad condition and the attention of the German artillery went now to the 3rd line. Also many of the communication trenches were gone.

At 19.51 hrs an attack follows by the naval infantry of the III Marine Division, supported by planes. It took the first German wave only two minutes to take the first British line! Some reports still talk about the Seesoldaten taking the lines, although this was a referral to the Seebataillone, which officially stopped to exist by the end of 1914. Surprised by their luck they stormed the second line directly and took it in a matter of minutes and the third was taken in a hand grenade battle. It seems the German artillery had a hard time following the fast attack (in other words, probably some marine personnel died from friendly fire). Flamethrowers were used to destroy the last British defences in the dug-outs etc. However, further east, the naval infantry was not that lucky, but again

Map of the area between Lombardsijde and the Yser river. The Allied troops had the entire Eastern Shore – about a depth of about 750 metres under control. The 'Seekessel' lay in the so-called 'no man's land'. Operation 'Strandfest' changed this situation. The German soldiers took over the area up to the Yser river brook. (Photo E. Mahieu)

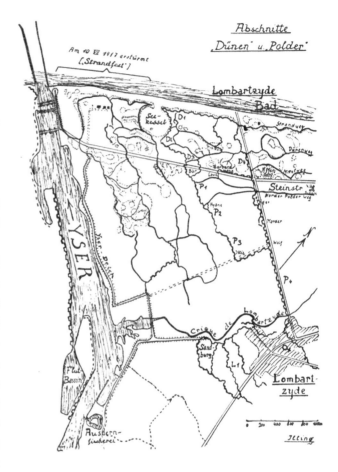

German reports tell us that the goals that had to be reached were achieved by 21.00 hours.

Also flamethrowers were used in this attack. The 6th and 12th Kompagnie of the Garde Reserve Pionier Regiment (Flammenwerfer) used large (model Grof) and twenty-six light (model Wex) flamethrowers. According to Bob Lembke, who's father participated in this, the flame attacks were very well planned. The Grof models were used in the opening phase of the attack, as they were not mobile, but had a longer range then the other models. The twenty-six others were used to make the first defence line collapse, but this would not have been that difficult as we have already seen not much remained of these lines.

A group of German soldiers posing by the conquered British lines. In the background we see the heavily battered jetty of Nieuwpoort at the Yser river brook. The photo was taken shortly after the operation 'Strandfest'. (Photo E. Mahieu)

10 July 1917: British soldiers are taken away from the battlefield by Germans

According to German sources 1,300 POWs were taken, of which seventeen were officers including the Regimental CO. The British opponents were the 1st Northamptonshire and 2nd KRRC of 2nd Brigade, 1st Division.

The total British casualties amounted to approximately 3,126 of all ranks, killed, wounded and missing. Of these, fifty officers and 1,253 other ranks belonged to the two battalions of 1st Division. He also mentions that four officers and sixty-four other ranks managed to reach the west bank of the Yser. It is not clear how high the German casualties were, but we know it was not a large number, which is also supported by the small number of graves that can be found marked 10 July 1917 on the German military cemeteries in Flanders.

In the most easterly sector of the attack there was a British counter-attack which was able to retake the 250 metres of ground they had lost in that area, but this was insignificant to the Germans, who had reached their goals to the west, and would retain them until the retreat in October 1918.

A report said that the observer planes and also the Kampfgeschwader with Rittmeister von Richthofen, had played an important role in the action. The POWs were taken to Oostende and Brugge, where there was a parade for Admiral von Schröder. One of the participants in the operation Strandfest and a lieutenant in the future Marine Sturmabteilung was a certain Bernard Hermann Ramcke, who certainly is known as the famous World War Two Fallschirmjäger General.

Lt. Bernard Hermann Ramcke (1889–1968). In 1916 he was decorated with the Iron Cross second class and later the Iron Cross first class. After a defensive action against three British attacks he was decorated with the Prussian Golden Merit Cross, the highest decoration for non-commissioned officers in the German Imperial Forces.

This is what can generally be found on the matter of the aerial part of the attack:

> The III Marine Infanterie Division attacks, supported by planes. The western bank of the Yser is bombarded by 24 C-type planes, and a plane from II MFFA co-ordinates the battle from the sky with its wireless, meanwhile two Schusta 29 planes protect the plane. KG I planes bombarded the coastal line between Nieuwpoort and Oostduinkerke. Jasta 17 planes do air cover for the whole operation during which a Sopwith is shot down.

Here is a detailed report of what happened day to day before and on the day of Operation Strandfest.

The following units participated : I, II MFFA – FA A 293b, A 231, 48b - Schustas 1, 16, 29, Marine Jasta, Jasta's 7, 8, 17, 20, Kasta 23 + the 4 elite fighter units of Jagdgeschwader I and the 6 Kastas of Kampfgeschwader I, saying that the unit left its airfield at Ascq for it to go to Gistel.

Most of the reports were written by Capt. Lt. Alfred Ritscher, who was the Kommandeur of the Feldflieger Abteilungen of the Marinekorps Flandern.

Ritscher issued a very clear order for the crews before and during the operation. No cards, notices or orders were to be taken with them in the plane. If taken prisoner they were to saying nothing about the operation, even when in prison, because of the danger of the enemy listening to conversations among prisoners.

The plane was to be burned if forced to land in enemy territory,

Capt. Lt. Alfred Ritscher was skipper of the 'German Arctic Expedition' of 1912–1913 and made reconnaissance flights in support of Marine units in Flanders during World War One.

and for this purpose a special device was build into the aircraft. All participating units had to place an experienced observer by the telephone as Officer with a specific duty.

No planes were to take off from an airfield unless they were on the schedule made by Ritscher, otherwise they needed an OK from Ritscher himself. Every loss of personnel or material, or personnel not able to operate, planes with engine trouble or other problems were immediately to be reported to Ritscher. The crews were also told to take enough negatives, maps without positions, signalling and machine-gun ammo, etc with them.

During the preparations for the operation and during Strandfest itself a Jagdstaffel was flying 'Sperrzeit' while another one was in 'Bereitschaft'. The last unit was to be in the air within twenty minutes after the command was given of heavy enemy activity that could endanger the operation. Meanwhile the Jagdgeschwader Richthofen was kept in reserve and could be used every day from 08.00 hours. Refuelling and reserve airfield for this unit were the aerodromes Snellegem and Varsenare (in fact the northern and eastern side of the Jabbeke aerodrome). Between 5.00 and 6.30 Jasta 20 was on duty with the Marine Jasta in reserve. 6.30 till 8.00 was for Jasta 17 and Jasta 7 in reserve. 8.00 till 9.30 the Marine Jasta and Jasta 8. 9.30 till 11.00 Jasta 7 and Jasta 20. 11.00 till 12.30 Jasta 8 and Jasta 17. 12.30 till 14.00 Jasta 20 and Marine Jasta. 14.00 till 15.30 Jasta 17 and Jasta 7 as reserve. 15.30 till 17.00 Marine Jasta and Jasta 8. 17.00 till 18.30 Jasta 7 and Jasta 20. 18.30 till 20.00 Jasta 8 and Jasta 17. 20.00 till 21.30 Jasta 20, no reserve. 21.30 till darkness Marine Jasta, no reserve.

Kasta 23 bombed the station of Adinkerke on the night of the 8 and 9 July. Kagohl I was moved from Ascq to Gistel aerodrome on the 7 July. The unit was to operate during the night before the operation and to bomb railway stations, aerodromes and fortified positions behind the front lines. They were also to bomb Dunkirk the night before, but this had to be cancelled because of low clouds.

A German plane ready for take-off at Gistel aerodrome

During the days before the attack, observation planes were recording all enemy traffic on the roads and railways leading towards the sector. Concerning the other units involved, these were their operations on the 10th, a day which was very clouded and stormy:

Marine Feldflieger Abteilung I
From 05.00 till 10.00: Photographing results of the artillery on Allied targets. This artillery had been led from the air to their targets by the same unit the previous day. From 10.00 till 20.00 Helping the artillery to find targets. From 20.00 till 23.00 Observation on enemy artillery activity and locations, observing of the 'Sperrfeuer', barrage artillery and reporting on the matter.

Marine Feldflieger Abteilung II
From 05.00 till 20.00 Long distance observation, afterwards photo recon flights.

FFA 293 05.00 till 20.00 same operations as MFFA I

Schusta 1 : 05.00 till 20.00 Protection flights on demand of the I Marine Feldflieger Abteilung.

Schusta 29 : 05.00 till 20.00 Idem Schusta 1 but for the A293

Kasta 23 : Around 09.00 bombing flight on the Allied aerodrome at Bray Dunes

FFA 231 : 05.00 till 20.00 stationed at the Flugplatz Vlissegem and operating on demand of the I Marine Feldflieger Abteilung.

FF48b and Schusta 16 were kept in reserve.

When the attack started at 07.51 hours, two Schusta planes were flying at low altitude over the storming infantry and were reporting the progression of the troops to the artillery and HQ. A total of six planes were used for wireless telegraphy during the operation and with full success.

Four C-type planes from Kogohl I were used as Sturmflieger, and were flying at altitudes between 20–50 metres attacking the enemy positions with machine-gun fire, operating just in front of the infantry. The principle of Stormflieger was completely new, and reports also mention that some British soldiers were so terrified by the attack that they were surrendering, hands in the air, even before they were reached by the Marine Infantry! The planes themselves were very slightly damaged, only a few bullet holes were found. Kagohl I was also very happy about the results and discovered a new way of warfare in it, calling them the Infanterie-Kampfflieger. They even made a task description: Their goal was to help the hard fighting infantry in attacks or defences, by deep flying, so strengthening the own troops and weakening the enemy by bombing and machine-gunning them. Needed were fast and very maneuverable planes with at least two MGs, capable of dropping bombs and with a light armour. Construction of special bombs with shrapnel or even gas was desirable.

The use of these tactics was only adequate when the planes attacked at the right moment, exactly as the troops are leaving the trenches attacking the enemy, so that they are under attack already from the air. It was even said that a good pilot, used in this way, had tactical more value than a Jasta pilot shooting down an enemy at high altitude…

Reports also say that between 20.00 and 22.00 all available planes were used to bomb targets in the area and to strafe them with machine-gun fire on the western side of the Yser river, making the Allies unable to bring along any reinforcements or to give any support to their colleagues under attack on the other side of the river. The Jastas on the other hand did over seventy war flights, but Allied air activity was extremely low due to the weather conditions. Before noon only one enemy plane was sighted, and during the afternoon a total of only four.

Jasta 17 was protecting Kagohl I during its flights and they shot down a Nieuwpoort plane. This probably was not a Nieuwpoort but very probably a Sopwith Camel N6361 of 4 Naval Squadron, shot down between Pervijze and Ramskapelle at 7.50 p.m., killing Flight S. Lt. E. W. Busby, who was the first Sopwith Camel casualty due to combat. It is said that it crashed south of Nieuwpoort and that the wings had already broken off in the air. A terrible death…

On the 10 July 1917, during the Strandfest operation, Kagohl I was bombing during three operations at Oostduinkerke-Bad and Nieuwpoort, targeting ammo and troop concentrations in that area. They claim that during the first raid they made an ammo dump explode near Oostduinkerke. It seems that between 8.00 and 10.00 in the evening they dropped over 6000 kg of bombs for this operation. Unfortunately nobody could confirm if the story was true regarding the destruction of the ammo dump. Later that night the railway station, harbour installations and aerodrome of Dunkirk were bombed, as were the railway station of Adinkerke, De Panne and Koksijde. This was again a total of 1500 kg of explosives.

Concerning the artillery this was their activity:

From 05.00 results are ok: Battery Pommern (1 x 38 cm gun), Moere (in fact Koekelare) was to open fire on the railway station of Adinkerke

Battery Deutschland (4 x 38 cm guns) at Bredene had Zielgruppe 3, an unidentified target (probably targets along the Yser river)

Battery Tirpitz (4 x 28 cm guns) at Stene, Oostende, was to fire at the Veurne railway station

At 08.00 five railway guns (21 or 28 cm, not specified) was to open fire on various targets

A drawing to show how the German 'Marineinfanterie' pushed the British troops into the Yser river
brook. A number of soldiers try to get away by wading through the water. On 10 July 1917 a total of 1,250
British soldiers were taken as POWs. (Photo E. Mahieu)

Between 10.00 and 12.00 the Pommern gun had to fire at Adinkerke in general and between 14.00 and 16.00 targeted again the railway station and the same location. Even after darkness they were firing on their targets...

They were assisted by A293, A231, and very curiously, a unit unnamed before A204... Curious thing is that the unit is only mentioned once in a list on the artillery flights, while the others are named frequently, and that FA A204 is not even mentioned in the list of units that participated. I think they only did some recon over the French targets during the operation.

The photos taken of the results, were immediately taken to the Generalkommando Gardekorps (Marinekorps) and to the III Marine Infantry Division by a motorcyclist. It is clear that the operation was the first of its kind and opened the way for a completely new way of warfare, which is still used with success by modern forces.

(Thanks to Johan R. Ryheul Jabbeke, Flanders for his research – 11 July 2005–22 July 2007)

A. O. K. 4.
Ia/e Nr. 266/Juli.
Geheim!

A. H. Qu., den 11. Juli 1917.

Marinekorps
Generalkommando
B.Nr. 4297. Ia. v. 13/7. 17

Eingeg. am 13. VII. 1917.
B. Nr. 2120 Anl. -3-

Armeebefehl

1.) Seine Königliche Hoheit der Oberbefehlshaber der Heeresgruppe Kronprinz Rupprecht von Bayern haben nachstehendes Schreiben an mich zu richten geruht:

„Euer Exzellenz spreche ich für das wohl vorbereitete und glänzend durchgeführte Angriffsunternehmen an der Dünenfront meine ganz besondere Anerkennung aus und bitte, diese Anerkennung auch dem Marine=Korps, dem Gruppenkommando des Garde=Korps, der 3. Marine=Division und allen beteiligten Truppen zu übermitteln.

Der Oberbefehlshaber
gez. Rupprecht
Kronprinz von Bayern
Generalfeldmarschall."

Indem ich diesen Erlaß der Gruppe Nord zur weiteren Bekanntgabe zugehen lasse, spreche auch ich allen an dem Unternehmen beteiligten Kommandobehörden und Truppen meinen warmen Dank und meine vollste Anerkennung aus. Insbesondere gilt mein Dank auch den Fliegern, welche auch bei dieser Gelegenheit trotz Ungunst der Witterung vortreffliche Dienste geleistet haben.

On 11 July 1917, the day after operation Strandfest, Crown Prince Rupprecht of Bavaria sent a letter with his congratulations for the successful attachment to the general command of the German Marine Corps. In this letter he socially thanked the members of the 3rd Marine Division.

Crown Prince Rupprecht achieved the rank of Generalfeldmarschall in July 1916 and assumed command of Army Group Rupprecht on 28 August that year, consisting of the 1st, 2nd, 6th and 7th armies. Rupprecht has been considered by some to be one of the best Royal commanders in the Imperial German Army of World War I, possibly even the only one to deserve his command. Rupprecht came to the conclusion much earlier than most other German generals (towards the end of 1917), that the war could not be won, seeing an ever-increasing material advantage in favour of the Allies.

CHAPTER THIRTEEN
TESTIMONY OF BERT FEARNS, 2/6 LANCASHIRE FUSILIERS 342970 D COMPANY, B PLATOON, 197 INFANTRY BRIGADE, 66TH INFANTRY DIVISION

END JUNE – BEGINNING JULY 1917

After Givenchy we were sent to the coast, the coast of Belgium where the French had been in charge for a long time. It was dead quiet; farmers were still working the fields just a mile or so behind the line.

That changed very quickly when the British arrived because, I believe, the Germans had heard we were planning attacks on the coast. Something like that – the news had got out. Anyway, each week the shelling got heavier.

There was a – well, not much bigger than a village really, a little seaside town on the beaches; I forget the name, and our trenches ran right across here – you got to the front through the town. We were right on the beaches in places, the tide nearly came into the front line!

The French had left the place in a hell of a mess. Filthy trenches, all falling in, and no cover from shelling.

A few pillboxes, that's all. I don't believe they needed much cover because

Bert Fearns (right) was an 18-year-old soldier in Nieuwpoort in 1917. (He lied about his age to be able to serve at the age of 17)

it had been so quiet. You could see they had been living in the houses, just as if there was no war on. When we arrived we used the cellars, broke through from one to another along the streets.

The Germans had heard of our plans, as I had already told them, and they made an attack against our lines on the north side of the river – we held a bit of ground over there. They drove us back across the river, which wrecked our plans of using boats and pontoons to allow the troops to go into the attack.

Oostduinkerke, a few kilometres from the front, exudes calm as if there was no war. This is how Bert saw the region when he arrived

It was all sand there. At first we thought it was wonderful to get out of the mud near Le Plantin – it was bad down there, trench foot and that, but then we found the sand – there was nothing but sand you see, we were in a big belt of sand dunes, no soil. But it got into everything with the wind blowing it in. You had sand in your tea, your bread, your Maconochie, your eyes; oh, it was terrible when the wind got up. I believe the veterinary people had trouble with horses eating sand in their feed; killed them, I think, they couldn't digest it, just sat in their stomachs. Sand in the rum even! I remember we were given lime juice in the trenches at Nieuwpoort – I'd never had it before.

Nieuwpoort-Bad as Bert found it on his arrival

And there were flies too. Oh Lord, the flies. Not the big houseflies – bluebottles – we had in the other place – they were there too of course – but clouds and clouds of little black biting things, like big midges. There was nothing the MO could give you to keep them away, so we got bitten to hell and back. I was not so bad, the bites got scabby and itchy, I was covered in them, but it made some of the lads really sick. They probably got the same as usual – a dose of castor oil! Break your arm and they'd give you castor oil. I think it was scabies people got from the flies, I don't know. We were never free of lice of course – they followed us everywhere!

It was a bit like Southport on a small scale. You didn't have to go far back for a drink and to find shops. We went into a shop once and I was told to occupy the shop girl by asking her to get something down from a top shelf, whilst someone else stole a box of cigars. But there was a sergeant outside looking in and as soon as we came out he made us take them back in again and apologise.

Our lot had an agreement when we went to an estaminet. The rule was that everybody would pay for a round, and no round would be the same. I'd come out into the sea air blotto, could hardly stand up. I wasn't used to drinking.

The landlady used to give us lectures about sex life in England – I don't know how she knew – and how in France they were more liberal and organised. There were red lamps in every town and

The last point of the western front at Nieuwpoort-Bad. It was known as 'Barrel Post'

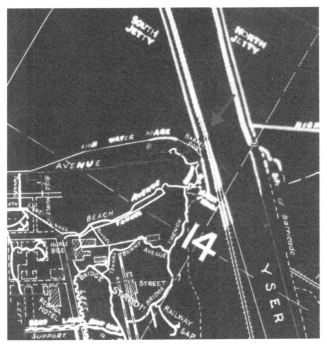

Location of 'Barrel Post'

the girls were inspected every week, she said. We'd had no warnings about women, although at Seaforth Camp I remember we had a wired off area for men with venereal disease. I don't recall any warnings about women. I was too frightened anyway. Ninety per cent of us must have been virgins. I never knew about sex until I saw it in France, didn't believe about brothels until we saw them in Bethune – and the queues! I was scared of three things – getting shellshock, losing my eyesight and having to use the bayonet. (Bert lost an eye during the battle on Passchendaele).

We'd go back to rest at other towns along the coast. May have been Dunkirk, I remember we all stripped off and went swimming in the sea to get rid of the lice. When we came out the whole promenade was covered in women looking at us.

The lines ran right up to the high water mark on the beach. That was the end of the Western Front really, although we never looked at it like that at the time. I remember it was a pile of barrels right on the prom. There was a huge jetty, like Southport, but without a pier end. You could see

The damaged piers at Nieuwpoort

footprints on the beaches, and these were made by men at night. You daren't go there in the day because of snipers. The Germans – and us I suppose – had them on their side of the river and on the jetty. We used to say the footpath was where they went over for whist drives!

After a while the shelling got heavier. We had more and more men coming in to prepare for the attack. Jerry saw this of course, and shelled us to hell. A lot of gas, I remember. Terrible inconvenience – and bloody uncomfortable – wearing a gas mask all day in hot weather. Difficult to eat and drink. They tried out new gases on us there. This was gas in shells, of course. I was lucky, never got a dose. Pure luck because it was a daily thing. All that happened to me was that I lost my voice for while.

Just on the other side of the dunes was a big town, Nieuwpoort, and I hated going into the line there. The lines were on the other side of the river – just a small salient which we hung onto. To reach the river you had to approach the town from behind. All the main streets ran straight towards the German lines, and you had to walk up them to reach the river, the bridges, rickety things, and the lines beyond. The Germans had an observation balloon and as soon as you turned the corner into the streets, there it was.

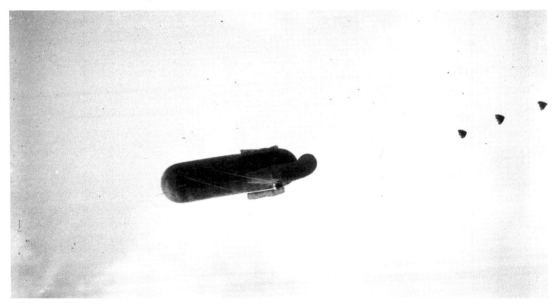

The German observation balloon at Nieuwpoort

You knew they could see you, and you knew the shells would arrive any minute. So it felt like walking into a shooting gallery. It wasn't the shells which did the damage but the flying bits of brick and stone when they hit the houses. My spirits used to sink as we approached the back of Nieuwpoort. I was really frightened there as anywhere else because it sort of built up inside as you reached the town. Attacks are all chaos and noise, and the adrenalin and your duties keep your mind off the fear. This was different though.

Inside view of a French 'cut and cover' trench in Nieuwpoort-Bad, 12 August 1917

Then in a little while the RE arrived and dug tunnels from the back of the town, under the houses and streets to the river. They were bloody marvellous. I don't think they were deep so a shell could easily have blown them in, but you couldn't see that bloody balloon any more, that was the great thing.

We hated that place. They had other one's which were just deep trenches covered with camouflage; it was illogical but you felt safe there too. It was as bad a spot as Ieper

Below: A 'trench' neatly laid out by the 2nd Australian Tunneling Company that leads to the entrance of a tunnel in Nieuwpoort-Bad, 14 November 1917

Nieuwpoort – blown to hell by the time we left. I think the French and Belgian Army had left a few men there to work with the Tommies.

At the same time they were putting in dug-outs on the coast. I never lived in any of them, but there were thousands of men there waiting for the call to attack, and you couldn't live with all the shelling, big guns, little guns, gas, shrapnel, they threw the lot at us. So they lived underground during the day – just as we did later in the Salient.

BERT FEARNS
2/6 LANCASHIRE FUSILIERS

Bert Fearns shortly before his death in 1996

CHAPTER FOURTEEN

THE CURRENT DAY RESULTS OF THE TUNNELLING IN 1917
OVERVIEW OF THE RESEARCH AT MODERN NIEUWPOORT

THE IMMEDIATE CAUSE

In December 1999 Mr B. Vandenberghe noticed some settling cracks in the front of his property at P. Braeckelaan 41, Nieuwpoort. He had bought the house only a few months previously, and saw no harm in the settling. Mr Vandenberghe, who is a building contractor himself, repaired the cracks and thought the problem was solved.

Early in 2000 the settling continued at a higher rate. The wall between the back yards of P. Braeckelaan Nos. 41 and 39 subsided. There had been an old repaired crack in this garden wall, but this time the damage was not confined to the garden wall, but the whole back of the building at P. Braeckelaan 41 had subsided. At the same time the houses at P. Braeckelaan 37, 35, 33, 31, 29, 27, 25 and 23 were all subsiding.

In March 2000 the settling continued even more rapidly, to the point that the house at No. 41 was declared unfit for human habitation by the Mayor, based on article 135 of the Belgian New Municipalities Act. The building had to be shored up at the side. No. 37, owned and occupied by Mr and Mrs Haemers-Devroe, showed a lot of settlement, resulting in cracks in the living room and the subsidence of the rear of the house, causing the doors to jam and the tiles to fall off the roof. The rear of the building had to be shored.

At the site of the biggest subsidence a leak was diagnosed after hearing that there was a heavy flow of water through the water supply. On 21 March 2000 a second leak was found in front of No. 23. In 1998 the pavements of the P. Braeckelaan and the J. Van Clichthovenstraat were totally renewed and nothing was seen that could point to a break in the water pipes. During the renovation of the pavements no work was done to the water pipes, and stabilised sand and concrete were lavishly used. The result of this was that because of the leak in the P. Braeckelaan the flow of water created a hollow underneath the pavement and the foundations of the nearby house,

The shored up building belonging to Mr Vandeberghe on the corner of the Van Clichthovenstraat and the Pieter Braeckelaan in Nieuwpoort.

Detail of the crack formation

View of the damage to the adjacent plots

The rear building of the P. Braeckelaan building 37

without the pavement showing any signs of subsidence. The flagstones of the pavement and the underlying stabilised sand formed an arched vault over the leaking water pipe.

THE RESULT

All this resulted in a juridical battle concerning the liability for the damage. Mr H. Declerq, civil engineer and architect, and Mr I. Deconinck, civil engineer and architect, were appointed as experts by order of the Chairman of the Court of First Instance of the county court at Veurne.

On 25 April 2000 the destructive examination was started to find the most obvious reason for the subsidence and the leak in the water pipes. The pavement of the Van Clichthovenstraat, near the corner house P. Braeckelaan 41, was opened up. The water pipes were located and uncovered. A break was found at some 70 cm to the right of the first window of the outbuilding next to the small gate and the subsided garden wall. The break happened in the upper half of the pipe.

It was decided that De Ruyter Building Contractors would carry out some manual digging in the immediate vicinity of the affected

Bert Vandenberghe shows the cavity that appeared under the foundations of his house

buildings in order to get a correct evaluation of the soil and the composition of the subsoil.

A trench was dug in the back yard of the house at P. Braeckelaan 41. When probing with a metal rod there was clearly less resistance where the worst subsidence of the building and the garden wall had taken place.

The infamous cracked cast iron water pipe

Next a pit was dug near the subsided gate of the garden wall. A horizontal fissure was found in the foundations, at a depth of 40 cm under the ground level. The foundations had separated by 8 cm. After probing with the metal rod almost no resistance was found up to a depth of 3 metres.

This issue received extensive media attention. The results of the surface collapse triggered the interest of Johan

Vandewalle, an experienced specialist concerning WWI underground warfare. He remembered the story of soldier Bert Fearns, who talked about the tunnelling in Nieuwpoort. The images of the damage were similar to various cases in the area around Ypres, where buildings subsided as a result of the nearby underground constructions from World War One.

On 13 May 2000 the Municipal Council of Nieuwpoort, Mr A. Coulier, legal representative for the affected inhabitants, the Association of Local Communes Water Company of Veurne-Ambacht (IVWA) and the Court of Veurne received a letter from the Association for Battlefield Archaeology and Conservation (ABAC) which contained the following points.

Although the research of ABAC has till now been focused on the underground war in the area of Ypres, we do dispose of important British data concerning tunnelling in Nieuwpoort-centre. During the second half of 1917 two British and one Australian Tunnelling Company worked on an extensive network of communication passages and headquarters, which were accessible through the cellars of the shelled houses. Within the limited current historic research ABAC has already found deep tunnel systems at less than 150 metres from the damaged houses. A thorough investigation of the archives will probably reveal more about what is below the P. Braeckelaan. During a working visit to the affected site, we found all known symptoms of an excavation by a straight 'subway' with some branches, probably used for accommodation. In view of the urgency to do something and to prevent further damage, we propose an urgent meeting with the Municipal Council, the water company, the owners and the experts appointed by the Court, in order to further clarify the questions.

The letter also proposed to start a historical examination in depth to find the location, size, depth and building of the corridor system in the British and Australian archives, and possibly some research into the earlier French building works of 1916 and early 1917.

A localisation at the site was also proposed, with test drilling and or scanning of the soil, geological and geophysical research, and following on a search for the remains of the complex itself, and stabilisation with foam concrete where possible.

It was made clear that this situation was a warning to enter in to a preventative policy on those sites where no big problems had yet manifested themselves.

On 17 and 24 May 2000 ABAC receives confirmation of delivery from the IWVA and from Mr Coulier. The Court and the Municipality never officially answered.

On 8 June 2000 ABAC sent an estimate of the costs for the historical research in London and for the Geophysical research at Nieuwpoort to the judicial experts H. Declercq and I. Deconinck.

On 19 June 2000 ABAC received a letter from the experts asking to supply as soon as possible the necessary documentation showing the presence of underground constructions. Strangely enough, all following efforts of Peter Barton to arrange a meeting with the judicial experts were negatively received and the requests remained unanswered.

On 8 July 2000 the experts received a letter from Peter Barton (ABAC UK) giving more details about the remaining underground constructions present.

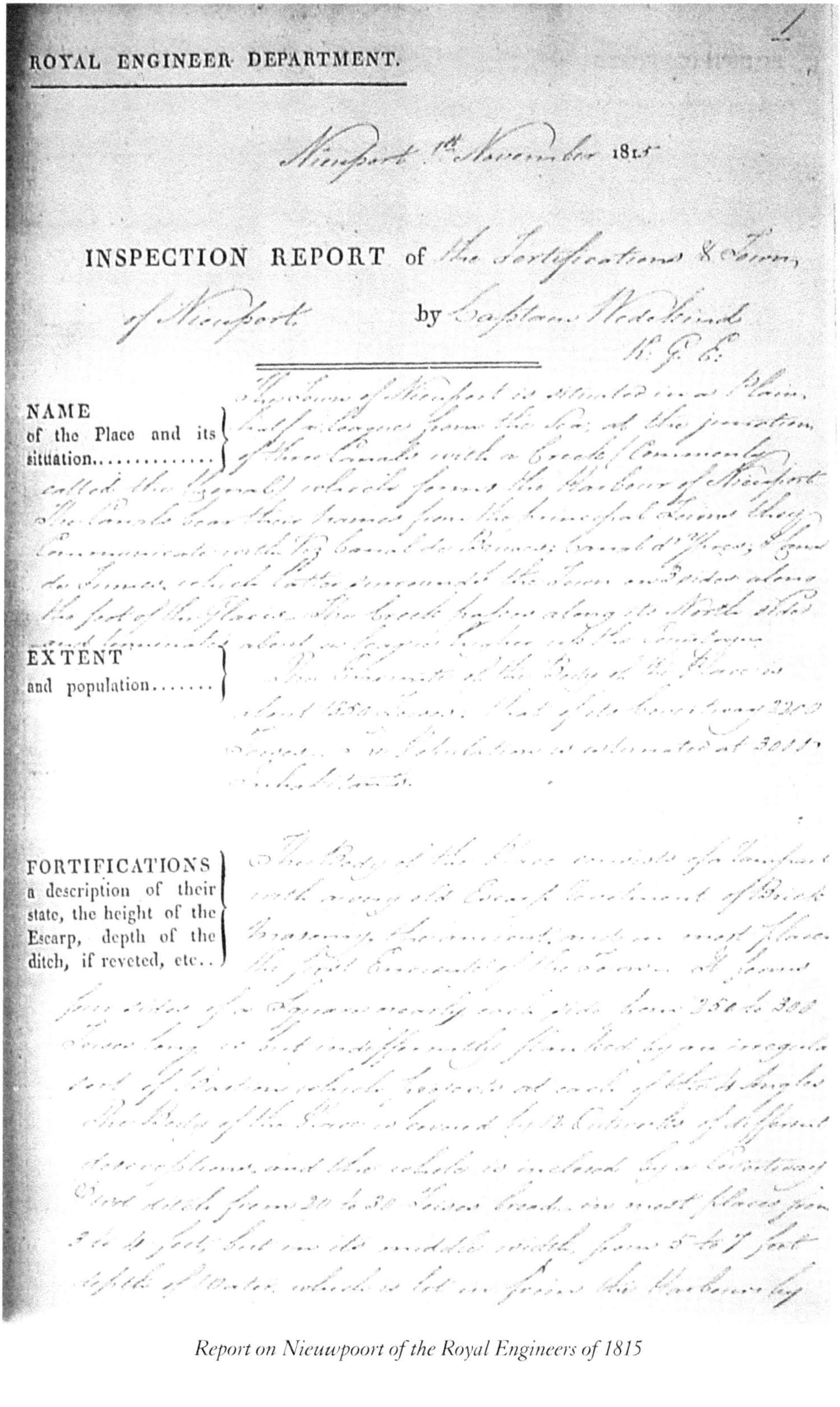

ROYAL ENGINEER DEPARTMENT.

1

Nieuport 1st November 1815

INSPECTION REPORT of the Fortifications & Town of Nieuport by Captain Wedekind K.G.E.

NAME of the Place and its situation............ The Town of Nieuport is situated in a Plain half a League from the Sea, at the junction of three Canals with a Creek (commonly called the [illegible]) which forms the Harbour of Nieuport. The Canals bear their names from the principal Towns they communicate with, viz Canal de Bruges, Canal d'Ypres, Canal de Furnes, which latter surrounds the Town and passes along the foot of the Glacis. The Creek passes along its North side and [illegible] about a League farther into the Country.

EXTENT and population....... The Circuit of the Body of the Place is about 1850 Toises. That of its covert way 2200 Toises. Its Population is estimated at 3011 Inhabitants.

FORTIFICATIONS a description of their state, the height of the Escarp, depth of the ditch, if reveted, etc.. The Body of the Place consists of a rampart with a very old Escarp revetment of Brick masonry, [illegible] and in most places the [illegible] of the Town. It forms four sides of a Square nearly each side from 250 to 300 Toises long, [illegible] indifferently flanked by an irregular sort of Bastion which projects at each of the 4 Angles. The Body of the Place is covered by 12 Outworks of different descriptions, and the whole is inclosed by a Covert way. Wet ditch from 20 to 30 Toises broad, in most places from 3 to 4 feet, but in its middle width from 5 to 7 feet depth of Water, which is let in from the Harbour by

Report on Nieuwpoort of the Royal Engineers of 1815

On 16 July Peter Barton wrote to H. Declercq and I. Deconinck that, according to the report of the Royal Engineers in 1815, the Vauban fortifications do not contain tunnels at the site of the subsidence, and that this strain of thought can be ignored.

On 1 September 2000 Peter Barton gave, in a three-page letter to the experts, information concerning the latest developments in the ABAC research. The results of the field research done by Professor Peter Doyle (Professor of Geosciences, School of Earth Environmental Sciences, University of Greenwich) were explained in detail.

The subsidence at and around the house at Kokstraat 54 was linked to the tunnelling works of the 257th

Professor Peter Doyle

Tunnelling Company Royal Engineers, as described in their Weekly Progress Report of 31 October 1917, recording that a brick lined water pit had to be broken into in order to locate the Dressing Station Tunnel. This caused a delay in the planned tunnelling works. The letter also mentioned that ABAC would like to share all information with the experts and would not publish the findings without consultation with them.

Still there was no reaction or answer from the experts H. Declercq and I. Deconinck.

Between 11 and 17 October 2000 attempts were made, via telephone and email, to organise a meeting of the experts, Professor Doyle and Peter Barton, without result.

On Wednesday, 20 September 2002, Mr I. Deconinck declared in an e-mail that because of circumstances outside their control the different parties are not prepared the pay the proposed costs of the historical research. He also stated that he was able to have a meeting with ABAC. In an answer to this on 21 September by Peter Barton, it was proposed to minimise the cost of the research by integrating it in the production budget of a documentary. A personal meeting is requested.

No answer to this was ever received, nor to the email of 26 September 2000, in which ABAC asks for an informal meeting in order to present the results of the research.

THE REPORT BY THE EXPERTS

On 27 October 2000, all parties receive a copy of the 'Experts Report, Part 1 – Pre-report'. On page 44 of this report a provisional conclusion concerning the possible cause of the subsidence is given:

VII. CAUSE OF THE SUBSIDENCE

In view of the clear lines in the damage, the gradual evolution of the subsidence, which has been going on for at least 5 to 10 years, and which continues to evolve at increasing speed, and in view of the fact that there were important underground infrastructure work during World War One, we are of the opinion that the external cause of the damage must be found in the presence of tunnels, the stability of which has been decreasing and the collapsing of which is causing the damage to structures above ground.

Concerning this we refer to the letter of 13/05/00 by the Association for Battlefield Archaeology and Conservation (ABAC) sent to the IWVA.

It must be noted that this conclusion was reached by the experts without them having access to, or having seen, any military archive map, dairy or other document held by ABAC.

Nobody at ABAC was informed about this conclusion or received a copy of this report.

PRESS CONFERENCE AT THE UNIVERSITY OF GREENWICH

Tuesda 12 December 200 a press conference was held at the University of Greenwich, UK, concerning the research on underground constructions at Nieuwpoort.

Professor Peter Doyle (Professor of Geosciences, School of Earth Environmental Sciences, University of Greenwich), Professor Mike Rosenbaum (Department of Civil and Structural Engineering Nottingham Trent University), Peter Barton (Association for Battlefield Archaeology and Conservation, UK) and Johan Vandewalle (Association for Battlefield Archaeology and Conservation, Belgium) informed the press of the result of the research concerning tunnel complexes present in and around Nieuwpoort.

Professor Luc de Vos, Professor of Military Science at KU Leuven and Military High School

The same evening Professor Luc de Vos, Professor of Military Science at the KU (Christian University) Leuven and the Military High School, appeared on television at VTM (Flemish television channel) where he took another view. The consequences of this reaction, both for ABAC and for Professor de Vos, would be greater than expected.

Professor Luc de Vos in the VTM news programme on 12 December 2000:

'In the area around Nieuwpoort or Diksmuide the groundwater level is so high that if you stick a shovel in the ground you hit water. So you have to pump considerably. Besides that the tunnels in that area were either above ground using sandbags, bags of earth, boards and stones. So if you will, two walls above the ground, or exceptionally there were trenches in dykes.

I think the British are letting themselves be misled by the situation around Ieper and at the Somme, where one could indeed dig deep and dig tunnels. In the area of Nieuwpoort and Diksmuide it is so damp that you can only build trenches and tunnels above ground. That this has to do with underground corridors seems unacceptable to me. I don't believe a word of it (grinning). After World War One, when the town had to be rebuilt, they have of course pushed all the rubble together, and have flattened it out, so to speak.'

In the newspaper *Het Laatste Nieuws* of 13 December 2000 we read the following:

Luc de Vos, Professor War Craft:
'Theory of researchers is twaddle'
Brussels – 'In Nieuwpoort you cannot dig an underground tunnel. The town is situated in the flat low-lying polders. If you put one shovel in the ground your feet will be wet. The ground water level is too high.' Luc de Vos, Professor War Craft at the KU Leuven and the Military School does not believe the theory of Vandewalle and the British. According to him only buttress walls were built above ground, with sandbags. 'In other great battle fields such as the Somme and around Ieper you can find hospitals or quarters underground. That is precluded in Nieuwpoort.'

According to De Vos the subsidence is due to back-filling of the soil after the war. 'In order to speed up the rebuilding the ground was levelled. On some sites the unstable ground is sinking.' Or another possibility: 'In 1870 a new system of sluices was designed for Nieuwpoort. Many small canals were filled in. If there are houses standing on that subsidence is possible.'

At the request of the Canvas television programme 'Ter Zake' (To the Point) a meeting takes place with ABAC, Professor Luc de Vos and Mayor Roland Crabbe of Nieuwpoort. Upon arrival of the members of ABAC (Prof. Peter Doyle, Peter Barton, Johan Vandewalle and Kristof Jacobs) at the office of the Mayor they are not exactly welcomed with open arms. No seating is offered and all maps, charts and documents must be elucidated whilst standing. It was the first time Prof. de Vos saw the British and Australian maps. The documents which motivated his point of view were the book *Nieuwpoort 14–18* by Commander Robert Thys, some photos and a map of the Belgian Army.

After fifteen minutes the people who had already been present resumed their discussion,

Commandant Robert Thys

Above: Soil subsidence at the lock complex between the Dunkirk Canal and the Noordvaart

Left: Johan Vandewalle examines the construction in the presence of Professor Peter Doyle and Peter Barton

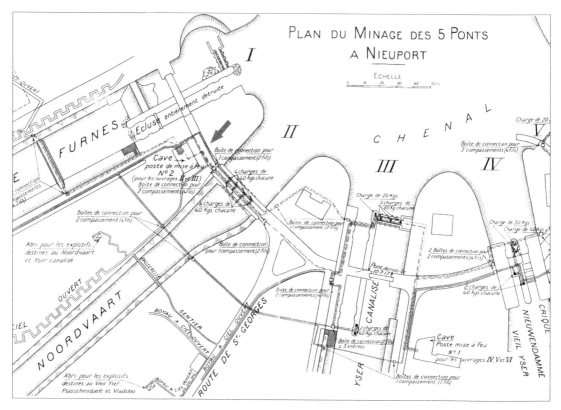

The location of 'Cave poste de mis à feu No. 2'

ignoring the ABAC members, who then left the office.

During the night of 14 to 15 December 2000, a new small subsidence happened in Nieuwpoort. This time the subsidence was situated at the Goosefoot near the locks complex between the Dunkerque Canal and the North Canal. The press printed all sorts of articles about this event. It varied from 'a collapsed tunnel' to 'shelter of the lock-keepers'. None of these proved correct.

After researching the construction it proved to be 'Cave poste de mise à feu N° 2' (Cellar of firing station number 2).

The construction can be found on the map in the book *NIEUWPOORT 1914–1918* by Commander Robert Thys, 1922, Henri Desoer, Liege.

SHORT BACKGROUND

In 1916 preparations started for the total destruction of the locks complex at Nieuwpoort in case a German attack would be launched. The Germans had already seriously damaged the sluices of the Vladsloo Canal and the Passchendaele Canal through accurate bombing with heavy-calibre shells. These bombardments of the sluices and of the paltry little bridges which connected the town with the

Redan and front lines to the north, were a constant worry to the engineers who had to continuously repair all damages and if necessary rebuild certain parts.

Their new task (preparing to blow up the locks) was not exactly undertaken with joy by the Sappers – Pontoon builders – in the knowledge that they had maintained and repaired the complex for more than a year.

By mid-1916 most of the original locks had been demolished by shelling and the engineers had constructed massive dams out of sandbags in order to maintain the essential 16 km flooding, which stretched all the way to Diksmuide.

Repairing these dams and the remaining sluices was extremely dangerous work. The installation of permanent explosive charges was the main cause of the risk to the troops during the work to the sluices. Only one German shell would have sufficed to hit a group of charges and the results would have been catastrophic. The Belgian engineers therefore proposed a plan.

The planned schedule of work would follow, and in February 1916, 400 kg of explosives arrived in the sector. Awaiting the finish of the remaining infrastructure work they were stocked at Veurne to avoid accidents.

Access to the sluices was the easiest part of the assignment for the Belgian troops tasked with the maintenance of the sluices. The Belgian engineers were able to reach the sandbag dam, one of the crossing points of the Veurne Canal, protected by a British tunnel which ran under the full length of the Langestraat.

The connection of the Langestraat with the sandy dam of the Veurnevaart

This tunnel, which connected to other British tunnels and French sunken boyaux, was part of a complex of underground passages in and around Nieuwpoort, mainly built by British and French engineers.

An offshoot of the tunnel network in the W. Deroolaan

The tunnels stretched out over various kilometres, and the Belgian troops generally knew them as 'Le Metro' (the Underground). The Langestraat-tunnel had various spurs very near the sluices which were connected to cellars made from reinforced concrete. These were used as accommodation for the Belgian 'Compagnie de Sapeurs-Pontoniers' (Engineers) and the Cyclists Corps, as well as kitchen and explosives store.

During an emergency situation the explosives were to be set of from the safe 'Cave des Officiers' (Officers' cellar) situated in a reinforced concrete cellar on the southern side of the Langestraat (abreast of house number 137, which today houses the offices of architect J. Bonquet). Canalising the cabling, positioning the charges and the watertight connections, and the construction of connection boxes was complicated and was carried out with the help of the British Royal Engineers. It was decided that detonation of the explosives would be electrical. Various circuits of eight leads were installed in order to have a better chance of successful detonation, and all cabling, connections and connection boxes were buried one metre below the surface in order to reduce the risk of breaks and failure due to German shelling as much as possible.

DECEMBER 2000

The subsidence which occurred near the Goosefoot on 14 December 2000 was due to the collapse of part of this infrastructure destruction of the Great War. The collapse brought to light a small underground shelter of about 4 metres by 3 metres, some 1.6 metres high, known as 'Cave poste de mis au feu number 2' (Cellar detonation post No 2). Cables ran underground from the 'Cave des Officiers', through the sandbag dam which closed off the Veurne Canal at the end of the Langestraat to this post. From this post they were distributed through the various spurs and also through Post No. 1 (located in the headland between the Creek Nieuwendamme and the Yser River) to the charges which had been placed on every lock gate of the following five canals: Noord Canal, Yser, Creek Nieuwendamme, Plassendale Canal and Vladslo Canal.

The subsidence was examined by Professor Doyle (University of Greenwich), Johan Vandewalle, Peter Barton and Kristof Jacobs (Association for Battlefield Archaeology and Conservation) on Friday 15 December. They established that the construction was built in brick. The roof vault was made of a double row of bricks placed sideways, with small pine struts. Wood rot in these struts was probably the cause of the collapse. The wall had been tarred in order to keep the space as dry as possible. The investigators referred to the same method of tarring they had found in various dugouts which they had examined previously, and which had been used for signalling. The relatively dry condition of this connection box was remarkable.

Photo from inside the partially collapsed 'Cave poste de mis à feu No. 2'

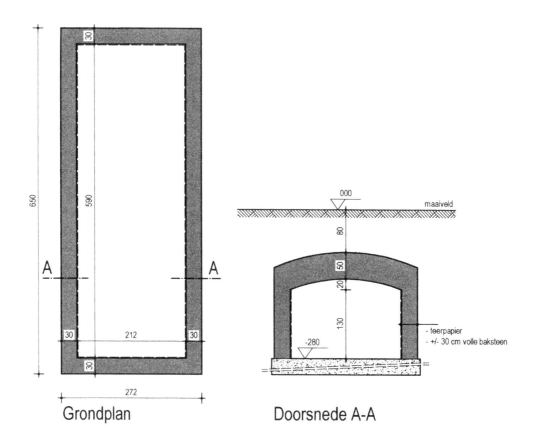

Plan showing the measurements of the 'Cave poste de mis à feu no. 2'

After this case of subsidence the cat is completely out of the bag and all kinds of stories and theories about the underground network in Nieuwpoort are circulating.

In the weekend edition of the newspaper *Het Volk* (The People) of Saturday and Sunday 16 & 17 December 2000 another theory is advanced.

WAR HOSPITAL OF SPANISH SEWERS?

NIEUWPOORT – According to professor Luc de Vos the most delicate point in Nieuwpoort is the intersection of the Kokstraat and the Havenstraat. A complete war hospital should be located under the houses there.

According to de Vos: 'From June to November 1917 British soldiers were working here. Afterwards, until Februay 1918, they were replaced by the French and afterwards by the Belgians. The plans, of which we dispose, date from June 1918. They show us covered trenches, one at ninety degrees to the the Yser, and a second one parallel to the Langestraat towards the Yser. These are trenches which the British dug in the summer of 1917. That was done during a dry period. Afterwards parts were filled in and the ground level of all of Nieuwpoort was heightened by 1.6 metres due to the war rubble.'

The only possible explanation of the current subsidence is, according to de Vos the combination of water and those historic corridors. 'Don't forget that the subsoil of all Nieuwpoort is very unstable due to the rubble, and can easily shift.'

It is very remarkable that Professor de Vos talks here about a complete underground war hospital, while in his interviews of 12 and 13 November he had qualified this as 'rubbish' of which he does not believe one word.

Dr P. Van Wanzele

In the meantime de Vos had had the opportunity to consult the maps and documents of ABAC, which could be an explanation of his departing from his previous standpoint.

In the same article a certain P. Van Wanzele from Gits appears, with a theory about Spanish drains in Nieuwpoort. Using a map dating from the Middle Ages, found at the documentation centre at Ieper, he postulates that the subsidence under the houses is due to the presence of old Spanish drains. 'The Spanish probably installed a system of sewers and drains at the then ground level, and afterwards raised the soil. Also the current underground contains much rubble from the Spanish periods.

This postulation shows that Mr Van Wanzele never visited the sites in order to compare his claims to reality. The site where the P. Braeckelaan and the J. Van Clichthovenstraat are now was waste ground during the Middle Ages, laying half in and half outside the town walls. This can also be seen on the map of the documentation centre at Ypres.

At the bottom of the article appeared a photo of Mr Van Wanzele speaking on the telephone. The caption read: 'Many worried inhabitants of Nieuwpoort telephone P. Van Wanzele for more information concerning the Spanish theory.'

Speaking with the various owners and inhabitants of the houses involved it turned out that nobody knew Mr Van Wanzele, let alone who would have contacted him.

During a press conference at the town hall of Nieuwpoort, on Thursday, 21 December 2000, Mayor R. Crabbe declares that the investigation

Mayor R. Crabbe shows on a copy of the map from ABAC where tunnelling was performed

commissioned by the Municipal Council has not produced any substantial results.

The Municipal Council appointed the company Georad Technology from Niel in order to investigate the presence of cavities in the subsoil of Nieuwpoort at certain points. The technology used was GPR (Ground Penetrating Radar). It works on the principal of electronic waves being sent into the ground of which the resistance is measured and placed on a diagram.

Some years ago Engineer Stefaan Van Nuffel, of the company Georad, offered his services for the detection of dug-outs around Ieper. In order to verify the technology Johan Vandewalle (ABAC) took Mr Van Nuffel to a pasture where the GPR-machine could be demonstrated. The machine showed there were no cavities in the soil. Next Mr Vandewalle took Mr Van Nuffel to the far end of the meadow, where the entrance of the already explored dugout, on which the machine had just stood, was located. According to Mr Van Nuffen the type of clay and the fact that the construction was filled with water caused the non-detection of the construction.

In view of the fact that the French military archives show that the deep tunnels present at Nieuwpoort were already decommissioned in November 1917 because of the presence of at least 60 cm of water, and in view of the high ground water level in Nieuwpoort during the winter months, it is not impossible that the results of the GPR investigation were slightly different from the actual condition of the subsoil.

A second series of scans were carried on Friday 19 January 2001, resulting in some cavities being found in the Hoogstraat.

Georad carries out GPR scanning in the Hoogstraat in Nieuwpoort

Above: The research was followed by the international press (Sky-TV Australia)

Right: Orange markings were placed on the street by Georad. Strangely enough these are 3 feet wide and follow a straight pattern

The company Georad made markings in different places on the street. Each time the distance between the two lines was 90 cm (3 feet = standard width of a tunnel).

Asked about these markings, Georad did not wish to give an answer.

On Friday, 29 December 2000, the Belgian newspaper *Het Laatste Nieuws* (The Latest News) published an article entitled 'Eyewitnesses describe underground tunnels'. It contained the story of Mr Jean Schotte of Sint-Kruis, Brugge, a fervent collector of old manuscripts, who found a description of the tunnel system below Nieuwpoort in a chronicle dating from 1918. He immediately contacted the Municipality of Nieuwpoort, but did not receive a reaction. He then decided to contact the press. Shortly after, Mr Schotte was contacted by Kristof Jacobs (ABAC), who was cordially received at Brugge, where he could study the documents.

Jean Schotte from Sint-Kruis Brugge finds an article for the tunnels under Nieuwpoort in an old war chronicle

The chronicle described the story of a certain A. Hans, who as a newspaper journalist (probably for the Dutch *De Telegraaf*) was travelling through the area immediately after the armistice. Nieuwpoort is described in a passage of the chronicle (underlining K. Jacobs):

… A few people are looking at a destroyed house, and when I ask if I can reach Nieuwpoort: 'There is no road, sir; you must go via Veurne.'

This does not tempt me; why would I not try? It cannot be so terrible. A bit further I meet another person. 'But, sir,' he says, 'you will not find any people at Nieuwpoort!'

'I am not going for the people, but for the things.'

'You can cross the canal; there is a cork bridge – you must go through the German trenches. One of my boys came back from Nieuwpoort; he had become a lump of mud.'

So I can get through… The landscape becomes a real wasteland; the meadows that were so fertile have now become clay, and show hillocks and hollows, where the water from the inundation has remained; the reeds are growing on all sides and the gulls are having a great time across the immeasurable, dreary plain. The German shelters start to rise out of the ground; on my map I see that Mannekensvere was located here. The roads become solid mud; it is a fat sticky clay; those who have cycled through Zeeuws Vlaanderen (the present Zeeland, south western Province of The Netherlands) during the beet harvest, and who imagine that it is a hundred times worse here, will have a small idea about the condition of the roads.

The Yser: on both sides lay the Germans; at the railway Nieuwpoort-Diksmuide lay the Belgians; between them the inundated part.

I climb on top of the trenches to find the bridge and if possible the old road to Nieuwpoort. There is the cork bridge, laid by the Belgian soldiers; with some trouble I lift up my bicycle across the trenches and walk across the river. I find myself in a new network of partly shelled and destroyed defences; in the narrow little corridors are wooden gangways, which have reasonably been preserved. Where to? Climb out again and look around. What a destruction, what a destruction: everywhere sallow clay soil, water and reads; here and there a piece of tree. Look, here is a whole row of copped distorted tree trunks; this must have been the old road: that is where I should go.

It becomes a very arduous trip; I have to follow the gangways of the boyaux, which snake continuously; if you have two metres of straight, you become cheerful! Everywhere are traces of heavy shelling, which amongst others are betrayed by the absence of planking and the presence of pits filled with water. My bicycle becomes a thing which cannot be handled: the clay sticks between tire and mudguard, so the wheels do not wish to turn any longer. I lift my bicycle up by the luggage rack and push it that way; I walk in the mud besides the planks, in order to leave them free for my bicycle, only on there can I keep it moving; behind this I have to give up because of all sorts of barbed wire. I come up to ditches with only a narrow plank across; I try to remove the clay from my shoes, hoist the bicycle on my shoulders (how heavy it is!) and risk it; I slip even before I am at the plank, have to restart several times; after incessant trouble I make it across the ditches. My shoes and leggings are a single clump of mud; my black bicycling suit is slowly taking on the same grey colour; my hands are completely covered in mud. And still the same bends follow one after the other. My bicycle becomes every heavier, the clay is running along the spokes and possibly the wheels have become solid, I have to push my little cart with all my strength, when it slips of the gangplank I have work to free it from the clay.

I have crossed the Yser three quarters of an hour ago and I climb the parapet to see how far I have progressed. The river is there at maybe four hundred metres, quiet and shiny now under the rays of the mild autumnal sun. When will I ever get to Nieuwpoort… will I actually get there! I am exhausted, the sweat runs of my. What if I ate! There is a crate of German hand grenades, on which I sit down and eat… What a terrible life it must have here for the soldiers; now it is armistice; finally I am walking here for my pleasure, and the weather is excellent … I imagine how it must have been during rainy weather under a hail of metal and fire, with pestiferous gas for air, and this for long years. Come on; I feel a little better. The awkward walk restarts? O, this mud, this mud! I realise that I will walk easier on tip of the trenches, but everywhere grenades have hit I have to descend again. I now also get a stupendous mess of all sorts of barbed wire, over which I have to climb with my bicycle.

A man comes towards me from the direction of Nieuwpoort. 'Sir, it is as bad as here for another two hundred metres – I would go back'. – Let's just continue.

What is that? Horrible – a body of a Belgian soldier; the khaki colour is just about recognisable. The man is mummified: it seems brown leather is stretched over the skull; the eye sockets stare bewildered at you, the mouth grins in a terrible rictus and the white teeth gleam like a star in the night; one hand lays away from the arm … a large grey raven flies towards it!

Come on… It is starting to get better; once in a while I can cycle some twenty metres along the grenade pits, the clinker bricks of the old road appear here and there. Along the road a small heap of rubble: that used to be the village of Saint Joris! In the distance the silhouette of something strange appears; it seems like a massive mound of rubble and stones, from which many long arms are raised to the sky: Nieuwpoort.

I have seen one of the most fertile parts of the old Flanders.

A. Hans reports on his visit to Nieuwpoort itself:

'After a terrible journey through mud, between barbed wire, often step by step on loose stone, planks, beams, I have finally arrived in Nieuwpoort, in the middle of the heart rending ruins and I feel very strange in a place which I know so well that I have described them on various occasions during peace time. Where is the Langestraat, where is the market place, where should I look for the ruins of the church, where for those of the Drapers' Hall? And the surroundings feel so astounding when I see here and there a civilian, a Belgian soldier or a German prisoner of war appearing from behind the rubble as out of a hole. They should create some order in this chaos and feel helpless against these huge mounds of ruins.

I would ask them not to change anything, to cart nothing away, to disturb nothing, but to keep

German prisoners of war are being deployed in Nieuwpoort during reconstruction

Nieuwpoort like that, like a museum that will portray to us and those after us the martyrdom of Belgium and of Belgium's heroism, the loyalty of the allies and the vandalism of the German militarism.

But no, we know the character of our people, and however impossible it seems at this moment, soon new life will rise here. At last I find the remains of the church and I recognise it by some Gothic window embrasures, some sculpted stones which still make the art of our forefathers recognisable between chalk, charred wood, lumps of iron and granite. The house of prayer dates from the 13th century when Nieuwpoort flourished thanks to the fishing industry, and it was a noble Gothic building. Where the old cemetery was some stumps of trees remain, and under the long grass that grows abundantly even amongst the rubble, many brave men are buried.

I first read: 'Ici repose Mohomed ben Abdallah' (Here lays Mohomed Abdallah); and thereafter inscriptions which remind me of the unrivalled courage of the French marines and fusiliers, some of whom I have met a short while ago on the coast, their caps adorned with the word 'Nieuwpoort'. Where could be the remains of the beautiful Dunnenhuus, where Albert and Isabella staid during the siege of Oostende in 1600; and to no avail I search for the Drapers' Hall, which lifted its slender

Above: The partly destroyed graveyard in Nieuwpoort City

Below: The station in Nieuwpoort City

tower so elegantly above the red roofs. A piece of the façade of the station still stands, bearing a board with black lettering:'Nieuwpoort stad'.

How I miss the bold templar's tower which stood just outside the town. Where could all the inhabitants have gone to?

The remainder of the 'Duvetorre'

So I wonder, and it is as if I can still see them in their good and genial hometown with the picturesque harbour. Where is the 'Vierboet', one of the first Flemish lighthouses, on top of which wood was burnt and which therefore fitted so well within the worn fishing town. I see nothing but ruins through which some streets have been cleared, and along the Yser mouth near the trenches some miserable threadbare trunks of the once so elegant trees.

I descend a staircase and arrive in the underground Nieuwpoort. Strong corridors made of wood run in all directions under the small town. I see abandoned kitchens and depot and phone dens, and rest now and then in front of a look-out window, from whence I notice the plain of Veurne-Ambacht, or hear the Yser murmuring. I am alone here, where thousands of men have lived for long months, while above them the shells burst. Nieuwpoort could not be lost, as this astonishing underground town also testifies, in which it is so eerily silent. 'Write that everything must remain as it is,' my friend the Major said to me yesterday, and with fervent conviction I repeat his words. Here is the most important sector of the famous Yser River. We see a lot this morning. The sluices, the electricity works, the trenches, at last the shelters in heaps of rubble, the wide Yser plain, across which the rain drives. No tree, no farm, no house can be see amongst the grenade pits and the great stretches of water.

From here on the Belgian Army, led by Albert, undertook their victory march to liberate the tormented country. And therefore the wide loneliness, the great silence, is all the more stirring.

I follow the muddy paths and arrive back at the German fortifications, along blown up batteries, exploded ammunition depots and across emergency bridges, and the reach the village of Slijpe, the first one in this sector which has not completely been flattened. I am all alone again and the silence is only disturbed the wind… And in this way A. Hans continues his journey towards Roeselare.

On Friday, 9 February 2001, the geophysical investigation commissioned by the Municipality is stopped. In the Belgian newspaper *Het Laatste Nieuws* of 10 and 11 February 2001, Mayor R. Crabbe declares that the searches have been stopped, as they found nothing more than some small cavities. Lawyer A. Coulier deplored that the research was stopped without scanning the private real estate, especially the back yards of the most damaged houses.

ABAC sent a request to the Municipality and Georad for access to the results of the GPR scanning, in order to have them analysed by Professor Peter Doyle.

On Wednesday, 28 February 2001, the Court of Veurne decided during a summary procedure that the Belgian State, through the Fund for War Damage, must be involved in the judicial procedures concerning the damaged houses in Nieuwpoort. The summary proceedings were taken by the eleven owners of the houses with subsidence in J. Van Clichthovenstraat and P. Braeckelaan. The Judge at the summary procedure also extended the commission of the experts appointed earlier, H. Declercq and I. Deconinck. In order to get more clarity excavations would have to be carried out.

Journalist Kris Callier writes in the Belgian newspaper *Het Volk* of 21–22 April 2001 a striking article titled 'World War One Tunnel discovered'. We cite Callier:

'In Nieuwpoort the first real tunnel dating to World War One has been discovered. At least, that is what Mayor Roland Crabbe confirms. The subject is a construction of some 80 metres long between the Hoogstraat and the Astridlaan. The tunnel runs from the basement of a house in the Hoogstraat and goes under the Kokstraat. The construction is shored up with wooden beams.'

He also writes: *'Mayor Roland Crabbe has seen the tunnel. As far as is known he is the only eyewitness? He does not doubt that this is an authentic construction from World War One. 'I did not enter it completely, but it is clearly a war tunnel. It is not built in brick, but propped up, in the way used in the war, with wooden beams. The tunnel is even still in good condition. I believe this is because the water level has remained constant and the beams have not rotted,'* says Roland Crabbe.

A few days later, in a telephone call with Kristof Jacobs (ABAC), Mayor Crabbe denies having seen this tunnel in the Hoogstraat, and certainly having entered one. He does confirm that some tunnel-like constructions were found some years previously during foundation work for a bank building in the Astridlaan.

This clearly shows the part of the press in this affair. Some journalists were specialists in the manipulation of witness statements or declaration of both ABAC and the Municipal Council, which means these constantly contradict each other.

The house to which the article refers is Hoogstraat 69.

It was owned by the Catholic Church of Belgium, and a retired city clerk had lived in it for years. When, in September 2000, Prof. Peter Doyle (University of Greenwich), Peter Barton and Kristof Jacobs (ABAC), visited the resident in order to ask him if he had not seen something unusual in his basement, they were promptly dismissed with the message 'those tunnels are fine there, if you want to know something you should go to the town hall'. Later efforts of ABAC to start a dialogue with the resident were negatively received.

The construction concerned was the Dressing Station Tunnel.

DRESSING STATION TUNNEL

From the weekly reports of the 257th Tunnelling Company Royal Engineers it is clear that the Dressing Station Tunnel is located at about 130 feet from the corner of the Ankerstraat and the Kokstraat. At about 15 feet next to it there is a short tunnel to a machine-gun emplacement. The size of the Dressing Station Tunnel is

The building Hoogstraat 69 where, according to the plans of the Royal Engineers, the 'Dressing station tunnel' is underneath and a machine-gun post once stood

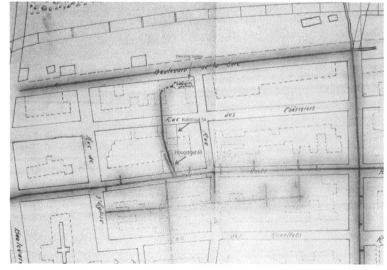

The location of the Dressing Station Tunnel on the map of the 257th Tunnelling Company Royal Engineers

6 ft x 3 ft (90 cm wide and 180 cm high), and the depth various between 3 and 5 metres.

The tunnel constitutes a link between the Rue Haute Tunnel which runs under the Hoogstraat loopt and the dressing station situated on the corner of the Astridlaan and the Ankerstraat. The dressing station was an underground field hospital where the wounded brought back from the front lines were given first aid. The hospital lies at a depth of about 3 metres below the current ground level, half of it under the apartment building 'Spaderyke', the other half under the garages behind the building.

The apartment building 'Spaderyke' on the corner of Ankerstraat and Astridlaan

The space is approximately 25 metres long, 9 metres wide and 2 metres high. The roof is made of a slab of reinforced concrete 50 centimetres thick. The concrete slab, combined with the 3 metres of sand which was placed on top of ensured that the dressing station was bombproof.

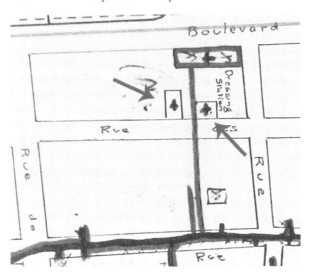

A map of the Australian Electrical and Mechanical Mining and Boring Company, which in 1917 electrified the tunnels built by the 257th Tunnelling Company Royal Engineers, shows that near the dressing station two small bunkers were built. They were built in brick, and 3 x 3 metres large. These shelters were bulletproof, but not bombproof.

Map of the Australian Electrical and Mechanical Mining and Boring Company

During World War Two a large concrete bunker stood in the Ankerstraat (near the corner with the Astridlaan, where garages can now be found). Various inhabitants of Nieuwpoort sheltered from the British bombers in this bunker. At the end of the seventies the bunker was demolished by the building firm Vandenberghe from Nieuwpoort in order to build an apartment building on the site. During the demolition an underground construction made of brick and with a brick vaulted roof was found. In view of the construction method it clearly was a construction predating 1917. Probably this construction was used as part of the dressing station.

Top left: The location of the Dressing Station for the construction of 'Spaderyke'
Bottom left: The demolition of the World War Two bunker
Top right: The tunnel structure is clearly visible
Bottom right: A corridor with brick vault is exposed

When, some years later, the building firm Vandenberghe dug the foundations for garages behind the 'Spaderyke' building they found a slab of reinforced concrete. By using a large hydraulic pickaxe on an excavator they managed to make an opening some 50 cm across in the slab. Under it they found a large empty space. In view of the stability of the concrete slab and the anticipated trouble to fully destroy it, it was decided to use the slab as foundation for the garages.

The garages are well founded on the concrete slabs used for the Dressing Station

Due to the location and dimensions of the concrete slab it is possible to state with some certainty that this was once the ceiling of the dressing station.

When, in early September 2000, the ABAC team undertook field research in Nieuwpoort in order to compare the British and Australian Military maps to the situation on the ground, it was obvious that at nearly all sites where the maps show constructions under the ground, there had been subsidence. Arriving at Kokstraat 54, where the map shows that the Dressing Station Tunnel runs, the sagging gate and the various repaired cracks in the front façade were immediately visible.

The owner of the house, Mr Willy Pyliser, testified that the house, and especially the garage, continued to sink. Kristof Jacobs, assistant-architect (ABAC), inspected the house and determined that the load-bearing wall between the garage and the living area had already sunk several centimetres. In the basement it was clear to see that the right side of the house was pulling away

Damage to the house at Kokstraat 54   *Cracked garden wall right in front of Kokstraat 54. The arrows show the extent of the damage*

from the remainder of the building. The hinging point of the subsidence is in the diagonal crack in the floor of the cellar which runs from the middle of the building on the street side to the right hand far corner of the building. Mr Pyliser stated that the floor of the garage had sunk by about 50 centimetres some years previously. The cause was thought to have been a break in the water pipes. The water company had paid for all repairs. The supposed break in the water pipes was never really surveyed. The settling of the building continues to evolve.

Mr Pyliser also mentioned that he filled his well with all the building rubble and broken up floor pieces, as the well was unusable anyway. Both the former owner and Mr Pyliser could never use the well because the water was not fit for consumption. The fluids from the septic tank, about 1 metre from the well, ran into it without any discernible cause, causing the pollution.

The Weekly Progress Report of the 257th Tunnelling Company, 7 November 1917, mentions tunnelling works at this site.

We can presume that in view of the location of the brick-lined septic tank as well as the location of the Dressing Station Tunnel, combined with the description in the report, that here the tunnelling works are also the cause of the structural problems. The subsoil under the house of Mr Pyliser was

Weekly Progress Report of the 257th Tunnelling Company from 7 November 1917

pierced by the 257th Tunnelling Company, and shored up with a wooden frame. After the war, when there was no more pumping, the tunnel was exposed to the variations of the ground water, causing the loading capacity of the wood to deteriorate. The problem here is the crumbling of the soil behind the wall boards of the construction, just as in the case of the dugout constructions in the area around Ypres. As a result the underground passage is compressed by the movement of the subsoil and variations in the water table. The underground slide was the cause of the burst septic tank. The sewage found a way out and finally ran into the well next to the septic tank. This explained the impossibility to use the well.

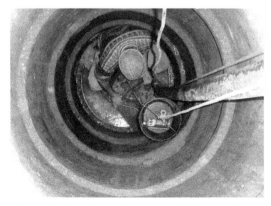

Johan Vandewalle carries out test drilling at a depth of 5 meters

One of the drill holes

In May 2005 Johan Vandewalle made various bore holes from inside the well belonging to Mr Pyliser. At a depth of 5 metres underground level a layer of disturbed earth was discovered, as well as remains of decayed organic matter. It is likely that, after the war, parts of the underground construction were dismantled and used as building materials by the local population. No attention was paid to thoroughly fill back or stabilise the underground hollows, causing the current problems.

JUDICIAL DIGS

On Friday, 27 April 2001, the experts H. Declercq and I. Deconinck gave orders to dig up some of the back garden of the damaged house at P. Braeckelaan 41. To start with a small digger opened the area indicated by the experts. The excavated materials soon made it clear that the subsoil was composed of rubble, ashes and other fill, which did not aid the stability of the soil.

Judicial excavation without any safety measures

Johan Vandewalle (ABAC), who was present, had proposed another part of the garden for digging, based on the British Army maps of 1917. This was not taken into consideration. When the digger had reached a depth of about two metres, the hole filled completely with swirling water, appearing out of nowhere, in less than a second. As the wall of the hole started increasingly to cave in because of the water, digging became very difficult. The remaining procedure was to install a concrete well-ring in the hole, after which the contaminated water was removed with a bucket.

One can but wonder at the amateur fashion in which this dig was undertaken. The photos make it clear that within the immediate reach of the digger's arm up to twelve people are present. No one is wearing a hard hat or safety shoes. Eight people are standing at the edge of the digging trench, which was dug without any form of shoring, which, in view of the unstable subsoil, carries a serious risk of soil slides. Health and Safety regulations were obviously not adhered to.

No water pump had been set up around the hole, resulting in a man with a bucket being sent down to drain it. In view of all these facts the question arises if the results of an investigation in such circumstances are actually reliable.

After arriving at a depth of 2.5 metres, the water became uncontrollable, the research was stopped, and the result was published as: 'no construction found'.

ABAC's research shows that a cut and cover trench, as built in Nieuwpoort, had a depth of

Men stood around watching the excavations without any apparent consideration for health and safety

1.60 to 2 metres. The excavated soil was placed back on the wooden ceiling. If the trench was being dug in a street, the street cobbles would be stacked on top of the soil. The advantage of this was that shells fired by the Germans tended to ricochet off the cobbles, but the trench was certainly not bomb proof. It was a bullet proof communication passage.

It is very unlikely that any remains of any constructions will be found at a depth of 2.5 metres, as the original ground level of the P. Braeckelaan was at least 2 metres lower, but has been raised by filling it with rubble throughout the town after the war. In the after war period wood was scarce, and all visible parts of trenches were dismantled by the locals and used as fuel or as building materials. The trenches were filled with rubble and the streets were rebuilt. This makes it very improbable that an intact cut and cover trench could be found today. The only things of which remains can be found are the pegs which were used to anchor the ground plate and the stiles. In P. Braeckelaan these should be, taking into account the back fill, at an actual depth of 3.6 to 4 metres. Therefore it is logical that the dig ordered by the juridical experts did not find anything.

K. Jacobs was finally invited by the juridical experts on Saturday, 29 September 2001, and was asked to display various documents.

Documents from the archives were presented, and the experts confirmed that they had considered this as an additional factor to the cause of the damage for quite some time.

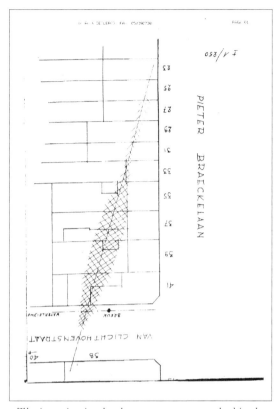

The investigation by the court excerpts resulted in the recording of this damage line

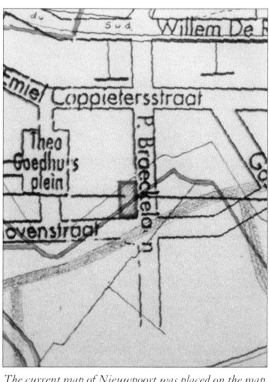

The current map of Nieuwpoort was placed on the map of the Royal Engineers 1917 by ABAC, with this result. This deviates 15° from the line of the excerpts

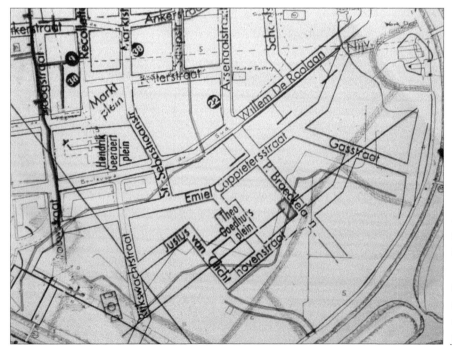

It is striking that everywhere where the green lines (covered trenches) intersect the buildings, cracks are present in the façades

In the experts' report Part II dated 04.01.2002 we can read the following:

'As the various maps and plans of diverse origin and appearance register the same configuration of tunnels and covered trenches, it is clear that there were tunnels and half dug covered tunnels (covered boyaux) in Nieuwpoort during World War One, when these details were mapped.

The lines of the covered boyaux and the configuration of the old Vauban defences match the data in the report of Mr Vandenberge dated 02/11/01, but he interprets the linear outlines visible on the ground on an aerial photograph of 17/07/1917 as town canals. When looking at the picture shown, dated 27/07/1997 in detail one can see that the supposed town canals do not connect to the canal, and even end before the canal. In the photograph real canals also appear which have a darker colour and which effectively connect to the canal. The canals prove to use that the constructions which run across the Braeckelaan and the Van Clichthovenstraat are not canals, but trench constructions.'

The case was handed over the judicial system, causing things to remain becalmed for some months.

On 2 December 2004 the newspaper Het Volk reported:

NIEUWPOORT – At the Court of First Instance of Veurne the case of the subsidence of houses in the Vanclichthovenstraat and the Pieter Braeckelaan in Nieuwpoort was heard. The five owners of houses in that location jointly demand 1,237,781 euro from water company IWVA. According to the owners the damage to their houses was caused by a leak in the water pipes. The water company maintains that the leak was the result of the subsidence of the houses.

Solicitor Alain Coulier, representing the owners and residents, says: 'The water company IWVA was warned on 21st March 2000 about the problems, and shut down the water supply. When the pipe was uncovered a large crack was identified.'

Solicitor Alain Coulier

UNDERGROUND TUNNELS

'Shortly after the subsidence manifested itself, Nieuwpoort buzzed with stories about underground tunnels, historians presented aerial photographs and in Belgium, as well as in Great Britain and Australia specialists were called in to support the war theory. However, a real wartime tunnel has not been found during any of these digs. But for financial security we have summoned the Belgian State in order to possibly make an appeal to the Fund for War Damage,' according to Coulier. 'Besides, at the end of 2002, after repairs to the crack in the water pipe, the subsidence has stopped and no further cracks or tears have appeared.'

Remarkably the judicial experts described the subsidence since 1999 as continuously evolving, but that the solicitor for the duped persons puts forward that no evolution of the damages has occurred since 2002.

On 18 May 2005 the Belgian newspaper De Standaard reports:

Archaeologists will not be able to research a World War One tunnel in Nieuwpoort. Notwithstanding agreements with the building company and the municipality, the works to the sewers in the Kokstraat were carried out without notifying the archaeologists.

On account of the planned work the members of the 'Association for Battlefield Archaeology and Conservation' (ABAC) and the Flemish Institute for Heritage Real Estate (VIOE) had asked to be allowed to search for remains of wartime tunnels. Although promises had been made to notify when the street was to be dug up at the intended site, this did not happen.

A representative of ABAC stated: 'We had, before the repairs to the Kokstraat, an agreement with the VIOE that the building company would notify us two days before the start of the works. We know that under the Kokstraat there was a tunnel to an underground field hospital. However, one day we received a telephone call from a local resident letting us know that the works had started. I needed three hours to finish at my place of employment and to drive back to Nieuwpoort. But during those three hours the builders had already installed a new waste pipe and had concreted over it… only on the probable site of the tunnel. The remainder of the street was still open. Furthermore, Mayor Crabbe forbade the VIOE to dig a test trench next to the new piece of sewer. Why?'

Kris Carlier (Newspaper *Krant van West Vlaanderen*): 'Cover-up'
New museums, new educational routes and the success of the In Flanders Fields museum demonstrate that the interest for World War One has never been greater. Only in Nieuwpoort the war of the past must remain covered. Strange, did the town not plan to install a war museum in the 'Bomb free'? Strange also, that the information from wartime documents may not be verified on the terrain. Not only for the historical value, but also for practical purposes: imagine building your house or a sewer on top of a covered trench in order to find out, a couple of years later, that the subsoil is only an underground amalgamation of rubble and rubbish.

Mayor Roland Crabbe: 'Tunnels are not a priority'

'Let us be realistic,' Mayor Roland Crabbe reacts. 'Some years ago we carried out some test boring in the Hoogstraat. These showed that there are no hollows. Furthermore the VIOE itself does not consider the tunnels as a priority. If that had been the case they would have supplied funding for a test trench in the Kokstraat. You cannot just dig a hole of six–seven metres deep. That should be done with pilings, otherwise the houses will crack. If Kristof Jacobs really wants to research those tunnels,

he must convince the VIOE to fund this. Because if the VIOE does not consider those tunnels a priority, why would I have to furnish 12,500 euros from the municipal coffers to dig a hole? We do not need the information for our museum. The museum will concentrate on the inundation. And for this we have sufficient materials.'

THE REFURBISHMENT OF THE HOOGSTRAAT 2005–2006

The refurbishment of the Hoogstraat at Nieuwpoort was started in autumn 2005. The sewerage network present was also replaced. In advance, the infrastructure department of the town contacted ABAC, requesting to be allowed to consult the maps from the archives, particularly because of the earlier presence of the 'Rue Haute Tunnel' under the Hoogstraat. In view of the fact that the sewage pipes were at least 1.5 to 2 metres above the roof level of the tunnel, the change of finding the former World War One construction during the works was zero. When comparing it with the first sewerage plan of the town from the 1920s it stood out that the sewage pipes always ran down the middle of the road, apart from at the start of the Hoogstraat, near 'Het Kasteeltje' |the little castle|. In that spot the sewage pipes run in a great detour, partly under the private houses. The explanation by the head of the infrastructure department was that in those days there were bomb craters there. When we compare it with the map of the 257th Tunnelling Company Royal Engineers from 1917 we can see on that site contained a heightened enlargement of underground accommodation which is not present in the rest of the street. This proves again that the work of the Royal Engineers was already known in 1920 and possibly caused soil disturbance, and the reason why the sewage pipes were laid around this sensitive site.

During the research into this matter in the last five years an old inhabitant of Nieuwpoort

recounted that he knew about the underground constructions, and that his father had always warned him about them. He testified that in the 1930s there had been a large surface collapse at the crossing with the Ankerstraat. A hole of some metres deep appeared in the road. At the time, the cause was said to be the collapse of an old 'sappe' (old dialect for tunnel). At the time the hole had been filled with a few lorries full of dune sand.

During the infrastructure works in the Hoogstraat at the site of the Ankerstraat during late December 2005, it was determined that a demarcation was clearly visible in the colour of the subsoil. Within

On the corner of the Hoogstraat and Ankerstraat, the traces of demarcation from the 1930s emerge when the street was redeveloped in 2005

the grey-brown subsoil a vertical strip of pure dune sand showed up, thus attesting to the statement about the collapse above.

The Municipality has known about the tunnels for more than forty years.

On 19 August 1963, the then acting Mayor Demarcke received a letter from Major H. V. Braker, asking what remained of the 1917 British defences.

The letter was answered on 29 August 1963 with the statement that the site was now a yacht club.

On 27 April 1967, the Mayor of Nieuwpoort received a letter from Major D. O. Dixon of the Machine Gun Corps, asking what remained of the defences the Corps built in 1917. Attached to his letter was an in-depth description of the situation in 1917, and he mentions that the miners dug hundreds of metres of underground passages in Nieuwpoort.

This letter was presented at the Municipal Council Meeting of 6 May 1967.

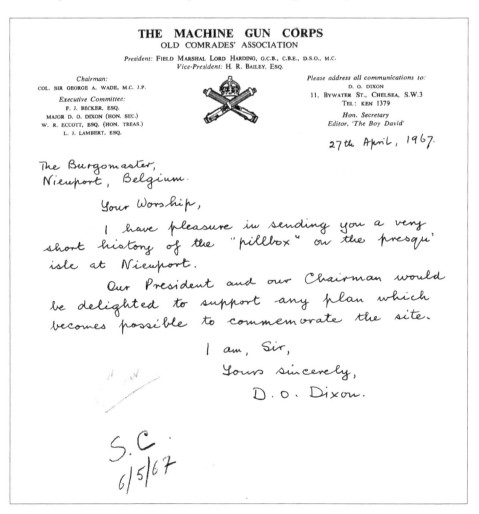

Letter from Major D. O. Dixon of the Machine Gun Corps to the Mayor

From: Major D.O. Dixon
      (Hon Sec, MGC/OCA)
- - - - - - - - - - -   tel: 01.589-1379.

A UNIQUE SITE AT NIEUPORT (BELGIUM).

For almost the whole of the 1914-18 war, the tip of the peninsula which now encloses the yacht-basin at Nieuport was the most advanced ground held by the Belgian and Allied forces in that area. The nearest German post was only 200 metres away.

If during that time it had been possible to place a machine-gun post on the raised ground at the t**i**p of the peninsula, such a post would have commanded the German front line inland for several kilometres.

The military engineers, however, said it was impossible to construct such a post. As soon an any work began, it would be observed and obliterated by the German artillery.
- - - - - - - - - -
In the spring of 1917 a young lieutenant of the Machine Gun Corps offered himself and his section -- all volunteers -- to construct such a post secretly.

Some of the men were coal-miners. They worked every night making an underground passage over 500 metres long from the trench at the base of the peninsula, removing the "spoil" before daylight. When the passage reached the tip of the peninsula , they excavated and shored-up a cavern 6 metres square, with only 50 cm of undisturbed earth on top.

Inside the cavern they laid a **concrete** floor 2 metres thick. On this they erected a steel framework, and finally built up the walls and roof with concrete 2 metres thick.

The work was finished in one month. Nothing of it was to be seen from outside, except finally the embrasure which was opened towards the German lines; and this too was successfully camouflaged.

For the rest of the war, this unique "pillbox" played a commanding role on the Nieuport sector both in attack and defence.

The "pillbox" is still there and is intact, but is now hidden beneath more than 2 metres of "spoil" dredged-up from the river to raise the level of the peninsula. The only sign of its existence is the former embrasure in the river-wall, marked by a patch of concrete.
- - - - - - - - - - - - - - - -
The peninsula is now under consideration by the Authorities in Nieuport for development in connection with modern facilities for the Yacht Haven.

It could perhaps be possible to include in the plans a means of access to the "pillbox" ?

Future visitors could be invited to descend to the "pillbox" and view throu the embrasure the commanding view of the former German positions along the Yser
- - - - - - - - - - - - - - -
The young officer was Lieut H.V. Barker, Madhine Gun Corps, commanding no 2 Section, 127th Company, Machine Gun Corps. He became a professional engineer, and is still alive.

The Machine Gun Corps existed only during the first world war. 160,500 officers and men served in the Corps, and suffered 62,049 casualties. All the survivors are near or past 70 years of age, but over 700 of them still subscrib to the funds of the Old Comrades Association.

The Old Comrades' Association would gladly co-operate with the Authorities of Nieuport in promoting any suitable commemmoration of this unusual site, and would provide funds for a memorial tablet, and make worthy arrangements for any desired observance of this feat of a former Company of the Machine Gun Corps.

D.o Dixon

27th April, 1967.

The explanatory annex to the letter from Major D. O. Dixon

THE PROVISIONAL DECISION ABOUT THIS CASE

The judicial procedure about the subsided houses is still ongoing. The duped parties have not yet received any recompense for the damages, and some have been forced to demolish a part of their home and rebuild it at their own expense, awaiting a verdict which may someday be handed down. No further research at the site has been carried out. The judicial case is only concerned with responsibilities and who will finally pay the damages. The point of view of the Municipality is that there are no problems with World War One tunnels in the town. Things are left to run on … and Nieuwpoort continues to slowly sink.

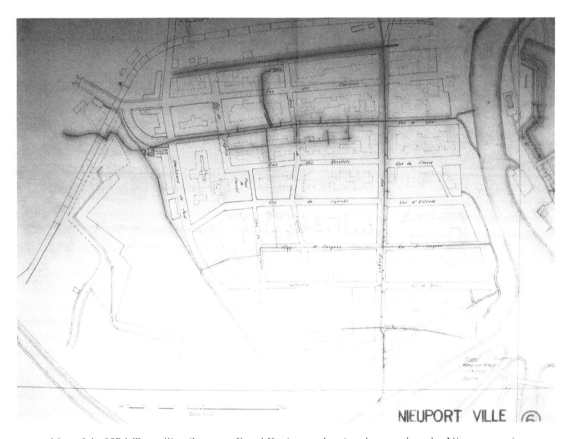

Map of the 257th Tunnelling Company Royal Engineers, showing the tunnels under Nieuwpoort city

Many young men fought here, worked here, tunnelled here and died here, far away from home, for a common cause.

THIS MAY NOT BE DENIED NOR FORGOTTEN.

CHAPTER FIFTEEN
DUGOUT AND TUNNEL DATABASE

In the past six years ABAC carried out research into the various present underground constructions of the sector Nieuwpoort which are the subject of this work. The constructions are of British and Australian origin and vary from observation posts, machine-gun posts, communication posts, accommodation for troops to wells. Using documents from the British and Australian archives all these constructions were located and geo-referenced on the actual topographical map.

Currently everything is being geo-referenced further in a GIS system in order to achieve a practical database which can be consulted for the prospection for building projects, archaeological and historical research.

Number	Name	Map Reference	Information	Started	Ended	Occupation	Total Length
	184 TUNNELLING COMPANY **Royal Engineers**	**184 TC**	**184 TC**	**184 TC**	**184 TC**		
96,125	Troops	R32 a 9.8		28.9.17			
2	KENT CAMP	R 33 d 2.7		> 20 Sept			
3	NORFOLK CAMP	R 23 c 3.2		> 20 Sept			
4	BRISBANE CAMP	X 3 b 1.6		28.9.17			
5	EAST SURREY CAMP	R 32 b 7.9					
156	Troops DO	R 33 a 5.3		21.9.17			
157	Troops DO	R 33 a 8.0		21.9.17			
158	Troops	R 23 c 8.4		21.9.17			
1	SURREY CAMP	R 32 a 7.7					
	257 TUNNELLING COMPANY **Royal Engineers**	**257 TC**	**257 TC RE**	**257 TC RE**	**257 TC RE**		
	OOST DUINKERKE	X 3 b 8.5					
	REDAN – Nieuwpoort	M 28					
	Nieuwpoort	M 28					
	Divisional HQ	X 4 a 2.9		18.7.17			
	LA PANNE HQ	W 14 d					
	LA PANNE SHELTER	L 3 d (sh.19)					
	DRESSING STATION TUNNEL	M 34 a 60.75					
6	PLAETSBURG DUNES	X 3 b 2.7		17.10.17			
155	Well	X 3 b 8.5					
	2ND. AUSTRALIAN **TUNNELING COMPANY**	**2nd ATC**	**2nd ATC**	**2nd ATC**	**2nd ATC**		
	SUBWAY Nieuwpoort BAINS	M 14 c	Infantry subway under s N-Bain				3910 feet
134	BOPPY MOUNTAIN	M 20 a 5.4	acc. dug-outs 5 inclines	12.10.17	14.11.17		1089 feet
136	BROKEN HILL	R 24 c 15.70		?		24 + 4	537.5 feet
137	SYDNEY RIDGE	M 19 d 05.00	Acc. 38 men	5.9.17	17.10.17	38 +	421.5 feet
183	MG Position	R 24 a 6.0	MG post	?		24 +	
140	BATHURST POST	M 19 d 1.5	1 off. no bunking	13.9.17	31.10.17	1 Officer	247 feet
149	COBAR POST	R 29 b 8.4		10.10.17		nil	575.5 feet
139	KURSAAL DUGOUTS	W 14 central	Corps HQ (xv)	14.9.17	3.10.17		422 feet
141	ADELAIDE POST	M 19 b 69.59	Accommodation 8 men	8.9.17	24.10.17	8?	333 feet
142	MELBOURNE POST	M 19 b 78.27	Accommodation 8 men	8.9.17	24.10.17	8+	171.5 feet
148	BALLARAT POST	M 19 d 4.5	1 officer, 33 men	8.9.17	31.10.17	33+	177 feet
147	KANGAROO POST	M 20 c 19.85	Accommodation 16 men	8.9.17	17.10.17	16 +	162 feet
151	SPOIL BANK	M 21 a 75.35		24.10.17	7.11.17	?	
145	MANLY POST	M 19 d 55.45	MG. Accommodation 33 men	5.9.17	31.10.17	33 +	376 feet
154	RIGHT RESERVE	M 20 a 95.32		24.10.17	31.10.17	125 +	517.5 feet
150	Left reserve MG post	M 19 a 9.8	connection to DO system	2.11.17	24.10.17	7.11.17	207 feet
153	HURLE BISE	M 14 c 60.75	MG pos. connection to subway	31.10.17	14.11.17	?	77 feet
146	Dune 18 Artillery Positions	M 19 b 1.2	Art. Group HQ. Acc.100 men	29.8.17	2.9.17	100 +	387 feet
144	ADV. DIV. HQ O-D Bains	R 27 c 8.3	11 shelters C&C sunk 12′ 6 x 23′	29.8.17	10.10.17	large	1385.5 feet
160	STATION TUNNEL DO'S	M 14 c 8.8		25.7.17	8.8.17	28 +	122 feet
135	Boche Close Support DO	M 21 a 75.35		?	10.11.17		316 feet
152	Left reserve DUGOUTS	M 19 a 9.8 area		?		large	1057 feet
159	MG Dugouts	R 29 a 76.78		10.10.17			
161	Mined dugout	M 20 b 2.7		14.7.17	15.8.17		
162	Left reserve dugout	M 20 a 0.9		14.7.17	29.8.17		
163	Mined dugout	M 20 a 8.9	see 9.9 # 35	14.7.17	22.8.17		
164	Mined dugout	M 20 a 0.5		?			
165	OP plus MG	M 20 a 6.4	Troops DO begun 17.10.17	?	1.8.17		
166	OP	M 19 b 8.2	check # 142	?			
167	OP	M 20 a 4.0		?	29.8.17		

168	MG Dugouts	M 19 b 65.60		5.9.17		
169	MC Dugouts	M 19 b 05.45		5.9.17		
170	MG Dugouts	M 20 c 45.75		5.9.17		
171	Broken Hill Post MG positions	R 24 c 20.65	MG Company HQ	1.9.17	7.11.17	
172	MG Dugouts	M 19 d 3.3		5.9.17		
138	MG Dugouts	R 24 c 75.95		5.9.17		
173	Tunnel under railway embankment	M 14 c 9.5		?	14.11.17	
	Tunnel under road N-B	M 14 c 4.6		?	12.9.17	72 feet
174	MG Dugout	M 19 b 80.45		?		
175	MG Dugout	M 20 c 5.8		?		
176	MG Dugouts	M 19 d 49.42		26.9.17	31.10.17	
177	MG Dugouts	R 24 c 55.65		?	7.11.17	
181	Bendigo Post MG positions	R 24 c 55.85		1.9.17	17.10.17	
	Test Bore Holes - Nieuwpoort	M 28 c 87.50		2.9.17		
	Station Tunnel Dugouts	M 14 c 5.7	connection to subway			
	256 TUNNELLING COMPANY Royal Engineers	**256 TC RE**	**256 TC RE**	**256 TC RE**	**256 TC RE**	
7	HA GROUP OP	R 24 c 2.3		14.7.17	22.8.17	
8	Signal Dugout	R 27 c 3.4			25.7.17	
9	Signal Dugout	R 33 c 3.6			25.7.17	
10	Signals	R 30 a 40.75 (4.8)	ext. begin 31.10.17		25.7.17	
11	Signals	S 8 a 4.2			25.7.17	
12	Signals	M 34 d 1.1			25.7.17	
13	Signals	M 35 c 2.8			25.7.17	
14	TM	M 21 c 85.90				
15	TM	M 14 c 8.1		25.7.17	1.8.17	
16	Well	R 32 c 6.5				
17	Corps HQ plus Artillery dug-outs	X 3 central	HQ finished 1.18.17	25.7.17		
18	OP	M 20 a 6.2		25.7.17	1.8.17	
19	'F' Coy Re dugout	M 21 a 8.0		25.7.17	1.8.17	
20	35th HAG	X 4 a 3.6		25.7.17	15.8.17	
21	Artillery dugout	R 28 b 3.8		I	5.9.17	
22	54 Siege Battery	R 34 a 3.3				
23	45 HAG dug-outs	R 27 c 0.3		25.7.17		
24	135 Siege Battery	R 28 d 9.6		25.7.17	8.8.17	
25	135 Siege Battery	R 28 d 6.5		25.7.17	8.8.17	
26	Finley Well	R 36 a 4.7				
27	Camp Well	X 2 a 8.8				
28	Decauville well	X 7 b 2.9				
29	Camp well	R 31 d 1.4				
30	54 HAG dugout	R 34 c 0.7		25.7.17		
31	35 HAG dugout	R 34 c 9.5		25.7.17		
32	54 Siege Battery	R 34 a 3.3		25.7.17	15.8.17	
33	TM	M 14 d 1.4		?	1.8.17	
34	TM	M 14 c 6.3		?	8.8.17	
35	Two TM dug-outs	M 20 a 9.9		1.8.17	8.8.17	
36	Power Station Well	R 32 c 7.3				
37	Camp Dugout	R 32 c 5.5				
38	Camp well	R 32 c 6.5				
39	Divisional headquarters	X 4 a 2.9		?	22.8.17	
40	Camp Well (b)	X 31 d 4.5				
41	Marsh Well	R 32 c 8.3				
42	227 Siege Battery	R 34 a 72.10	ext. begins 31.10.17	8.8.17	22.8.17	
43	Mined Artillery dugout	R 29 c 35.70		?	29.8.17	
44	C and C do 61 Siege Battery	R 34 b 5.1		?		
45	Leonards Well	R 32 c 8.2				
46	Marsh Well (c)	R 32 c 7.5				
47	25 Siege battery	R 34 d 35.61			22.8.17	
48	268 Siege Battery	R 29 c 2.4		8.8.17		
49	45 HAG Well	R 28 c 1.3				
50	32 HAG dugout	R 34 c 3.3	double dug-outs	12.9.17	26.9.17	

51	140 Siege Battery	R 29 c 4.7		?	
52	268 Siege Battery BC Post	R 29 c 3.3			
53	268 Siege Battery Fighting post	R 29 c 1.8		?	
54	TM	M 20 a 7.9		?	15.8.17
55	312 Siege Battery DO	R 28 b 5.9	ext. begins 26.9.17	?	3.10.17
56	54 HAG Well	R 33 d 95.80			
57	45 HAG Dugouts and Well	R 27 c 1.3		29.8.17	5.9.17
58	330 Heavy Battery	M 19 d 3.5		22.8.17	
59	331 HB	M 19 b 6.8		22.8.17	
60	66th. Div. HQ	R 34 c 6.5			
61	268 Siege Battery	R 29 c 6.4	ext. begins 17.10.17	?	29.8.17
62	268 Siege Battery FP	R 29 c 2.7		pre-29.8.17	5.9.17
63	330 Siege Battery DO	M 19 d 3.5		pre-29.8.17	12.9.17
64	32 HAG DO	R 34 c 3.2	extensions begin 19.9.17	pre-29.8.17	26.9.17
65	54 HAG extension	R 34 c 15.10	ext. begins 10.10.17	?	31.10.17
66	54 HAG Well	R 34 c 10.20			
67	18 Australian FB	M 20 c 2.8	extensions 26.9.17	29.8.17	3.10.17
68	222 Siege Battery	M 34 c 9.7		29.8.17	12.9.17
69	140 SB dugout	R 29 b 12.18		29.8.17	5.9.17
70	4th. Field Survey Company	R 34 c 48.12		29.8.17	5.9.17
71	331 Siege Battery	M 19 b 6.8		?	5.9.17
72	Y Corps HAG	X 3 a 95.50		pre-29.8.17	7.11.17
73	45 HAG small DO	R 26 d 7.2		29.8.17	5.9.17
74	TM DO	M 14 c 35.50		?	29.8.17
75	114 Heavy Battery	R 28 a 5.2	ext. from 3.10.17	?	10.10.17
76	246 Battery	S 9 b 4.3		29.8.17	
77	45 HAG DO	R 27 c 1.3			
78	325 Siege Battery two dug-outs	R 22 d 8.1		29.8.17	
79	35 HAG, OP, plus FSC	R 23 d 9.6	ext. started 10.10.17	pre-Sept?	7.11.17
80	35 HAG	R 33 a 7.8		pre-Sept.	26.9.17
81	45 HAG dugout and well	R 27 c 0.3		25.7.17	
82	312 Siege Battery	R 28 b 5.9		22.8.17	10.10.17
83	122 SB	R 23 c 16.00	new do's begin 3.10.17	5.9.17	31.10.17
84	331 RFA	R 23 d 7.8		5.9.17	
85	Section dugout	R 32 c 1.2		12.9.17	
86	TM Dugout	M 20 a 8.6		12.9.17	26.9.17
87	138 HB	R 29 b 8.7		12.9.17	3.10.17
88	140 HB	R 29 c 42.90		12.9.17	3.10.17
89	331 RFA dugout	R 29 d 3.2		19.9.17	
90	158 B Battery DO	M 19 d 6.4		19.9.17	7.11.17
91	138 Battery Tunnel	R 30 a 3.7	ext. begin 3.10.17	19.9.17	14.11.17
92	1/1 Lowland Battery	R 34 d 70.45	more begin 19.9.17	29.8.17	31.10.17
93	Divisional HQ DO	Q 5 c 9.3		19.9.17	
94	Section Dugout	R 32 c 1.9	ext. begin 31.10.17	9/1/00	
95	RFA Battery	R 23 d 7.8			
96	Section dugout	R 32 a 9.8		12.9.17	
97	222 Siege Battery	R 34 a 60.42		19.9.17	10.10.17
98	222 Siege Battery	R 34 a 48.49		19.9.17	
99	Section dugout	R 32 a 6.4		19.9.17	
100	158 B Battery officers mess	M 19 d 7.5		19.9.17	
101	331 RFA 'A' Battery	R 29 d 3.8	see also # 112		
102	331 RFA 'B' Battery	R 29 d 5.9		26.9.17	
103	Divisional HQ	W 5 c 9.3			10.10.17
104	222 Siege Battery	R 34 a 48.69		?	10.10.17
105	'B' Battery 158 RFA	M 19 d 6.4			14.11.17
106	46 Battery RFA	M 19 d 75.64	Extensions	26.9.17	10.10.17
107	Section DO	R 31 b 9.1		3.10.17	24.10.17
108	Divisional HQ	W 5 c 9.3			
109	203 Heavy Battery	R 28 b 9.6		3.10.17	
110	122 Siege Battery	R 28 c 20.80		10.10.17	7.11.17
111	138 HB dugout	R 30 a 3.7	see also 91	?	24.10.17
112	A battery 331 Brigade	R 29 d 3.8	see also #101	10/1/00	
113	Connection to # 80 34 HAG + HQ	R 33 a 7.8	Conn. to nearby HQ, 17.10.17		5.9.17
114	61 Siege Battery	R 34 d 3.7		17.10.17	
115	O.P. for 34 HAG	M 20 a 60.40	see also 2 Aus.	17.10.17	14.11.17

116	312 Siege Battery 'Diana'	R 27 d 8.8	ext. begin 17.10.17	?	7.11.17
117	Naval Group. 'Carnac' dugout officers	R 33 b 6. 80		17.10.17	
118	'A' Battery 187 Brigade Artillery	R 29 c 95.75		?	24.10.17
119	61 Siege Battery	R 34 b 35.55		10/1/00	7.11.17
120	'B' battery 187 Brigade Artillery	R 29 b 85.30			31.10.17
121	268 Siege battery	R 29 c 3.6		?	24.10.17
122	Naval Group 'Carnac' Off. DO	R 28 d 20.69		24.10.17	31.10.17
123	Do signals 140 HB	R 29 c central		24.10.17	31.10.17
124	140 HB Ammo Chamber	R 28 d 85.15		31.10.17	7.11.17
125	No.3 section DO	R 32 a 9.8		10/1/00	
126	NZ Brigade DO	R 30 a 7.8	plus visual tunnel begun 7.11.17	31.10.17	14.11.17
127	61 Siege Battery	R 34 b 35.55	extra tunn. to DO begun 7.11.17		14.11.17
128	135 Siege Battery	R 34 b 10.90		7.11.187	
129	9th. NZ FA Brigade.	M 19 d 70.75		7.11.17	
130	C&C concrete DO for RN	B 21 b 2.3			
131	138 Siege Battery	R 29 b 70 .55		7.11.17	
132	135 Siege Battery forward	R 28 d 4.9		14.11.17	
133	C&C conc. DO for Navy	B 21 a 9.8			
21	Artillery dugout	R 24 c 1.2	ext. begin 17.10.17	29.8.17	
185	Pipeline for cables to Nieuwpoort	X 11 d 3.0	starting point	19.9.17	
178	Artillery dug-outs	R 23 d 8.7	not 7.8		26.9.17
176	Artillery Dugouts	M 19 d 55.45		24.10.17	7.11.17
48	Artillery dug-outs	R 29 c 2.6	ext. begin 24.10.17	?	31.10.17
179	Artillery DO	R 29 d 3.9			24.10.17
180	Extension to Artillery DO	M 20 a 6.4		7.11.17	
182	Artillery Dugouts	R 27 d 8.7 (not 8.8)			10.01.18

ND - #0174 - 090625 - C145 - 246/189/19 - PB - 9781910500880 - Matt Lamination